MODEL RAILROAD
Bridges & Trestles

The material in this book first appeared as articles in *Model Railroader* Magazine from 1962–1991

Library of Congress Cataloging-in-Publication Data

Model railroad bridges and trestles: a reprint from Model Railroader
Magazine / Bob Hayden, editor.
p. cm.
ISBN 0-89024-128-7
1. Railroads–Models. 2. Railroad bridges–Models. I. Hayden,
Bob. II. Model Railroader.
TF197.M58 1992
625.1'9–dc20

91-62805

CIP

First printing, 1992. Second printing, 1993. Third printing, 1996. Fourth printing, 1998. Fifth printing, 2001.

KALMBACH
BOOKS

Understanding bridge construction

Basic bridge types, engineering, and materials

BY HAROLD RUSSELL

A WELL-CONSTRUCTED bridge adds beauty and excitement to any railroad, prototype or model. As proof, readers of MR need only recall how often scenes dominated by bridges and trestles appear in Trackside Photos. Besides making model railroads of all scales look more interesting, these structures make them appear more realistic. Modelers adding bridges must choose the proper setting and be sure that all important features are correctly proportioned components arranged in a realistic manner. However, because they deal with a drastic compression of space they may depart from real life by placing railroad as well as highway bridges with greater frequency on their layouts.

All of this suggests that model railroaders have good reason to learn more about bridge and culvert design and why, depending on the location, some structures are better than others for carrying a railroad over a road or waterway, a ravine or other topographical depression. Luckily, we don't have to be civil engineers to understand the basic principles and specific applications of bridge construction.

As an introduction to bridge construction, I have prepared a series of articles, of which this is the first. Modelers seeking additional information should go out and examine and photograph real bridges.

PICKING THE APPROPRIATE BRIDGE

Building a bridge for a model railroad involves, first, determining the type of structure that is appropriate. In this series, we will try to follow the decisions of actual railroad engineers. That means selecting materials and forms used during whatever era you're modeling. For example, wood was used extensively through the 1870s, after which its use gradually declined. Therefore, a wooden Howe truss bridge would not be appropriate for a modern mainline steam or diesel operation. However, if you're modeling western United States narrow gauge, you could reasonably use wood for trestles and bridges well into the twentieth century.

We should not forget that real railroad engineers pay most attention to a site's characteristics and use when determining what type of bridge to build. That explains why, in places where the distance to be crossed is very great, they usually find it cheaper to use a series of short bridges supported by piers.

If building an intermediate pier seems impractical, engineers may use a long bridge, at least at that point in the crossing. This may occur on a river subject to periodic flooding, where debris would damage a pier, or on a navigable body of water where a mid-water support would menace boating. In other locations, engineers may determine that the soil is too swampy to support a pier.

A required clearance under a bridge will also influence what is constructed. Whenever navigable water is crossed there must be clearance for ships to pass beneath. In such a situation, a through-type bridge is generally preferable to a deck-type, whose depth could prevent boats from passing. Even so, engineers may decide to use a moveable span, such as a swing or a lift drawbridge.

An eastbound Erie Lackawanna passenger train crossing the Starrucca Viaduct in May of 1972. An extraordinary engineering achievement for its time, this masonry structure was built in 1847-48 for the Erie RR, and is still in use. It is 1200 feet long, 110 feet high, and 30 feet wide at the top.

Fig. 1 BRIDGE LOADS

E-30	Light service
E-50	Common loading in 1910
E-60	Common mainline loading in the 1920s
E-65	Modern mainline service with 100% diesel operation
E-70	Modern high-speed mainline service

Fig. 2 BRIDGE CONSTRUCTION

TYPE	BRIDGE MATERIAL	SPAN IN FEET		
		19th Century	20th Century	Modern
Beam	Wood	to 20	to 15	to 10
	Steel	–	to 20	to 40
	Concrete	–	to 10	to 20
Plate Girder	Steel	to 100	10-150	20-200
Simple Truss	Wood	15-150	15-150	–
	Steel	50-300	50-500	100-700
Arch	Wood	50-200	50-200	–
	Steel	100-700	100-1000	100 +
	Concrete	to 100	to 200	to 300
Cantilever	Steel	200-1000	300-1500	300 +
Continuous	Steel	–	300-800	300-800

Harold W. Russell

Fig. 3. This beam bridge constructed of "S" beams crosses a small stream. While engineers once relied on wood to build such structures, today concrete and steel are the preferred materials.

A BRIEF HISTORY

Prior to the 1840s, the bridges found in the United States were either masonry edifices or flimsy wooden structures. Railroads greatly changed bridge-building practices. With their heavy equipment and constant need for easy grades and gentle curves, they forced engineers to devise better ways for overcoming natural obstacles.

Builders first relied on traditional materials, and some rather sophisticated bridges of masonry appeared on the Baltimore & Ohio and other early railroads. Many of these structures, like the Erie RR's famed Starrucca Viaduct shown above, were built so well that they can still carry heavily loaded freight cars.

Iron first appeared as a building material in the early 1840s. Up to the 1860s, steel was used mostly for tension members and wood for compression. By 1869, however, bridges made entirely of steel were being erected. As steel became more economical to use, solid steel continuous spans were built, along with arches and cantilevers. By the end of the 19th century, the first lift drawbridges were being constructed, and concrete was replacing stone for masonry arches, supporting piers, and abutments.

Bridge construction slowed during the depression era of the 1930s, just as railroads began to decline. All the same, notable changes did take place, such as the replacement of rivet assembly methods by bolted construction. By the 1950s, all-welded construction was commonplace.

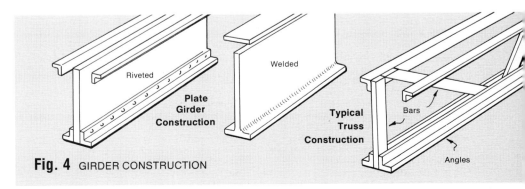

Riveted

Plate Girder Construction

Welded

Typical Truss Construction

Bars

Angles

Fig. 4 GIRDER CONSTRUCTION

Harold W. Russell

Fig. 5, above. The concrete pier at the center supports the ends of two deck plate girder spans. The pier was built to withstand the rapidly flowing floodwater that carries debris. The bridge has an E-50 load rating to support locomotives with a 50,000-pound load per axle. **Fig. 6, below.** A structure like this Baltimore & Ohio Warren truss is used where there is insufficient clearance and no room for an intermediate pier or support.

DESIGN AND LOAD SUPPORTING CAPABILITIES

Materials and methods of construction may change, but the factors involved in designing an actual bridge (sheer, stress, live and dead loads) remain the same. Thankfully, most are of little importance to the model builder, except when they are used to develop the charts and standards with which he can construct a properly proportioned model.

The supporting capabilities of any bridge are measured according to a system devised in the late 1900s called Cooper's Loadings. This system, which is still used, uses "E" numbers to indicate the individual locomotive axle loading that a structure will safely support.

Thus, E-60 indicates a capability of supporting a locomotive with a weight of 60,000 pounds per axle.

A bridge with a low E number (those found on early railroads) would have light construction members, while one with a high E number (later and contemporary practice) would have heavier members. Figure 1 is a chart showing the general E loadings for different periods.

An additional guide for bridge design and use is shown in fig. 2. It indicates the relationship between era, materials, and bridge span (length). Notice that most cantilever and continuous bridges are not well suited for the average model railroad layout when built full-scale size. A typical cantilever or suspension bridge would be around 20 feet

long in HO scale, which is longer than the largest dimension of an average home layout.

BEAM, GIRDER, AND TRUSS BRIDGES

Bridges fall into two general categories. A deck structure indicates a bridge with a supporting structure of girders or trusses positioned below the track or road. A through bridge has the supporting structure straddling the track or road.

Words such as "deck truss," "girder," "trestle," "beam," and "through" are adjectives describing bridge structure construction. By putting these words and other adjectives together in various combinations we can describe and name any bridge.

Beam bridges (the term "deck" is implied and seldom used here) use single

Fig. 7, above. Included in this Erie Railroad steel structure are trestle towers, long and short plate girder spans, two truss bridges, and stone piers.

Fig. 8, right. A fairly recent ballasted deck pile trestle on a lightly used branch line of the Seaboard Coast Line in Florida. Structures of this type, built with round pile or square framed supports, were once common as railroad bridges.

Fig. 9 below right. A culvert can be a simple large-diameter pipe or framed wood structure, or be grandiose, like this New York Central masonry structure. Culverts generally have several feet of earth fill between them and the roadbed.

heavy supporting members. Early beam bridges were made of wood. Later, steel beams were the common construction material. See fig. 3. When a member stronger than the largest rolled beam (36″ deep) is required, it is built up with plates and angles into a plate girder, as shown in figs. 4 and 5. When an even stronger support member is required, an open network is fashioned of structural steel members into a truss, as is shown in figs. 4 and 6.

Generally speaking, beams are members 12 to 36 inches in depth, girders are 36 to 170 inches, and trusses are 170 inches and higher. These categories overlap, however, so you may find a 24″-deep girder or a 144″-deep truss. Finally, different bridge types are often combined to make a single long structure that may include trestle, plate girder, and truss configurations. See fig. 7.

TRESTLES, VIADUCTS, AND CULVERTS

If a structure consists of several short spans that are frequently supported along the length (fig. 8), it is termed a trestle. Trestles are usually made of timber or steel, though making low trestles

Fig. 10. The Rainbow Bridge at Niagara Falls is an example of an arch span. Rapidly flowing water and winter ice prohibited the use of intermediate piers. The ends are anchored in solid rock. Spandrels, rising vertically from the arch, support the roadway. On arch bridges the roadway, or railroad roadbed, can be built at the top of the arch, entirely above the arch, or through it with portions both above (ends) and below (center).

out of precast concrete is not unheard of. When those structures are built from stone, as with Starrucca, they are called viaducts. However, viaducts can be made from materials other than stone or concrete.

A culvert is also considered a type of bridge. As shown in fig. 9, it is usually made by placing fill over a metal pipe or concrete box. Timber or stone can be used to construct a culvert, and sometimes a combination of materials is used.

ARCH BRIDGES

Arch bridges are one of several types used to cover distances of 400 or more feet. The Rainbow Bridge, shown connecting Niagara Falls, N. Y., and Ontario in fig. 10, is a good example. Supported at the ends, it curves upward in the middle. When a load is applied to push it down, the ends tend to spread apart. Thus, solid foundations must be constructed at the ends to resist the extreme forces exerted by the arch structure. Arch bridges require materials such as wood, stone, concrete, and steel that are strong in compression.

Engineers can vary the design of an arch bridge to have the deck pass above, below, or through the arch. Similarly, they can recommend that the arch be made of solid steel plate or trussed members arranged in a web.

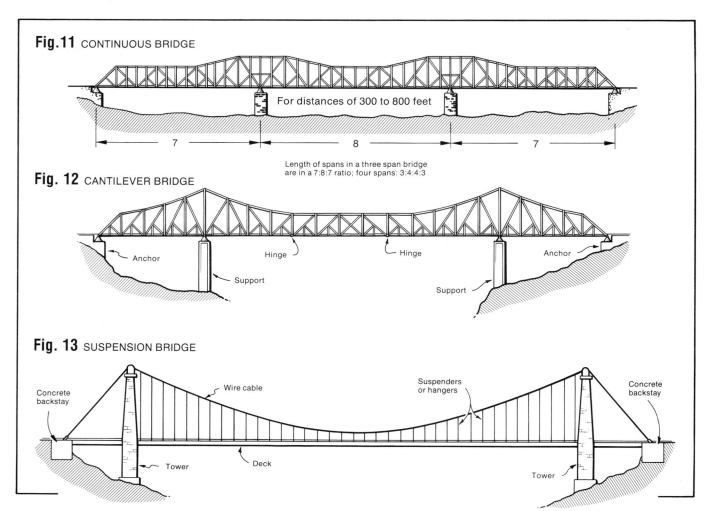

Fig.11 CONTINUOUS BRIDGE

For distances of 300 to 800 feet

7   8   7

Length of spans in a three span bridge are in a 7:8:7 ratio; four spans: 3:4:4:3

Fig. 12 CANTILEVER BRIDGE

Anchor   Hinge   Hinge   Anchor

Support   Support

Fig. 13 SUSPENSION BRIDGE

Concrete backstay   Wire cable   Suspenders or hangers   Concrete backstay

Tower   Deck   Tower

CONTINUOUS TRUSS BRIDGES

The other types of bridges are the continuous, cantilever, and suspension bridges. A continuous truss bridge is used to cover distances of 300 to 800 feet. As shown in fig. 11, this structure is really a single long truss with intermediate pier supports. The entire structure acts as a single truss, and its overall height is much lower than that of a series of individual simple trusses. A continuous truss can easily be identified by the high top portions that are located above the piers.

A continuous bridge with a single pier at the center is called a "two span." The bridge shown in fig. 11 is a "three span" and has two piers and span lengths with a ratio of 7:8:7. A "four span" bridge (three piers) has a span length ratio of 3:4:4:3.

CANTILEVER BRIDGES

A simple cantilever is a structure section supported at one end only. Figure 12 shows a variation of this principle that is incorporated into span bridges up to 1800 feet long. It consists of two cantilevers, each supported partway from the ends. The cantilever halves are fastened at the center portion and hinged so that no stresses are transferred between the sections.

In fig. 12, the high pointed portions of the piers identify this structure as a cantilever bridge. A truss has been hung between the cantilevers that requires two hinges. Note also that the center span is considerably longer than the end sections.

SUSPENSION BRIDGES

Suspension bridges have a series of cables in tension fastened to the shores at the ends and running over two towers, as shown in fig. 13. The floor is suspended from these main elements by smaller vertical cables called "suspenders" or "hangers." Suspension bridges are suitable for distances of several thousand feet. While suspension bridges are inherently flexible and thus not well suited to heavy railroad use, some have been constructed on eastern lines.

STRUCTURAL SHAPES USED TO CONSTRUCT STEEL BRIDGES

Structural steel members used in bridge construction are made of various grades of steel and strengths that are rolled in the mills to certain shapes and sizes. The sections shown in fig. 14 are representative of those commonly used in bridge construction. Other sizes and shapes exist, but those shown are enough for model builders. Note that the shapes are manufactured with various wall thicknesses. In model building this dimension is not significant, so we can work with available materials that have a single wall thickness per shape size.

Wide Flange Beams have the cross section of a letter H and are called "W" shapes. W shapes are generally preferred in bridge building.

Narrow Flange Beams, made in the shape of a letter I, are used less because they lack the strength of the W shape. Their technical designation is "S" beams.

Channels commonly range from 5" to 15" in depth and are called "C" shapes. The width of this shape is about one-half its depth.

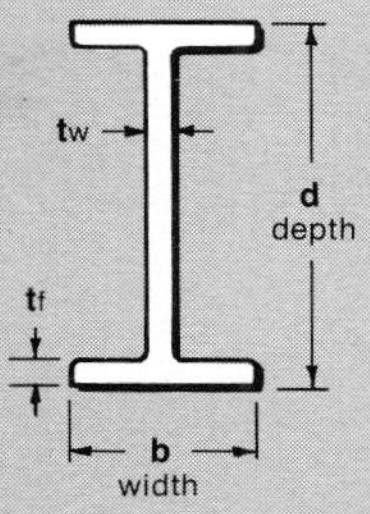

tw
tf
d
depth
b
width

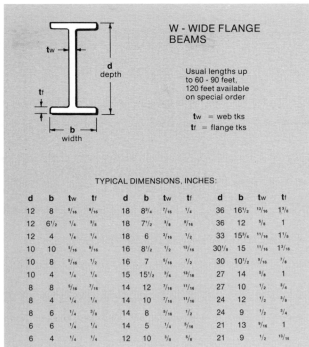

W - WIDE FLANGE BEAMS

Usual lengths up to 60 - 90 feet, 120 feet available on special order

tw = web tks
tf = flange tks

TYPICAL DIMENSIONS, INCHES:

d	b	tw	tf	d	b	tw	tf	d	b	tw	tf
12	8	5/16	9/16	18	8 3/4	7/16	1/4	36	16 1/2	13/16	1 3/8
12	6 1/2	1/4	3/8	18	7 1/2	3/8	9/16	36	12	5/8	1
12	4	1/4	1/4	18	6	3/16	1/2	33	15 3/4	11/16	1 1/8
10	10	5/16	9/16	16	8 1/2	1/2	13/16	30 1/8	15	11/16	1 3/16
10	8	5/16	1/2	16	7	5/16	1/2	30	10 1/2	9/16	7/8
10	4	1/4	1/4	15	15 1/2	3/4	13/16	27	14	5/8	1
8	8	5/16	7/16	14	12	7/16	11/16	27	10	1/2	3/4
8	4	1/4	1/4	14	10	7/16	11/16	24	12	1/2	3/8
8	6	1/4	3/8	14	8	5/16	1/2	24	9	1/2	3/4
6	6	1/4	1/4	14	5	1/4	5/16	21	13	9/16	1
6	4	1/4	1/4	12	10	3/8	5/8	21	9	1/2	13/16

S BEAMS

Usual lengths up to 60 - 90 feet

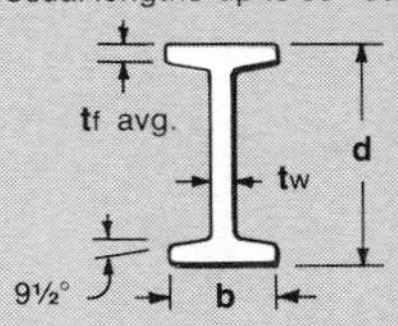

tf avg.
tw
d
9½°
b

TYPICAL DIMENSIONS, INCHES:

d	b	tw	tf
18	6 1/4	11/16	11/16
18	6	7/16	11/16
15	5 5/8	9/16	5/8
15	5 1/2	7/16	5/8
12	5 1/2	11/16	11/16
12	5 1/4	7/16	11/16
12	5 1/8	7/16	9/16
12	5	3/8	9/16
10	5	5/8	1/2
10	4 5/8	5/16	1/2
8	4 1/8	7/16	7/16
8	4	1/4	7/16
7	3 5/8	1/4	3/8
6	3 5/8	7/16	3/8
6	3 3/8	1/8	1/4
5	3	3/16	5/16

C CHANNELS

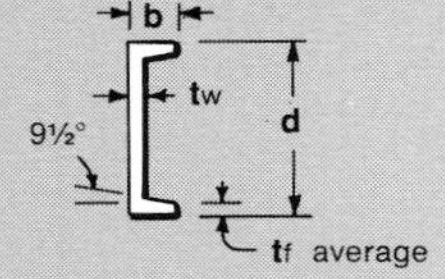

b
tw
d
9½°
tf average

TYPICAL DIMENSIONS, INCHES:

d	b	tw	tf
15	3 3/8	3/8	5/8
12	3	5/16	1/2
10	2 5/8	3/8	7/16
9	2 1/2	5/16	7/16
8	2 1/4	1/4	3/8
7	2 1/8	3/16	3/8
6	2	5/16	5/16
5	1 3/4	3/16	5/16

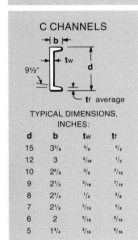

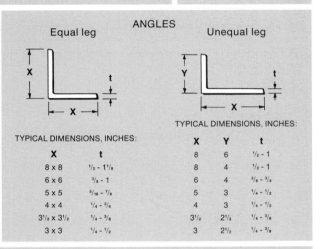

ANGLES

Equal leg

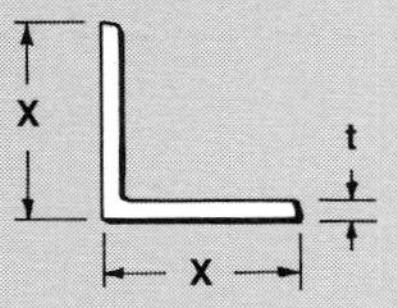

X
t
X

TYPICAL DIMENSIONS, INCHES:

X	t
8 x 8	1/2 - 1 1/8
6 x 6	3/8 - 1
5 x 5	5/16 - 7/8
4 x 4	1/4 - 3/4
3 1/2 x 3 1/2	1/4 - 3/8
3 x 3	1/4 - 1/2

Unequal leg

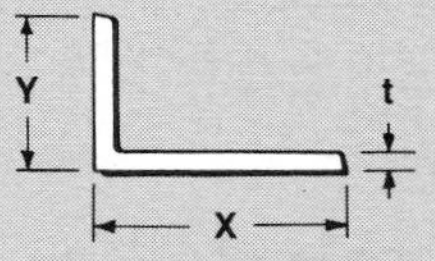

Y
t
X

TYPICAL DIMENSIONS, INCHES:

X	Y	t
8	6	1/2 - 1
8	4	1/2 - 1
6	4	3/8 - 3/4
5	3	1/4 - 1/2
4	3	1/4 - 1/2
3 1/2	2 1/2	1/4 - 3/8
3	2 1/2	1/4 - 3/8

PLATES

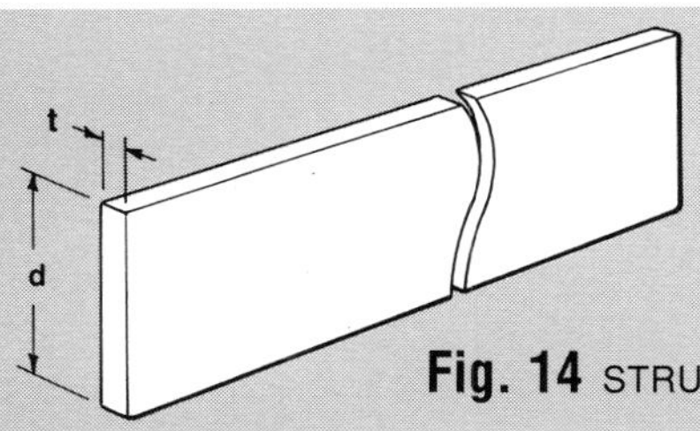

t
d

d	Increments	t
10" - 69"	1"	3/8", 7/16", 1/2", 9/16", 5/8"
70" - 170"	2"	3/4", 7/8", 1"
		for all depths

Fig. 14 STRUCTURAL STEEL SHAPES

Angles with equal legs are a commonly used structural material and are manufactured up to an 8" x 8" size. The smallest size used in bridge construction is 3" x 3", and the most common sizes are 4" x 4" and 6" x 6". Larger angles having unequal legs are also used in bridge construction, with 6" x 4" and 8" x 6" being the most common.

The last common shape is the Tee. It is cut from W shapes and ranges in size from 2" x 2" to 16½" across the flange by 18" deep. Most often, 6" and 8" are the sizes used.

Steel plates are used to construct plate girders and can serve as gusset plates for strengthening the junction of structural shapes. They are available in various sizes, ranging from 3/8" to 1" in thickness and 10" to 170" in width.

Now that we are familiar with some basic principles of bridge design and use as well as the specifications of construction materials, we can consider how these ideas and components are combined to make authentic looking structures ready to be placed in realistic model settings. We will start next month by discussing beam and plate girder bridges and bridge floor systems.

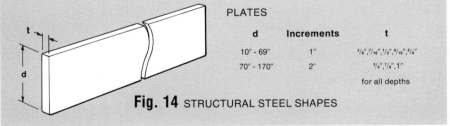

Beam and through plate girder bridges

Design characteristics and flooring systems
for beam, girder, and truss bridges

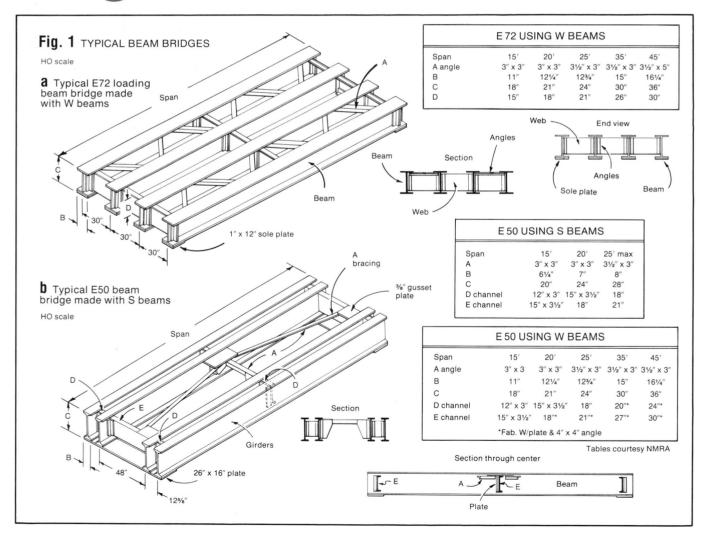

Fig. 1 TYPICAL BEAM BRIDGES

HO scale

a Typical E72 loading beam bridge made with W beams

b Typical E50 beam bridge made with S beams

HO scale

E 72 USING W BEAMS					
Span	15′	20′	25′	35′	45′
A angle	3″ x 3″	3″ x 3″	3½″ x 3″	3½″ x 3″	3½″ x 5″
B	11″	12¼″	12¾″	15″	16¼″
C	18″	21″	24″	30″	36″
D	15″	18″	21″	26″	30″

E 50 USING S BEAMS			
Span	15′	20′	25′ max
A	3″ x 3″	3″ x 3″	3½″ x 3″
B	6¼″	7″	8″
C	20″	24″	28″
D channel	12″ x 3″	15″ x 3½″	18″
E channel	15″ x 3½″	18″	21″

E 50 USING W BEAMS					
Span	15′	20′	25′	35′	45′
A angle	3″ x 3	3″ x 3″	3½″ x 3″	3½″ x 3″	3½″ x 3″
B	11″	12¼″	12¾″	15″	16¼″
C	18″	21″	24″	30″	36″
D channel	12″ x 3″	15″ x 3½″	18″	20″*	24″*
E channel	15″ x 3½″	18″*	21″*	27″*	30″*

*Fab. W/plate & 4″ x 4″ angle

Tables courtesy NMRA

Section through center

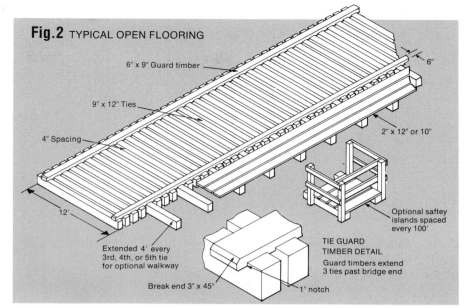

Fig.2 TYPICAL OPEN FLOORING

6" x 9" Guard timber

9" x 12" Ties

4" Spacing

12'

6"

2" x 12" or 10"

Extended 4' every 3rd, 4th, or 5th tie for optional walkway

Break end 3" x 45°

1" notch

Optional saftey islands spaced every 100'

TIE GUARD TIMBER DETAIL
Guard timbers extend 3 ties past bridge end

BY HAROLD RUSSELL

THIS PART of the ABCs of Bridges will deal with beam bridges, along with typical flooring systems and the general design of a through plate girder bridge. Included is a scale plan for a modern 70-foot plate girder bridge with a load rating of E72. Except for the rivet detail, these types of bridges are the easiest to model and can be used singly or in multiples butted together to make a long structure.

STEEL BEAM BRIDGES

Perhaps the simplest of all bridges is a beam type consisting of a number of steel shapes set parallel to the rails. There are two kinds of beam bridges: those made with wide flanges (W shapes) and those made with I beams (S shapes). Wide-flange beam bridges have a maximum length of about 40 feet and are used for spans with an E50 loading or greater.

Figure 1a shows the general arrangement and spacing of the components. The table indicates the beam and angle sizes used for spans from 15 to 45 feet. For load ratings of E50 and less, the arrangement shown in fig. 1b is employed. The tables indicate the sizes for E50 and E30 loading spans using S or W shapes.

To model these bridges you could use wood, brass, or plastic structural shapes. Larger W shapes can be fabricated using styrene strips and sheet or a combination of sheet and angle.

TRACK FLOORING

Conventional railroad roadbed uses steel rails spiked to wood ties with the ties set in ballast (stone) to anchor them and provide drainage. On a bridge another system can be used. Wood ties as large as 9" x 12" (earlier bridge ties were no more than 8" x 8") are fastened to the bridge structure and the rails spiked to the ties. Common bridge tie lengths are between 10 and 12 feet. This open flooring system can be applied to any wood or steel bridge. See fig. 2.

If the bridge is long, an outside walkway and a railing may be applied on one or both sides of the track. See figs. 2 and 3. If optional safety islands are used, they are spaced about every 100 feet. Every third to fifth tie is lengthened to support the 3- to 4-foot-wide walkway made of 2 x 10 or 2 x 12 planks. In fig. 3, crosswise planking is laid on top of the first longitudinal layer.

A second flooring method (known as ballasted flooring) consists of a large wood, metal, or concrete trough in which conventional ballast and ties are laid. See fig. 4. Ballasted decks are often found on beam and through plate girder bridges (see fig. 5), masonry structures, and some trestles. While open flooring is cheaper to construct, a ballasted floor is fireproof, permits easy rail alignment, and provides a smoother as well as a quieter riding surface.

Kalmbach Collection

Fig. 3, above. This open floor system on a deck truss bridge over the Cimarron River in Kansas was built in 1938 by the Rock Island. The walkway planks running the length of the structure are covers with an additional crosswise layer. Guardrails placed inside the running rails help to keep derailed wheels in line. **Fig. 5, below.** A through plate girder bridge with a ballasted floor built by the Baltimore & Ohio RR to eliminate a crossing over a highway. Ballasted flooring provides a smoother roadbed than open flooring.

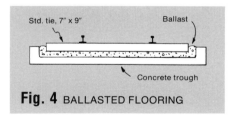

Std. tie, 7" x 9"

Ballast

Concrete trough

Fig. 4 BALLASTED FLOORING

Harold Russell

Harold Russell

Fig. 6. Guardrail ends are terminated in several ways. Looking from left to right, the rail ends are brought together and bent down into the ballast, one rail notched and the two bolted to a wedge-shaped casting to hold the pieces in position, and both rails bolted to a pointed metal casting.

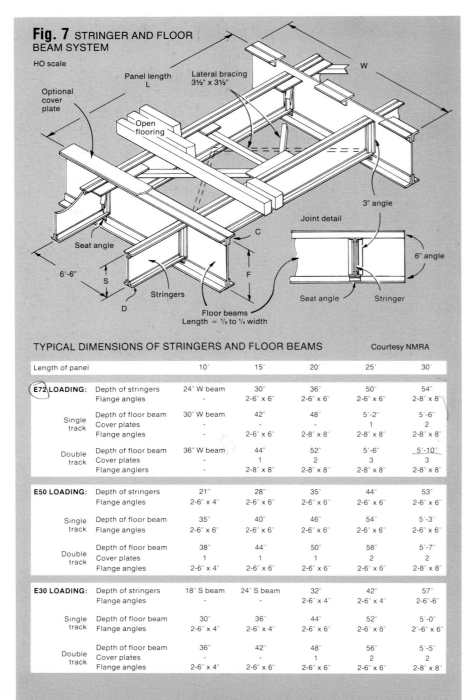

Fig. 7 STRINGER AND FLOOR BEAM SYSTEM

HO scale

Panel length L

Lateral bracing 3½" x 3½"

W

Optional cover plate

Open flooring

3" angle

Joint detail

Seat angle

C

6" angle

6'-6"

S

Stringers

F

D

Seat angle

Stringer

Floor beams
Length = ⅛ to ¼ width

TYPICAL DIMENSIONS OF STRINGERS AND FLOOR BEAMS

Courtesy NMRA

Length of panel		10'	15'	20'	25'	30'
E72 LOADING:	Depth of stringers	24" W beam	30"	36"	50"	54"
	Flange angles	-	2-6" x 6"	2-6" x 6"	2-6" x 6"	2-8" x 8"
Single track	Depth of floor beam	30" W beam	42"	48"	5'-2"	5'-6"
	Cover plates	-	-	-	1	2
	Flange angles	-	2-6" x 6"	2-8" x 8"	2-8" x 8"	2-8" x 8"
Double track	Depth of floor beam	36" W beam	44"	52"	5'-6"	5'-10"
	Cover plates	-	1	2	3	3
	Flange anglers	-	2-8" x 8"	2-8" x 8"	2-8" x 8"	2-8" x 8"
E50 LOADING:	Depth of stringers	21"	28"	35"	44"	53"
	Flange angles	2-6" x 4"	2-6" x 6"	2-6" x 6"	2-6" x 6"	2-6" x 6"
Single track	Depth of floor beam	35"	40"	46"	54"	5'-3"
	Flange angles	2-6" x 6"	2-6" x 6"	2-6" x 6"	2-6" x 6"	2-6" x 6"
Double track	Depth of floor beam	38"	44"	50"	58"	5'-7"
	Cover plates	1	1	1	2	2
	Flange angles	2-6" x 4"	2-6" x 6"	2-6" x 6"	2-6" x 6"	2-8" x 8"
E30 LOADING:	Depth of stringers	18" S beam	24" S beam	32"	42"	57"
	Flange angles	-	-	2-6" x 4"	2-6" x 4"	2-6"-6"
Single track	Depth of floor beam	30"	36"	44"	52"	5'-0"
	Flange angles	2-6" x 4"	2-6" x 4"	2-6" x 6"	2-6" x 6"	2'-6" x 6"
Double track	Depth of floor beam	36"	42"	48"	56"	5'-5"
	Cover plates	-	-	1	2	2
	Flange angles	2-6" x 4"	2-6" x 6"	2-6" x 6"	2-6" x 6"	2-8" x 8"

GUARDRAILS

Most though not all bridges have guardrails positioned 8″ to 10″ inside the running rails. They are generally lighter weight than the running rails and often are used material. See fig. 3. These rails are darker in color and tend to be rustier than running rails. Terminating 20 to 60 feet beyond the bridge's end, guardrails serve to catch an errant wheel of a derailed car and to center the trucks before the car passes over the bridge. As a result, the possibility of derailing and either crashing into the bridge structure or falling off is lessened. Figure 6 shows three typical end configurations for guardrails.

STRINGER AND FLOOR BEAM SYSTEMS FOR THROUGH BRIDGES

Flooring systems are placed on top of a beam bridge structure and fastened to it. On through bridges the flooring is carried by a network of structural steel called a stringer and floor beam system. Figure 7 shows a typical system.

Smaller floor beam systems use W or S shapes. With larger ones, the pieces are made from steel plate and angles. The depth of these sections usually is approximately one-fifth the distance between the supporting girders or trusses at the side for single-track bridges and slightly more for double-track ones. For a bridge having a span of 25 to 30 feet and a load rating of E72, one or two cover plates would be placed on the top and bottom of each floor beam as indicated in fig. 7.

The panel length between floor beams is usually about 15 feet for plate girder bridges and up to 30 feet for truss bridges. Stringers, used in pairs positioned 6'-6" apart, run between the floor beams parallel to the running rails. They are generally plate girders (built of plate and angles) and are set 6″ below the top of the floor beams to provide clearance for lateral angle bracing.

In calculating the dimensions of real floor beams, the sizes of the structural elements are rounded off to the next largest standard shape size (a calculated 33″ W shape becomes a 36″ shape). The table in fig. 7 lists typical dimensions of floor beams and stringer systems for various panel lengths and loadings.

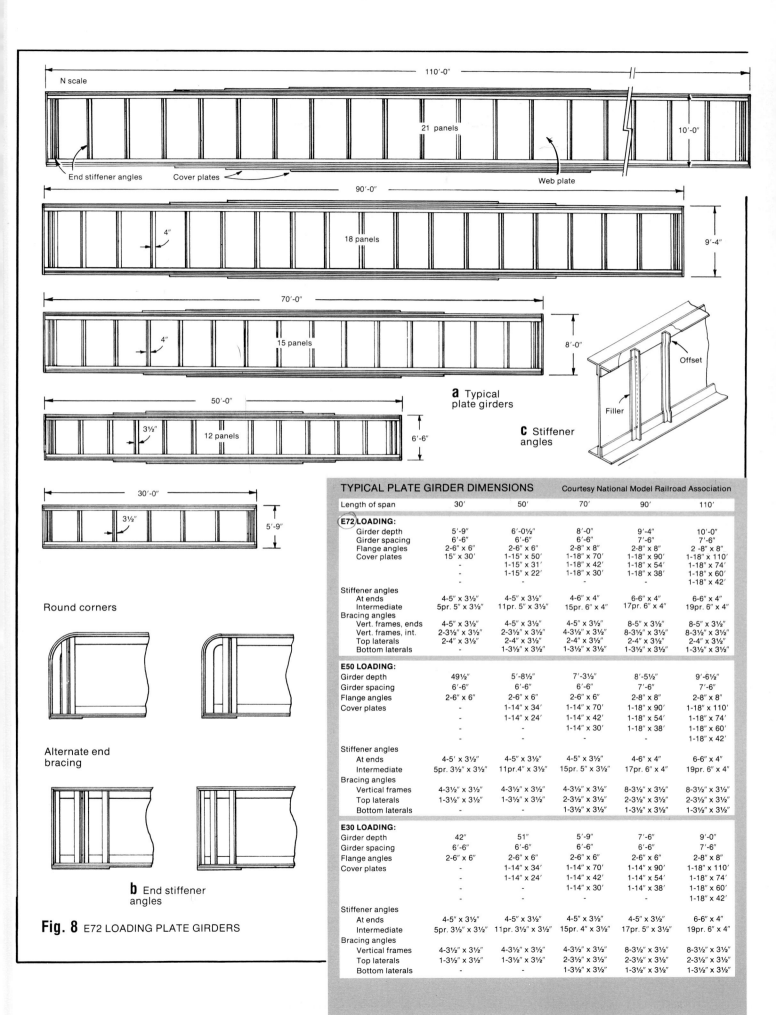

N scale

110'-0"

21 panels

10'-0"

End stiffener angles   Cover plates   Web plate

90'-0"

4"

18 panels

9'-4"

70'-0"

4"

15 panels

8'-0"

a Typical plate girders

Offset

Filler

C Stiffener angles

50'-0"

3½"

12 panels

6'-6"

30'-0"

3½"

5'-9"

Round corners

Alternate end bracing

b End stiffener angles

Fig. 8 E72 LOADING PLATE GIRDERS

TYPICAL PLATE GIRDER DIMENSIONS				Courtesy National Model Railroad Association	
Length of span	30'	50'	70'	90'	110'
E72 LOADING:					
Girder depth	5'-9"	6'-0½"	8'-0"	9'-4"	10'-0"
Girder spacing	6'-6"	6'-6"	6'-6"	7'-6"	7'-6"
Flange angles	2-6" x 6"	2-6" x 6"	2-8" x 8"	2-8" x 8"	2 -8" x 8"
Cover plates	15" x 30'	1-15" x 50'	1-18" x 70'	1-18" x 90'	1-18" x 110'
	-	1-15" x 31'	1-18" x 42'	1-18" x 54'	1-18" x 74'
	-	1-15" x 22'	1-18" x 30'	1-18" x 38'	1-18" x 60'
	-	-	-	-	1-18" x 42'
Stiffener angles					
At ends	4-5" x 3½"	4-5" x 3½"	4-6" x 4"	6-6" x 4"	6-6" x 4"
Intermediate	5pr. 5" x 3½"	11pr. 5" x 3½"	15pr. 6" x 4"	17pr. 6" x 4"	19pr. 6" x 4"
Bracing angles					
Vert. frames, ends	4-5" x 3½"	4-5" x 3½"	4-5" x 3½"	8-5" x 3½"	8-5" x 3½"
Vert. frames, int.	2-3½" x 3½"	2-3½" x 3½"	4-3½" x 3½"	8-3½" x 3½"	8-3½" x 3½"
Top laterals	2-4" x 3½"	2-4" x 3½"	2-4" x 3½"	2-4" x 3½"	2-4" x 3½"
Bottom laterals	-	1-3½" x 3½"	1-3½" x 3½"	1-3½" x 3½"	1-3½" x 3½"
E50 LOADING:					
Girder depth	49½"	5'-8½"	7'-3½"	8'-5½"	9'-6½"
Girder spacing	6'-6"	6'-6"	6'-6"	7'-6"	7'-6"
Flange angles	2-6" x 6"	2-6" x 6"	2-6" x 6"	2-8" x 8"	2-8" x 8"
Cover plates	-	1-14" x 34'	1-14" x 70'	1-18" x 90'	1-18" x 110'
	-	1-14" x 24'	1-14" x 42'	1-18" x 54'	1-18" x 74'
	-	-	1-14" x 30'	1-18" x 38'	1-18" x 60'
	-	-	-	-	1-18" x 42'
Stiffener angles					
At ends	4-5' x 3½"	4-5" x 3½"	4-5" x 3½"	4-6" x 4"	6-6" x 4"
Intermediate	5pr. 3½" x 3½"	11pr.4" x 3½"	15pr. 5" x 3½"	17pr. 6" x 4"	19pr. 6" x 4"
Bracing angles					
Vertical frames	4-3½" x 3½"	4-3½" x 3½"	4-3½" x 3½"	8-3½" x 3½"	8-3½" x 3½"
Top laterals	1-3½" x 3½"	1-3½" x 3½"	2-3½" x 3½"	2-3½" x 3½"	2-3½" x 3½"
Bottom laterals	-	-	1-3½" x 3½"	1-3½" x 3½"	1-3½" x 3½"
E30 LOADING:					
Girder depth	42"	51"	5'-9"	7'-6"	9'-0"
Girder spacing	6'-6"	6'-6"	6'-6"	6'-6"	7'-6"
Flange angles	2-6" x 6"	2-6" x 6"	2-6" x 6"	2-6" x 6"	2-8" x 8"
Cover plates	-	1-14" x 34'	1-14" x 70'	1-14" x 90'	1-18" x 110'
	-	1-14" x 24'	1-14" x 42'	1-14" x 54'	1-18" x 74'
	-	-	1-14" x 30'	1-14" x 38'	1-18" x 60'
	-	-	-	-	1-18" x 42'
Stiffener angles					
At ends	4-5" x 3½"	4-5" x 3½"	4-5" x 3½"	4-5" x 3½"	6-6" x 4"
Intermediate	5pr. 3½" x 3½"	11pr. 3½" x 3½"	15pr. 4" x 3½"	17pr. 5" x 3½"	19pr. 6" x 4"
Bracing angles					
Vertical frames	4-3½" x 3½"	4-3½" x 3½"	4-3½" x 3½"	8-3½" x 3½"	8-3½" x 3½"
Top laterals	1-3½" x 3½"	1-3½" x 3½"	2-3½" x 3½"	2-3½" x 3½"	2-3½" x 3½"
Bottom laterals	-	-	1-3½" x 3½"	1-3½" x 3½"	1-3½" x 3½"

Harold Edmondson

Fig. 9. Bridges with various configurations and lengths are often used in combination. This Southern Pacific structure has center-rounded corner girders as well as square-cornered girders at the ends.

Stringers are attached to the floor beams with angles that are typically 3″ x 3″ in size. Seat angles are placed under the stringers to support them. See fig. 7.

Using at least 3½″ angles, the stringers are lateral braced in a zigzag pattern at the top or bottom. These braces should be close to 45 degrees to the stringers. On deep beams this lateral bracing is applied to both the top and bottom of the beams. In fig. 7, the bottom lateral angles would be run at opposite angles to the top angles. Viewed from the top, the lateral bracing would form a series of X arrangements.

Extra lateral cross braces, made of angles and paralleling the floor beams, are occasionally used. They are positioned midway along a panel length at the point where the lateral support angles connect to the stringers.

THROUGH PLATE GIRDER BRIDGES

A girder bridge floor system by itself is structurally weak; hence, it must be strengthened by plate girders or trusses. Figure 8a shows some typical plate

Harold Russell

Fig. 10. Knee braces are used to brace the junction of the side girders and floor beams. Other details include the cover plates atop the girders, lateral bracing, gusset plates, and open flooring.

girder designs for several bridges with a load rating of E72 and spans ranging from 30 to 110 feet. The general dimensions of the girder components are listed in the table in fig. 8.

A plate girder consists of a solid steel sheet (called a web plate) reinforced with flange angles at the edges. The most commonly used sizes range from 6″ x 6″ to 8″ x 8″. To strengthen the girder assembly intermediate stiffener angles are used in vertical pairs on opposite sides of the web plate at each floor panel joint and at intermediate positions along the panel length. Equal spacing is shown, but uneven spacing is also used. A double set or sometimes more of end stiffener angles is used at the ends where the bridge structure is supported by shoes or pedestals. See fig 8b.

On through bridges the top end corners of the girders may be squared or, as shown in fig. 8b, rounded. Different lengths and configurations of plate girder bridges with both round and square corners are often used in combination, as shown in fig. 9. If the girder is used for a deck bridge these top corners are always squared.

At the point where stiffener and flange angles meet, the stiffener angles are either bent to fit over the flange angle, or a filler bar is placed between the stiffener and the web plate. See fig. 8c.

As the bridge gets longer sheet cover plates are added to the top and bottom of the girder. As you can see, these stacked plates get progressively shorter.

Steel shapes used to make plate girders are manufactured in specific lengths, usually 50 and 70 feet. To make longer plate girders the components must be spliced using similar shapes riveted over the main pieces. Plate girder splices are usually located one-third of the way along the length and never at the exact center. The splice design may vary, but will always have many closely spaced rivets.

The bridge girders in fig. 8 are for a load rating of E72. Consult the table for basic E30 and E50 loading girder dimensions. Stiffener angles are spaced exactly the same as for the E72 girders in fig. 8a.

KNEE AND LATERAL BRACING ON GIRDER BRIDGES

Figure 11 is a scale drawing of a 70-foot-long through plate girder bridge

that is designed for an E72 load rating. The girders in this bridge are spaced 17 feet apart, and the structure will accommodate track with a slight curve.

At the point where the floor beams are attached to the girders, additional structural support (called knee bracing) is used to keep the girders from buckling in or out. This is shown in figs. 10 and 11. These portions are fabricated of plate and angle material.

In addition to knee bracing, the bottom surfaces of the girders in fig. 11 are cross braced with 3½″ x 3½″ angles. This crossed lateral bracing is omitted on E72 loading spans 30 feet or less and on E50 and E30 loading spans 50 feet or less. Lateral bracing is usually connected to other members of the bridge assembly with steel gusset plates.

DOUBLE-TRACK BRIDGES

Double-track plate girder bridges are built in two ways. One style uses an additional central girder. For the bridge in fig. 11, such a central girder would be 12″ deeper (measured from the bottom) than the outside girders. The other style of construction uses only outside girders, but increases the depth of each by 12″.

SKEWED AND CURVED RAILROAD BRIDGES

When a bridge crosses over an obstacle at other than 90 degrees, a skewed or angled form of end construction may be employed. See fig. 11. Skewing is generally applied only to shorter spans and usually to both ends. Exceptions to this rule exist, however. For example, skewing is frequently used where a waterway is crossed at an angle and the center supporting pier of the bridge is aligned with the flow of the water to minimize damage during high water and flood conditions.

The offset distance of the shorter girder of a skewed bridge must be some multiple of the panel length, with the end meeting the girder at a stiffener plate. Notice that the double end stiffener angle arrangement is now applied at this point. Lateral bracing at the skewed end takes on a distinctive, asymmetrical shape. All the other parts remain in the normal configuration. The stringers extend beyond the end floor beam in both the squared and skewed end bridges. See fig. 11.

Railroad bridge girders are never curved. Individual straight bridge spans are arranged end to end to form a series of straight or tangent sections roughly conforming to the radius of the track curve. In model railroading the proportions of a two-girder double-track bridge can be used for a single curved track.

AVAILABLE MODEL BRIDGES

As mentioned before, modelers can construct beam and through plate girder bridges from wood, metal, or plastic structural shapes and styrene sheet and strip material. In addition, a number of bridge kits for several scales are available. Next month, we'll talk about various types of truss bridges. We'll pay close attention to their use as well as such important design characteristics as gussets, lacing, and rivet placement. ☼

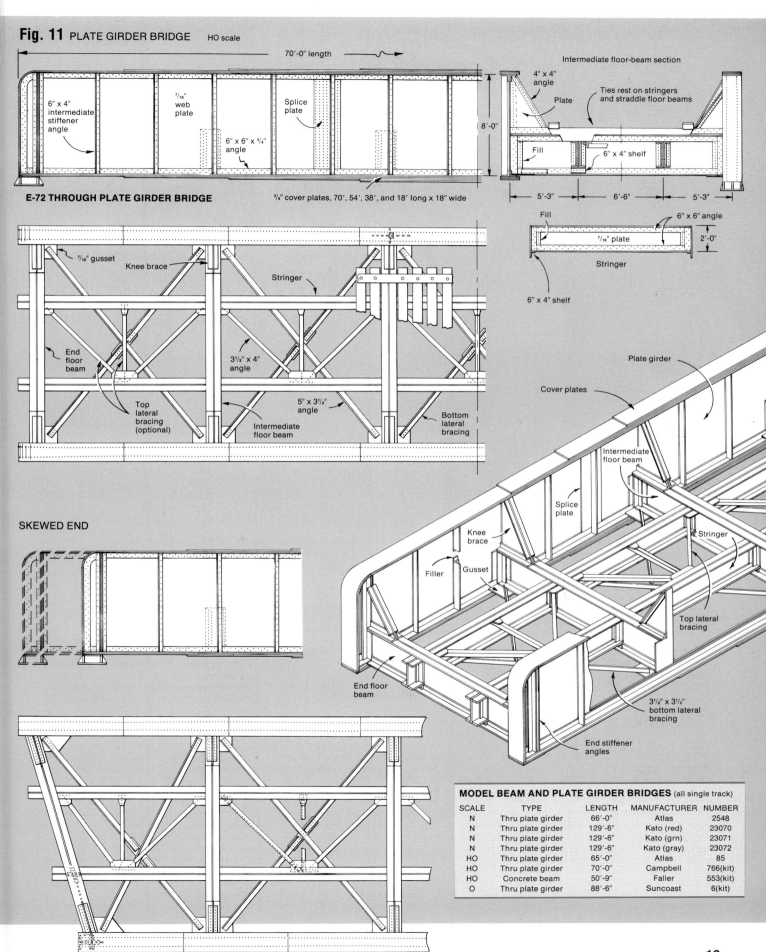

Fig. 11 PLATE GIRDER BRIDGE   HO scale

70'-0" length

6" x 4" intermediate stiffener angle

7/16" web plate

Splice plate

6" x 6" x 3/4" angle

8'-0"

E-72 THROUGH PLATE GIRDER BRIDGE

3/4" cover plates, 70', 54', 38', and 18' long x 18" wide

Intermediate floor-beam section

4" x 4" angle

Plate

Ties rest on stringers and straddle floor beams

Fill

6" x 4" shelf

5'-3"   6'-6"   5'-3"

Fill

6" x 6" angle

7/16" plate

2'-0"

Stringer

6" x 4" shelf

7/16" gusset

Knee brace

Stringer

End floor beam

3½" x 4" angle

Top lateral bracing (optional)

5" x 3½" angle

Intermediate floor beam

Bottom lateral bracing

SKEWED END

Plate girder

Cover plates

Intermediate floor beam

Splice plate

Knee brace

Filler   Gusset

Stringer

Top lateral bracing

End floor beam

3½" x 3½" bottom lateral bracing

End stiffener angles

MODEL BEAM AND PLATE GIRDER BRIDGES (all single track)

SCALE	TYPE	LENGTH	MANUFACTURER	NUMBER
N	Thru plate girder	66'-0"	Atlas	2548
N	Thru plate girder	129'-6"	Kato (red)	23070
N	Thru plate girder	129'-6"	Kato (grn)	23071
N	Thru plate girder	129'-6"	Kato (gray)	23072
HO	Thru plate girder	65'-0"	Atlas	85
HO	Thru plate girder	70'-0"	Campbell	766(kit)
HO	Concrete beam	50'-9"	Faller	553(kit)
O	Thru plate girder	88'-6"	Suncoast	6(kit)

WARREN, even number of panels (1850s)

WARREN, odd number of panels

Fig. 1 TRUSS TYPES

Charles R. Yungkurth

A Conrail pin-connected Pratt truss span at Williamsport, Pa. Lightweight tie bars are used for the tension members. The bottom chord changes from plate and lattice construction at the ends to tie bars at the center. Pin-connected bridges had the advantage of being easy to assemble at the site.

Through truss spans

The construction and proportions of through truss bridges

BY HAROLD RUSSELL

HAVING CONSIDERED beam and plate girder bridges last month, we'll now turn to truss bridges and see how truss members and through trusses are constructed. Several truss designs have emerged since the Howe truss bridge was introduced in 1840. Perhaps the most common of these is the Warren design, which dates from the 1850s. Some nineteenth-century Warren bridges, along with some Pratt and lattice designs, are still in service. Each type shown in fig. 1 has a basic style and arrangement of the pieces, though variations of each type exist.

There is a good mechanical reason for constructing truss bridges. As a bridge span increases, the depth (height) of a plate girder structure required to support it also increases. Eventually the depth becomes impractical, as governed by the rolling mills' limited manufacturing capabilities or the problems of transporting oversize materials. Then bridge engineers decide to use a truss, a fabricated structure better suited to long spans.

TYPES OF TRUSSES

Several truss bridge types are shown in fig. 1. For each basic type, the period of its first use (if known) is indicated. Probably the most common type is the Warren, which can easily be identified by the W shape of its diagonal members. It may or may not have vertical side members supporting the floor load. A simple though important variation is the quadrilateral Warren or Warren double intersecting truss, which is merely two superimposed Ws with two verticals at the end.

The Pratt truss has all diagonals sloping up and away from either side of the bridge center. On a Pratt or a Warren truss bridge with an odd number of panels the diagonals cross at the center panel. An example of this is shown at the beginning of this article.

The lattice truss, shown in fig. 2, is not as common as the Warren or the Pratt. It features many intersecting diagonals. The simple Warren and Pratt, in addition to the lattice and Whipple types, are common designs first built before 1900.

As railroad equipment grew larger toward the end of the nineteenth century,

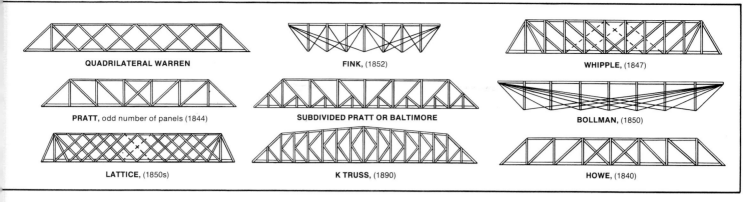

QUADRILATERAL WARREN

FINK, (1852)

WHIPPLE, (1847)

PRATT, odd number of panels (1844)

SUBDIVIDED PRATT OR BALTIMORE

BOLLMAN, (1850)

LATTICE, (1850s)

K TRUSS, (1890)

HOWE, (1840)

H. Christiansen

Fig. 2. A lattice construction bridge on the Chicago & North Western at Techny, Ill., in the 1950s. This late 19th-century design enjoyed limited use. The top bracing has laced members.

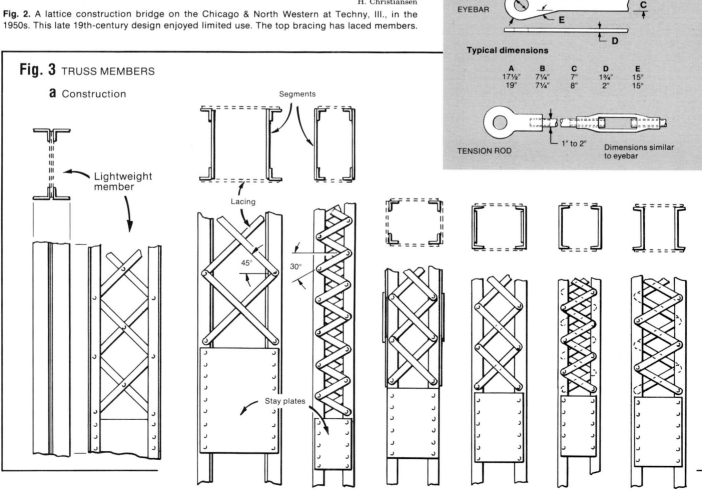

b Alternates to lacing

Perforated plates

Multiple stay plates

c Eyebars and tension rods

EYEBAR

Typical dimensions

A	B	C	D	E
17½"	7¼"	7"	1¾"	15°
19"	7¼"	8"	2"	15°

TENSION ROD — 1" to 2"   Dimensions similar to eyebar

Fig. 3 TRUSS MEMBERS

a Construction

Segments

Lightweight member

Lacing

45°   30°

Stay plates

bridge sizes increased and their general proportions got heavier. That meant that the panel lengths also had to increase. Consequently, since floor beams can attach only at a panel joint, the resulting floor system was very large and unwieldy. To keep the size of the flooring reasonable, the panel lengths were subdivided to provide more junction points. The subdivided Pratt is an example of this construction.

Since a truss requires more strength (and depth) at its center and less at the ends, engineers in the 1890s developed curved top chord bridge designs that can be applied to most trusses. As the K truss bridge design in fig. 1 shows, this top chord consists of a series of straight sections set at a slight angle to one another, rather than several curved pieces. K truss bridges can also have the diagonals face inward.

Some bridges use an additional diagonal called a counter. Counters are light tension members usually found at the bridge's center. By slanting in the opposite direction of the main diagonals they relieve compression stresses applied to the main diagonals.

The Howe truss, which was built of wood only, was common in the early days of railroading. Other early bridge designs were the Fink, and the Bollman, both of which used iron rods in tension to give them stiffness.

TRUSS MEMBER CONSTRUCTION

Truss members are usually made of channels, angles, bars, and plate sheets to form H-, I-, or box-shaped cross sections. The sides of these sections, called segments, are joined by lacing, intermittent stay plates, continuous plates, or continuous plates with cutouts. Small cross-section segments are made from channels, while larger ones are built up of plates and angles. Fig. 3 shows some configurations.

Lacing is accomplished with round end bars that are at least 3/8″ thick and about 2½″ wide. See figs. 3a and 4. The bar ends may be cut square to match the sides of the member and the intersection of the bars. When the segments are 15″ or less apart, single lacing is set at 30 degrees to the length of the segment. When their spacing is greater than 15″, double lacing set at 45 degrees is used. As close to the end of the section as possible the segments are secured with stay plates 3/8″ to ½″ thick and 1¼ to 1½ times as long as the width. Lightweight members like the I shape may have either single or double lacing.

Segments joined with plates along the entire length may have round, oval, or

Fig. 4. The flooring of this Warren truss bridge has been removed, revealing the details of the floor beam and stringer construction. Note the knee bracing used to strengthen the side truss and floor system joint. The lacing on the bottom chord has the diagonals run onto the stay plates.

Fig. 5. A 100-foot-long pin-connected Pratt truss span over the Peace River on the old Seaboard Coast Line at Zolfo Springs, Florida. The structure, which has now been scrapped, had very light construction, which included pin-connected truss rods for the top lateral bracing and counters.

Fig. 6 TRUSS MEMBER CONNECTIONS

a Gusseted joint

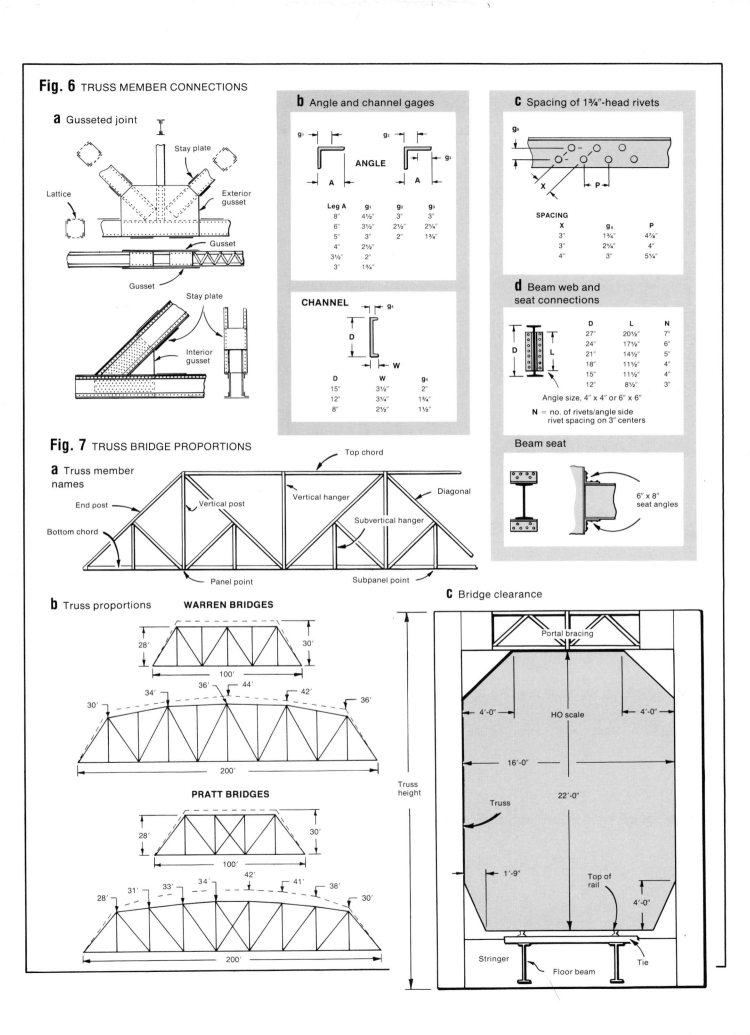

Stay plate

Lattice

Exterior gusset

Gusset

Gusset

Stay plate

Interior gusset

b Angle and channel gages

ANGLE

Leg A	g₁	g₂	g₃
8"	4½"	3"	3"
6"	3½"	2½"	2¼"
5"	3"	2"	1¾"
4"	2½"		
3½"	2"		
3"	1¾"		

CHANNEL

D	W	g₄
15"	3½"	2"
12"	3¼"	1¾"
8"	2½"	1½"

c Spacing of 1¾"-head rivets

SPACING

X	g₅	P
3"	1¾"	4⅞"
3"	2¼"	4"
4"	3"	5¼"

d Beam web and seat connections

D	L	N
27"	20½"	7"
24"	17½"	6"
21"	14½"	5"
18"	11½"	4"
15"	11½"	4"
12"	8½"	3"

Angle size, 4" x 4" or 6" x 6"

N = no. of rivets/angle side
rivet spacing on 3" centers

Beam seat

6" x 8" seat angles

Fig. 7 TRUSS BRIDGE PROPORTIONS

a Truss member names

Top chord

Vertical hanger

Diagonal

End post

Vertical post

Subvertical hanger

Bottom chord

Panel point

Subpanel point

b Truss proportions

WARREN BRIDGES

28'
30'
100'

30' 34' 36' 44' 42' 36'
200'

PRATT BRIDGES

28'
30'
100'

28' 31' 33' 34' 42' 41' 38' 30'
200'

c Bridge clearance

Portal bracing

4'-0"   HO scale   4'-0"

16'-0"

22'-0"

Truss height

Truss

1'-9"

Top of rail

4'-0"

1'-9"

Stringer

Floor beam

Tie

Gordon Odegard

Fig. 8. Above. A subdivided Pratt curved-top-chord double-track truss bridge on the Chicago & North Western in Wauwatosa, Wis. The approaches to this span over the Soo Line track and Underwood Creek are plate girder bridges. **Fig. 9. Below.** Typical bottom lateral bracing on a through truss bridge. The stringers are not as deep as the floor beams to allow clearance for the lateral bracing.

Harold Russell

rectangular holes cut in them. These reduce weight and make inspection and painting easier. Figure 3b shows some examples of this construction.

TRUSS MEMBER JOINTS

Trusses are assembled with pins, rivets, bolts, or welded joints. Bolting and welding are fairly modern techniques. Pinning, on the other hand, was popular prior to 1920 due to the ease of assembling the parts at the bridge site. As shown in fig. 3c, pin-connected truss

bridges contain tension members with eyebars and tension rods. Eyebars can also be seen on the Pratt truss bridge in fig. 5. Pins range from 6" to 12" in diameter, with 7½" being most common.

GUSSETS AND RIVETS

Members of a truss are joined together with ½"-thick plates called gussets. Rivets were originally the most common fastener, but now bolts are generally employed. Some typical gusset shapes are shown in fig. 6a, and you should see

some in the bridge photos in figs. 2 and 4. The shape is determined by the arrangement and number of pieces at the joint; the size by the number of rivets or fasteners required to carry the load.

A typical bridge rivet has a head from 1" to 2½" in diameter. Rivets (and bolts) are set in lines, called gage lines, that run parallel to the edge of the member they are fastened to. The distance between parallel gage lines is called the gage. Figure 6b shows typical gage line positions on angles and channels. Note that they are slightly off-center on the legs. The minimum spacing for a rivet with a 1¾"-diameter head (average size) is 2¼" center to center, with 3" being preferred. See fig. 6c.

Angles are the connecting shape commonly used to fasten a beam to the side of another member. Figure 6d shows typical rivet connections for beam to web, and beam seat angle to web connections. (For further clarification examine the floor beam and stringer assembly in the second part of this series, which appeared in the August MODEL RAILROADER.)

THROUGH TRUSS NOMENCLATURE AND TYPICAL PROPORTIONS

Trusses are built to definite sizes and proportions. Figure 7a identifies the various elements of a typical truss. Figure 7b shows the proportions of two Warren and two Pratt truss bridges, 100 feet and 200 feet in length. The dotted lines indicate the increased height required for double-track spans. Where there are more than two tracks, intermediate trusses must be used between the tracks.

GENERAL CHARACTERISTICS

There are some general design and proportion characteristics that, when followed, will allow you to design and construct a well-proportioned model of a truss bridge, even without exact plans.

Following the A. R. E. A. (American Railway Engineering Association) dimensions shown in fig. 7c (showing a typical portal construction), there must be a minimum clearance of no less than 22 feet. Also, no part of the bridge may fall inside the outline described. Thus, the overall height of a truss includes the minimum dimension of 22 feet plus the height of the floor system, rail, ties, and top bracing. The maximum depth of the average truss ranges from one-tenth of the span for older structures to one-sixth or one-seventh for modern bridges.

The width of a truss bridge is typically one-twentieth of its length, with a minimum inside clearance of 16 feet for single track. All panels of a span are the same length, with the diagonals set at 45 to 60 degrees to the horizontal. Bridges with an odd number of panels have a cross-braced panel at the center, and pin-connected bridges may have two or three center panels diagonally braced.

Truss bridges tend to be symmetrical about their vertical center line unless they're skewed. Those more than 150 feet long may have a curved top chord. Figure 8 shows a double-track Pratt curved-top-chord span with subdivided panels. Spans of 200 feet almost always have curved top chords.

Fig. 10 PORTALS AND TOP BRACING

a Portals

Pony truss
Knee brace
4" x 4" angles
Floor beam
Triangular-shaped bracing
Small trusses
Angles or small trusses
Top of rail
22'-0" minimum clearance

b Truss top chord bracing

TOP STRUT
TOP LATERAL

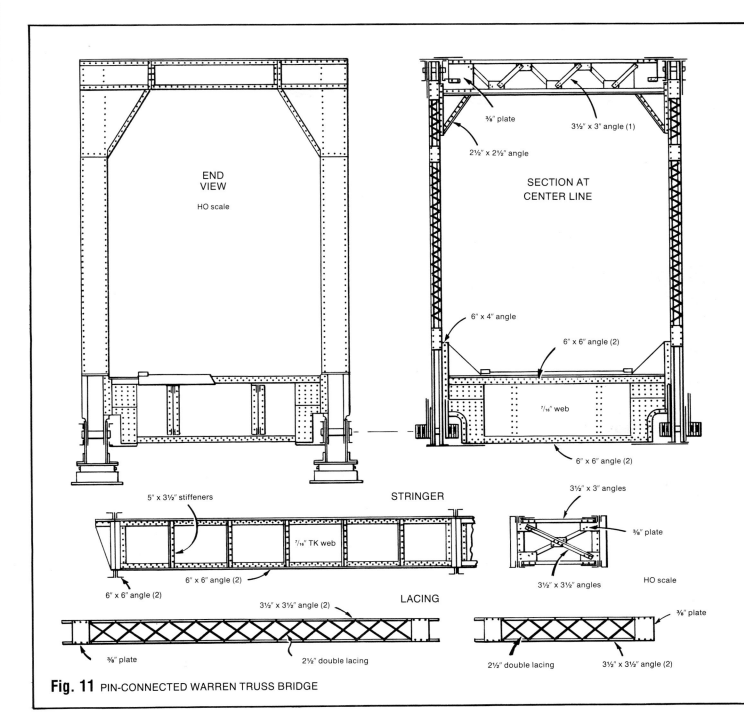

Fig. 11 PIN-CONNECTED WARREN TRUSS BRIDGE

Look carefully at fig. 4 to see how floor beams (which I described last month) and the necessary zigzag or cross bracing (usually 4" x 4" for truss bridges) are connected to the trusses at the panel points and, if they are used, at the subpanel points. The angle attachment and rivet pattern are pictured in figs. 6d and 9.

TOP AND KNEE BRACES, LATERAL STRUTS, AND PORTALS

When the height of the truss is such that the clearance exceeds the A. R. E. A. minimum, a system of bracing and lateral struts is used to connect the trusses at the top panel points, as shown in fig 10a. At the portals, the complexity of the bracing becomes more complicated as the height increases. The bracing starts with angles and develops into small trusses and large cross-braced panels. Plates or angles are used to form triangular-shaped bracing between the top and side trusses. See figs. 8 and 10b.

For spans less than 100 feet long, a short truss called a pony truss (see fig. 10a) may be used. The normal design proportions of such spans with top bracing would not be tall enough to provide the minimum clearance. For that reason, top bracing is omitted and the trusses are knee-braced. Knee braces are sometimes used on full-height trusses with top bracing, as seen on the vertical on the rear truss in fig. 4.

TYPICAL TRUSS BRIDGES

Figure 11 is a scale plan of a 160-foot-long single-track pin-connected Warren truss bridge that can be modeled in any scale. The side elevation and the bottom view are in N scale, and all the details are in HO scale. If this was a fully riveted bridge, each diagonal would be made of 13"-wide plate and four 6" x 4" edge angles. Also, the eyebars would be omitted on the lower chord, while the laced member at the end would extend the entire length of the span.

Next month, we'll turn to deck bridges and their construction, bridges on curves, information on abutments and piers, and movable bridge spans. ⚙

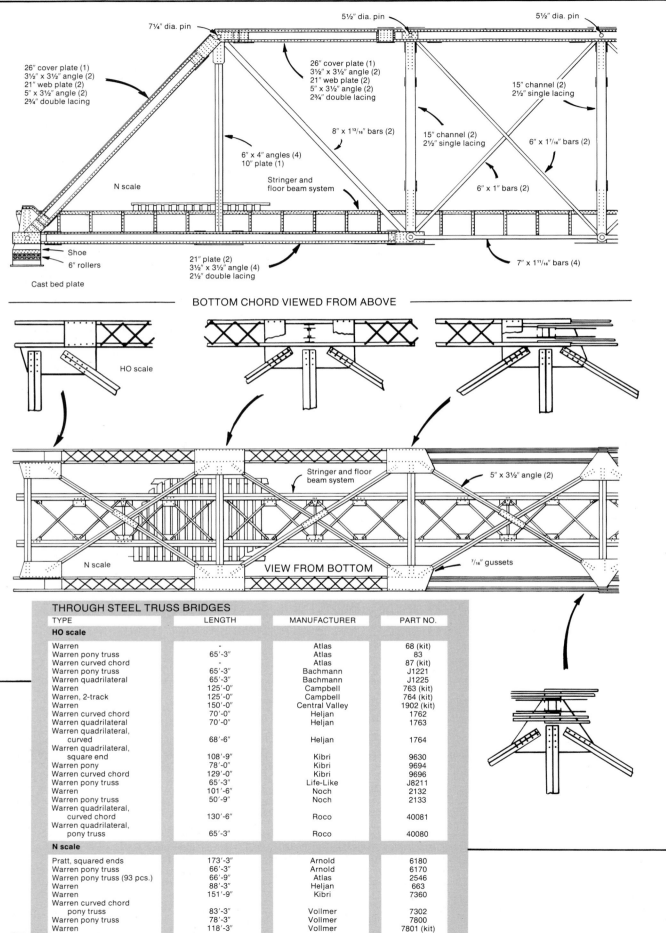

BOTTOM CHORD VIEWED FROM ABOVE

VIEW FROM BOTTOM

THROUGH STEEL TRUSS BRIDGES

TYPE	LENGTH	MANUFACTURER	PART NO.
HO scale			
Warren	-	Atlas	68 (kit)
Warren pony truss	65'-3"	Atlas	83
Warren curved chord	-	Atlas	87 (kit)
Warren pony truss	65'-3"	Bachmann	J1221
Warren quadrilateral	65'-3"	Bachmann	J1225
Warren	125'-0"	Campbell	763 (kit)
Warren, 2-track	125'-0"	Campbell	764 (kit)
Warren	150'-0"	Central Valley	1902 (kit)
Warren curved chord	70'-0"	Heljan	1762
Warren quadrilateral	70'-0"	Heljan	1763
Warren quadrilateral, curved	68'-6"	Heljan	1764
Warren quadrilateral, square end	108'-9"	Kibri	9630
Warren pony	78'-0"	Kibri	9694
Warren curved chord	129'-0"	Kibri	9696
Warren pony truss	65'-3"	Life-Like	J8211
Warren	101'-6"	Noch	2132
Warren pony truss	50'-9"	Noch	2133
Warren quadrilateral, curved chord	130'-6"	Roco	40081
Warren quadrilateral, pony truss	65'-3"	Roco	40080
N scale			
Pratt, squared ends	173'-3"	Arnold	6180
Warren pony truss	66'-3"	Arnold	6170
Warren pony truss (93 pcs.)	66'-9"	Atlas	2546
Warren	88'-3"	Heljan	663
Warren	151'-9"	Kibri	7360
Warren curved chord pony truss	83'-3"	Vollmer	7302
Warren pony truss	78'-3"	Vollmer	7800
Warren	118'-3"	Vollmer	7801 (kit)

Jim Shaughnessy

This long bridge across the Hudson River on the Boston & Maine RR consists of a series of equal-sized Warren deck truss spans set on piers.

Deck bridges and movable spans

Top-track-mounted and movable bridges and supports

BY HAROLD RUSSELL

AFTER SPENDING the first parts of this series describing through bridges, we'll now turn to the alternative configuration — the deck bridge. On deck bridges girders or trusses support the roadbed or floor from underneath rather than straddling it. A deck bridge is usually a simpler structure than a through design and requires less material. In some cases no network of floor beams and stringers is required. Deck bridges use the same basic open and ballasted flooring that was described in part two, which appeared in the August MODEL RAILROADER.

A deck bridge configuration can be used only where there is ample clearance beneath for highway, water, or railroad traffic. When crossing water sufficient clearance is also required for floodwaters and related debris. The construction of the girders and trusses for deck bridges is largely the same as for through bridges (refer to the second and third parts of the ABCs of Bridges), though some structural changes are necessary. Plate girders are used for deck bridges 20 to 150 feet in length and trusses for bridges more than

Rock Island Lines photo

Fig. 1. The deck plate girder spans at the center of this Rock Island Lines bridge over the Skunk River in Iowa are longer and deeper than the adjacent spans.

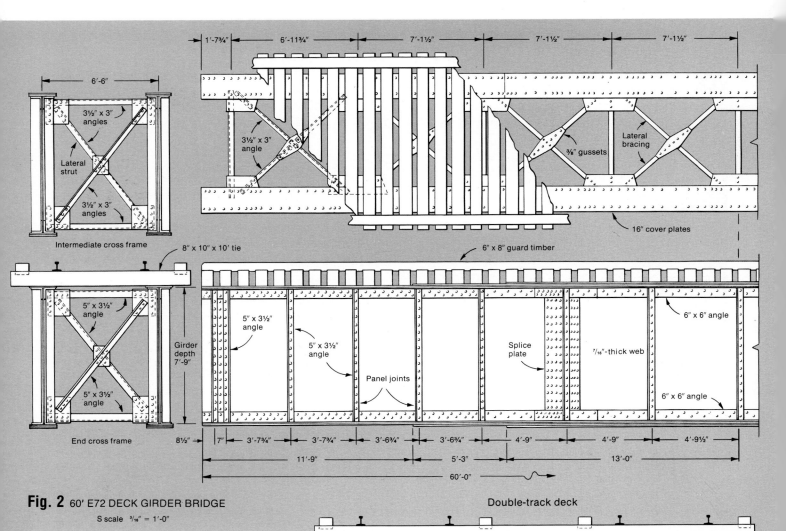

Fig. 2 60' E72 DECK GIRDER BRIDGE

S scale ³/₁₆" = 1'-0"

Intermediate cross frame

Lateral strut

3½" x 3" angles

3½" x 3" angles

3½" x 3" angle

⅜" gussets

Lateral bracing

16" cover plates

8" x 10" x 10' tie

6" x 8" guard timber

5" x 3½" angle

5" x 3½" angle

5" x 3½" angle

5" x 3½" angle

Girder depth 7'-9"

End cross frame

6" x 6" angle

Splice plate

Panel joints

⁷/₁₆"-thick web

6" x 6" angle

Double-track deck

Top bracing

Bottom bracing

100 feet long, for the same reasons given for through bridges last month.

Another bridge form to be covered is the movable span, which uses modified plate girder or truss supporting structures in either through or deck configuration. We'll discuss several basic motion designs used by bridge builders.

DECK PLATE GIRDER BRIDGES

Figure 1 shows a series of deck plate girder bridges and piers crossing a floodplain in Iowa. There are two different depths of plate girders, with longer spans at the center. Drawings of a typical 60-foot-long single-track span with an E72 load rating are shown in fig. 2.

For spans up to 70 feet long, the girders are spaced 6'-6" apart, center to center. For those more than 70 feet in length, the spacing is 7'-6". A series of horizontal- and cross-braced frames at the end and at each panel point is used to separate the girders. Consult the table in fig. 8 of part two for the necessary dimensions of these parts. Note that the bracing angles which separate the plate girders are referred to as "vertical frames, ends" if they relate to braces at the ends of the span and "vertical frames, intermediate" if they relate to those at the panel points. Returning to fig. 2, you'll

see an end view indicating a typical double-track bridge. It consists of two single-track spans fastened together with top and bottom lateral bracing.

DECK TRUSS BRIDGES

Model railroaders frequently turn a through truss bridge upside down to make a deck span. On prototype railroads, however, the truss construction is left in the same position as for a through bridge, but is modified by replacing, first, the floor beams with top lateral struts (the same pieces used on the deck plate girder bridge shown in fig. 2) and then, if necessary, the top lateral cross bracing with a system of floor beams as well as stringers.

In addition, some alterations have to be made to the ends of the trusses, as shown in fig. 3, and the end bracing. The top chord is always extended to the end of the bridge. For a Warren truss, where the open flooring rests directly on the top chord, an end post will be added to the extended top chord. The Pratt truss has two configurations shown. One has end posts and a square end, while on the other the lower chord is angled up to the top chord, leaving a space for the end support. The Pratt configurations are used mainly on long spans having trusses spaced widely apart for rigidity.

BRIDGES ON CURVES

Bridges for curved track cost more to

22

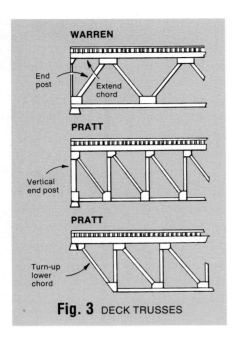

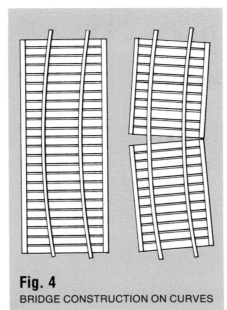

Fig. 3 DECK TRUSSES

WARREN
- End post
- Extend chord

PRATT
- Vertical end post

PRATT
- Turn-up lower chord

Fig. 4
BRIDGE CONSTRUCTION ON CURVES

build than those for straight track, which is one reason railroads avoid curves on bridges wherever possible. There is no such thing as a steel bridge with curved trusses; in fact, until quite recently no curved plate girder bridges existed either.

Two ways that railroads handle curves are shown in fig. 4. Sometimes the structure is made wider and the rails curved through the straight bridge. For long bridges engineers design a series of short spans that are joined at an angle at frequent intervals.

ABUTMENTS, PIERS, AND BENTS

An abutment is a structural support for the end of a bridge that is usually positioned with land against one surface. Abutments have been made of wood, stone, and concrete, and each material has its own advantages. Wood, for example, is cheaper than masonry, but does not last as long. Stone, which is more pleasing in appearance (especially on a model railroad), was the most common building material until around 1920. Since that time, concrete abutments have predominated. A typical abutment configuration is shown in fig. 5a, with a table of dimensions.

Although stone abutments have the same general proportions as concrete ones, their design is different. Most stone abutments have the tops of the wings (the angled sections reaching out on both sides of the portion to support the bridge structure) stepped, whereas the tops of concrete wings are usually sloped. On a stone structure using random or irregularly sized stones, the smaller stones are always placed near the top. Cut stone, which is trimmed to specific and regular shapes, may also be used. Supports or pedestals never rest directly over a joint between stones.

Fig. 5 ABUTMENTS AND PIERS

a Abutment dimensions

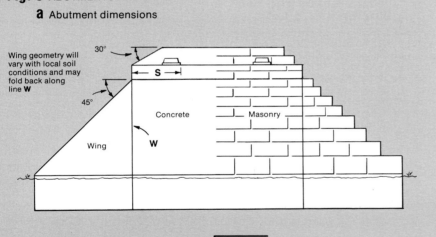

Wing geometry will vary with local soil conditions and may fold back along line **W**

30°
45°
Concrete
Masonry
Wing
W
S

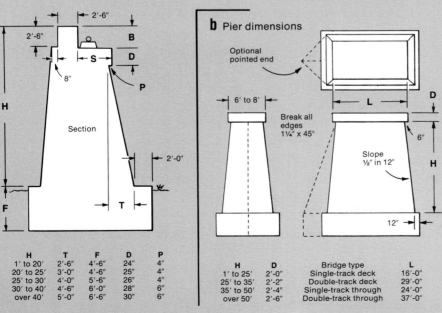

Section

H	T	F	D	P
1' to 20'	2'-6"	4'-6"	24"	4"
20' to 25'	3'-0"	4'-6"	25"	4"
25' to 30'	4'-0"	5'-6"	26"	4"
30' to 40'	4'-6"	6'-0"	28"	6"
over 40'	5'-0"	6'-6"	30"	6"

b Pier dimensions

Optional pointed end

6' to 8'

Break all edges 1¼" x 45"

Slope ½" in 12"

L

D

6"

H

12"

H	D	Bridge type	L
1' to 25'	2'-0"	Single-track deck	16'-0"
25' to 35'	2'-2"	Double-track deck	29'-0"
35' to 50'	2'-4"	Single-track through	24'-0"
over 50'	2'-6"	Double-track through	37'-0"

C Complex piers

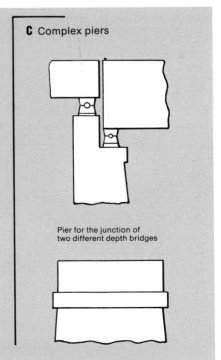

Pier for the junction of two different depth bridges

A pier is a solid structure, usually made from masonry, used as an intermediate support for a single bridge or the junction of two spans on a longer bridge. We may think of a pier as being located in water, but this is not always true. A typical pier is shown in fig. 5b, along with a table of dimensions. Piers can have square, round, or pointed ends. When used in water, the end that faces upstream may be pointed to deflect flood debris while the downstream end can be square or rounded. See fig. 6. Some piers have wood cribbing around them for added protection.

There are cases in which two bridges with different depths or styles use a common pier. The geometry of such a pier is shown in figs. 5c and 7.

At this point, I should also mention the bent, a trestle-like frame structure of wood or steel that supports a steel bridge in a manner similar to a pier. However, extended discussion of such structures must wait until the fifth part of this series.

PEDESTALS

Short beam and plate girder bridges as well as arch bridges all rest directly on simple supports at the ends. As a bridge's span gets longer and larger, engineers rely on a more complicated system of pedestals. Figures 8 and 9 show several styles.

The simplest pedestal consists of pairs of heavy steel base plates. The pair at one end is fixed, while that at the other end is allowed to slide to compensate for whatever horizontal movement is produced by expansion and contraction of the steel work and load stresses.

As a bridge increases in length, pedestals are built to distribute the bridge's weight onto the abutment or pier. Again, one end is fixed to its support with bolts, while the other has a movable mounting to accommodate movement caused by expansion and contraction of the structure and the forces applied to the span. Spans more than 70 feet in length will have a moving pedestal with a system of rockers or rollers.

Both photos by Harold Russell

Fig. 6. left: Bridge piers are usually pointed and tapered on the upstream side to deflect flood debris. Downstream ends may be square. An interesting detail is the lines left in the concrete by boards used for the forms. **Fig. 7. right:** Stepped piers are made to accommodate plate girder and/or truss spans of different depths. The end of the span at the left is the one secured to the pier with bolts.

SWING BRIDGE AND DRAWBRIDGE SPANS

When a bridge crosses a navigable waterway and does not have sufficient clearance for passing ships, a movable span is employed. It should be noted that water traffic has the right-of-way over railroad traffic. Figure 10 shows several configurations of swing bridges and drawbridges. The general construction of the plate girders and trusses follows the same principles as for fixed bridges, but these components are heavier in construction and have different supports. Swing bridges rotate around a vertical axis, while balanced drawbridges (also called bascule bridges) rotate up and down about a horizontal axis.

SWING BRIDGES

The concept of a railroad swing bridge is not a modern one, as railroad wood truss swing spans were constructed in the second half of the nineteenth century. Before 1910 the most common movable bridge was the swing bridge. Plate girder swing bridges (fig. 10a) are generally shorter than truss bridges (fig. 10b), with the latter ranging in length from 200 to 520 feet. Figure 11 shows an unusual offset swing bridge with a concrete counterweight at the left end. On most swing spans the structure is identical on both sides of the center. Turntables should also be considered a type of swing bridge.

When closed for railroad traffic, a swing bridge is locked into position at the ends and center, and the structure acts like two separate bridges with a common support at the center. For this reason, truss swing bridges have portal construction (see fig. 10 in the third part of this series) at the center as well as the

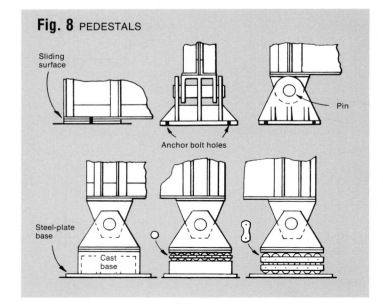

Fig. 8 PEDESTALS

Sliding surface

Anchor bolt holes

Pin

Steel-plate base

Cast base

Harold Russell

Fig. 9. Two different types of pedestals. The left one is a sliding plate version while the other one is rigidly mounted to the pier.

ends. The top chords of some swing bridges are pin connected at the center, which allows for tension and compression in the span halves when the span is unlocked and open or locked in the closed position.

The running rails are hinged at the ends of the swing bridge and are mechanically swung up before the bridge is moved. See fig. 10c. Also used are wedges located between the bottom of the bridge and the abutments, which support the bridge ends when the span is closed. Electric motors usually drive the mechanisms that control the rail lifts and wedges and turn the span. Their controls are located in a small house built on top of the bridge's center or off to one side at track level. See fig. 11. The locks, wedges, turning controls, and signals controlling the passage of trains over the bridge are often interlocked so they operate in the proper sequence.

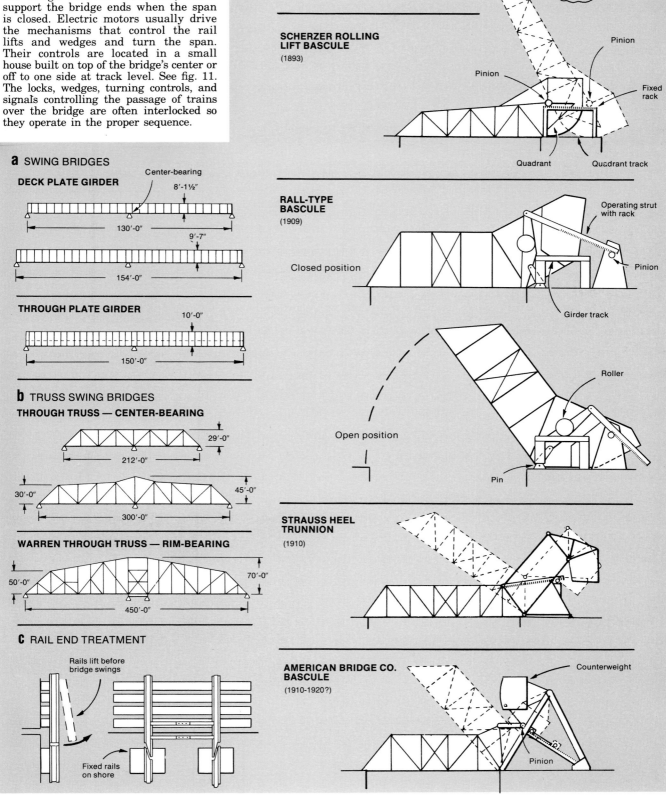

Fig. 10 MOVABLE BRIDGE SPANS

a SWING BRIDGES

DECK PLATE GIRDER

Center-bearing
8'-1½"
130'-0"
9'-7"
154'-0"

THROUGH PLATE GIRDER

10'-0"
150'-0"

b TRUSS SWING BRIDGES

THROUGH TRUSS — CENTER-BEARING

29'-0"
212'-0"
30'-0"
45'-0"
300'-0"

WARREN THROUGH TRUSS — RIM-BEARING

50'-0"
70'-0"
450'-0"

c RAIL END TREATMENT

Rails lift before bridge swings
Fixed rails on shore

d BASCULE BRIDGES

SIMPLE HEEL TRUNNION BASCULE (1894)

Counterweight
Pinion

SCHERZER ROLLING LIFT BASCULE (1893)

Pinion
Pinion
Fixed rack
Quadrant
Quadrant track

RALL-TYPE BASCULE (1909)

Operating strut with rack
Closed position
Pinion
Girder track
Roller
Open position
Pin

STRAUSS HEEL TRUNNION (1910)

AMERICAN BRIDGE CO. BASCULE (1910-1920?)

Counterweight
Pinion

Fig. 11. Built in 1904 for the Milwaukee Road, this offset center-bearing swing bridge over the Menomonee River in Milwaukee, Wisconsin, has a heavy concrete counterweight at the left to keep the bridge in balance.

A typical center-bearing swing bridge has a 12"- to 36"-diameter bearing at the center connected to the side trusses or girders by a crossed girder assembly. Eight or more balance wheels, each about 18" in diameter, roll on a circular track to prevent the structure from tipping. Most plate girders are center-bearing types.

By contrast, rim-bearing swing bridges are supported by conical rollers riding on a circular girder whose dimensions tend to surpass the bridge's width. Engineers use as many rollers as the geometry will permit. See the curved chord truss bridge in fig. 10b. Rim-bearing spans have a four-post tower (square formation) at the center, while center-bearing types have a two-post tower. Most long bridges are rim-bearing types.

The concrete pier on which the bridge rests is often long, narrow, and pointed at the ends. Wood piles are driven around the periphery to protect the support and bridge from damage from debris and water vessels.

BASCULE BRIDGES

Bascule bridges, with a movable span called a leaf, rotate on a horizontal axis or trunnion and have a large counterweight to offset the weight of the leaf. The opening action is one of lifting and/or rolling backwards in a singular motion. Design of modern practical leaf-type bridges began in 1894, with the construction of the Tower Bridge in London, a steel simple heel trunnion bascule bridge. This type consists of a truss or girder leaf counterbalanced with a weight, as shown in fig. 10d. All the different designs appear to have been conceived between 1894 and 1915.

A single-leaf bascule bridge has one movable section, while a double leaf has two that meet at the center and are hinged at the extremities. Double-leaf spans are often used for highways, where the quick opening and closing action is desirable, and precise end alignment is not critical. They are seldom used for railroads.

The most popular bascule bridge is the Scherzer rolling lift. As the pinion (a small driving gear) rotates along a fixed horizontal track, the bridge structure rocks or rolls back on the quadrant track (near track level), the leaf rises, and the counterweight lowers. See figs. 10d and 12.

Fig. 12. The Canadian National Rys. utilizes a pair of double-track Scherzer rolling lift bascule bridges to cross the Welland Canal. The independent spans use a common center pier. This style of bridge contains the simplest of the bascule mechanisms, which makes it the easiest to maintain. The approach spans are deck plate girder bridges.

Donald Sims

Harold Russell

Fig. 13. left: This Southern Pacific bascule bridge in Beaumont, Tex., was built by the American Bridge Co. Clearly visible are the struts to the top chord of the truss and counterweight, as well as the inclined rack.
Fig. 14. below left: Each of the towers on this vertical lift bridge over Canada's Welland Canal has both a drive mechanism and a counterweight. As the bridge is raised the counterweights block highway traffic. A railroad lift bridge would be a more substantial structure than one built for highway traffic.

MODEL DECK BRIDGES

kits unless noted RTR (ready-to-run)

Type	Length (in feet)	Manufacturer	Part no.
HO:			
Warren truss	70	Atlas	84 RTR
Plate girder	65¼	Campbell	165
Plate girder	50	Micro Engineering	501
Plate girder	30	Micro Engineering	502
Plate girder	65¼	Model Masterpieces	126
Lattice truss	50¾	Pola	808 RTR
HOn3:			
Plate girder	50	Micro Engineering	503
Plate girder	30	Micro Engineering	504
N:			
Warren truss	66¾	Atlas	2547 RTR
Plate girder	50	Micro Engineering	150
Plate girder	30	Micro Engineering	151

MOVABLE SPANS

N:			
Scherzer rolling lift plate girder	?	Model Power	1504 RTR

ABUTMENTS AND PIERS

O:		
Cut stone abut.	A. I. M.	100
Field stone abut.	A. I. M.	101
Random stone abut.	A. I. M.	104
Cut stone abut.	Thos. A. Yorke	1240
HO:		
Cut stone abut.	A. I. M.	100
Field stone abut.	A. I. M.	101
Random stone abut.	A. I. M.	104
Concrete abut.	A. I. M.	118
Cut stone pier	Atlas	825
Cut stone abut.	Chooch	7027
Cut stone abut., 2-track	Chooch	7028
Cut stone pier	Chooch	7030
Cut stone abut.	Chooch	7039
Cut stone abut.	Faller	547
Cut stone pier	Faller	549
Cut stone abut.	Faller	556
Cut stone piers	Heljan	1765
Random stone pier	Kibri	9690
Random stone abut.	Kibri	9691
Cut stone abut.	Model Masterpieces	133
Cut stone pier	Model Masterpieces	135
Cut stone abut.	Mountains in Minutes	825
Cut stone pier	Roco	40082
Cut stone pier	Vollmer	2530
Cut stone abut.	Vollmer	2531
Concrete abut.	Vollmer	4016
Cut stone pier	Vollmer	4512
N:		
Cut stone abut.	A. I. M.	200
Random stone abut.	A. I. M.	204
Cut stone piers	Arnold	6168
Cut stone piers	Arnold	6222
Cut stone piers	Arnold	6223
Cut stone piers	Arnold	6224
Cut stone pier	Arnold	7810
Cut stone abut.	Arnold	7820
Concrete piers	Atlas	2543
Cut stone abut.	Chooch	9520
Cut stone abut., 2-track	Chooch	9521
Concrete abut., 2-track	Chooch	9523
Cut stone pier	Heljan	664

When Rall-type bascule bridges are closed, they are supported by a pin with rollers raised off their girder tracks. See fig. 10d. To raise the bridge the pinions rotate against the racks on the operating struts. As the leaf begins to rise, the rollers contact the girder track and the bridge weight is transferred from the pin to the rollers. The entire leaf then rolls and recedes along the track.

A Strauss heel trunnion bridge has a single pivot or trunnion axis. The fixed position pinions rotate against the rack on the operating struts, which pulls the struts back and raises the leaf. The counterweight, attached to the top chord of the bridge with pivoted struts, swings down to offset the weight of the span.

The American Bridge Co. bascule in fig. 10d is similar to the Strauss heel trunnion. Here the moving pinion turns against a fixed rack and pulls the operating struts to raise the leaf. Figure 13 shows an example of this type of bridge.

VERTICAL LIFT BRIDGES

A vertical lift bridge raises its movable span up from both ends, much like an elevator. See fig. 14. The first modern example was a 130-foot-long span with a lift of 155 feet that was built in Chicago in 1892. Many more such bridges were built between 1910 and 1930.

Small vertical lift bridges have two supporting posts at each end, while larger bridges have four-post towers and may have a truss connecting the two towers at the top. The counterweights, one at each end, are attached to the lift bridge with many cables. A single power source is used to synchronize the movement of the cables so the span is lifted in a square attitude.

Vertical lift bridges are almost always single track. If multiple tracks are served, two or more lift spans are constructed side by side. Lift bridges are generally not skewed.

As usual, I have added a list of available models of some of the bridges mentioned. Next month, in the fifth part of the ABCs of Bridges, I will focus on trestles. Specifically, I'll discuss wood and steel trestles, trestle bent supports for steel truss and plate girder bridges, and viaducts. See you then. ✿

CP Rail photo

ABCs of bridges: 5

Trestles, arches, and viaducts

Bridge types that date from railroading's early days

BY HAROLD RUSSELL

ALTHOUGH THE TERMS "trestle" and "viaduct" are often confused, there is a distinction between the two, as this part of the ABCs of Bridges will explain. Also, the components of a trestle and the materials used to build these types of structures will be covered. All of this should help when you decide to add anything from a simple low trestle to an elaborate viaduct to your layout.

First, though, let's get our terms straight. A trestle is an open, braced framework, made of wood or steel, that supports the roadbed of a highway or railroad. It consists of a series of identical (or nearly so) vertical supports holding up a succession of short spans, as shown above in the Canadian Pacific photo. By contrast, a viaduct is a bridge resting on a series of reinforced concrete or masonry arches having high towers or piers, as shown in fig. 2. The dictionary also defines it as a steel bridge made up of short spans carried on high steel towers, a definition that, as I will show, could well include some steel trestles.

TIMBER TRESTLES

In the early days of railroading, wood was plentiful and the timber trestle was a commonly used structure, especially where deep canyons and ravines had to be crossed. Tall timber trestles have not been used on mainline railroads for some time. However, some roads have continued to build short and low wooden trestles. Such a trestle is shown in fig. 1. The timber used for present-day trestles is pressure-treated with a preservative; previously, the wood was treated with creosote.

There is no fixed or standard trestle design, and the construction has varied among different railroads. When building a realistic model, though, there are some general construction principles to follow. An important structural feature to remember is that all wood portions of a wood trestle or bridge are designed to be in compression and never in tension.

BENTS

The floor system of a trestle, which is like the open flooring used on steel bridges, is supported by structures called bents. See fig. 3. There are two types of bents. The pile bent has round posts or vertical members, usually 12" in diameter, that are driven directly into the ground. The frame bent has 12"-square posts and a horizontal bottom support member called a sill, and it rests on a separate foundation (fig. 3a). The number of posts in each bent and the spacing between bents are determined by the E load rating. Trestles with low E ratings have only four posts. More posts are added to compensate for higher E ratings, as indicated by the table in fig. 3.

Figure 3c shows the 12"-square cap found at the top of both pile and frame bents. On a single-track structure it tends to be 14 to 16 feet long. Figure 3f shows common post spacing. If, on a pile bent, a post's diameter is greater than 12", the top is angled to 12" to prevent water from collecting. Posts on frame

bents rarely exceed 12″ square; so they do not need such angling.

The center post or posts are always vertical, the outer posts "battered" or angled 2″ to 3″ per foot, and the intermediate posts battered 1″ to 1½″ per foot. The batter of the outermost posts should be twice that of the intermediate posts.

Limited by the length of available wood material (generally no longer than 60 feet), pile bents are not made higher than 30 feet. A prime reason is because each post is a single piece, and a sizable portion of the length must be driven into the ground for support. In addition, the round configuration is not easily adapted to the construction of tall trestles. Piles are always driven with the narrow diameter down.

Frame bents are also made shorter than 30 feet, though they can be built

Lackawanna RR photo

Harold Russell

Fig. 1. Above: A fairly recent timber trestle on the Family Lines south of Ft. Myers, Fla. Like most modern trestles, a ballasted deck is used for the track. **Fig. 2. Below:** Paulins Kill concrete viaduct near Harrisburg, N. J., was built between 1900 and 1910. The structure is 1100 feet long and 117 feet high.

higher. However, building any bent more than 30 feet high *requires* a framed construction as shown in fig. 3e. Such bents are divided into stories, separated by horizontal intermediate 12″-square sills, which in turn are separated by 10″ x 12″ purlins running the length of the trestle. The stories are further subdivided by pairs of 3″ x 10″ horizontal cross braces known as sashes. Purlins also serve as bracing between bents, since they attach to every bent. An alternative to purlins are 6″ x 8″ girts, which are horizontal timbers placed atop the sashes or sills (fig. 3g).

The bottom of a frame bent is attached to a 12″-square sill, which is then bolted to a concrete or masonry foundation. This sill may also be set upon a series of piles driven into the ground, with one directly below each post.

SWAY BRACING

Bents that are more than 10 feet high require 3″ x 10″ sway bracing for reinforcement. Such bracing is attached to the cap, posts, and sills at an angle somewhere between 30 and 60 degrees. Bridge engineers tend to prefer 45 degrees. Typical sway bracing is shown in figs. 3b and 3d.

Figure 4a shows typical timber connections using square-headed nuts and bolts, and flat- and cast-iron washers. Scale nut-bolt-washer castings can be used to simulate these joints in a model trestle. The cap is attached to the top of the bent with drift pins (1″ in diameter and 24″ in length), while bracing is sometimes secured with spikes having 1″-square heads. A flat washer is generally placed under the spike head. See fig. 4b.

Framed posts are secured to the bottom sill with drift pins driven in at an angle. See fig. 4c. The sill is secured to a concrete foundation with bolts that were set vertically in the concrete foundation as it was being poured. A pile foundation as previously described may also be used.

Sometimes a combination bent is employed on a tall trestle, with the lower story of pile construction capped with a sill and a framed story construction continuing upward.

PIERS

Trestles are rarely used to cross water more than a few feet deep. When they are, a bent is left out of the construction and a long wood or steel deck or truss bridge is inserted. Two to four bents are grouped together to form a pier to support both the trestle flooring and the bridge. Crisscrossed 12″-square timbers are placed on top of the piers to form a solid base to distribute the load. The Toledo, Peoria & Western RR bridge shown in fig. 5 nicely illustrates this.

BENT-TO-BENT BRACING

To make the structure rigid along the length, trestles more than 10 feet high are secured with girts or purlins as previously described. But, in addition to these elements, the structure is stiffened with wall bracing. This bracing lies parallel to the sides of the trestle and connects the posts of adjacent bents with

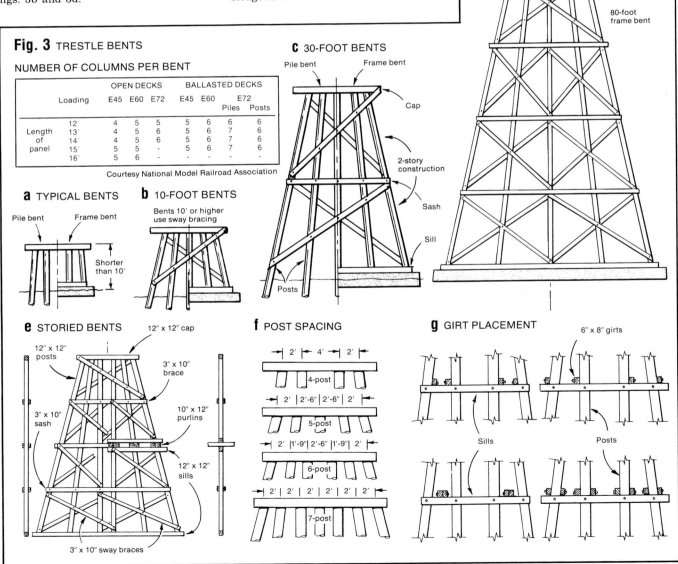

Fig. 3 TRESTLE BENTS

NUMBER OF COLUMNS PER BENT

		OPEN DECKS			BALLASTED DECKS			
	Loading	E45	E60	E72	E45	E60	E72	
							Piles	Posts
Length of panel	12′	4	5	5	5	6	6	6
	13′	4	5	6	5	6	7	6
	14′	4	5	6	5	6	7	6
	15′	5	5	-	5	6	7	6
	16′	5	6	-	-	-	-	-

Courtesy National Model Railroad Association

a TYPICAL BENTS

Pile bent Frame bent

Shorter than 10′

b 10-FOOT BENTS

Bents 10′ or higher use sway bracing

c 30-FOOT BENTS

Pile bent Frame bent

Cap

2-story construction

Sash

Sill

Posts

d 5-STORY BENT

80-foot frame bent

e STORIED BENTS

12″ x 12″ cap
12″ x 12″ posts
3″ x 10″ brace
3″ x 10″ sash
10″ x 12″ purlins
12″ x 12″ sills
3″ x 10″ sway braces

f POST SPACING

2′ 4′ 2′
4-post

2′ 2′-6″ 2′-6″ 2′
5-post

2′ 1′-9″ 2′-6″ 1′-9″ 2′
6-post

2′ 2′ 2′ 2′ 2′ 2′
7-post

g GIRT PLACEMENT

6″ x 8″ girts

Sills

Posts

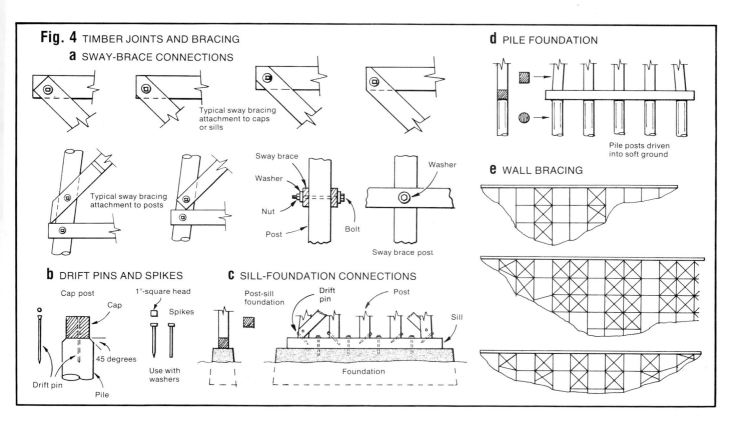

Fig. 4 TIMBER JOINTS AND BRACING

a SWAY-BRACE CONNECTIONS

Typical sway bracing attachment to caps or sills

Typical sway bracing attachment to posts

Sway brace
Washer
Washer
Nut
Post
Bolt
Washer
Sway brace post

b DRIFT PINS AND SPIKES

Cap post
Cap
1"-square head
Spikes
45 degrees
Drift pin
Pile
Use with washers

c SILL-FOUNDATION CONNECTIONS

Post-sill foundation
Drift pin
Post
Sill
Foundation

d PILE FOUNDATION

Pile posts driven into soft ground

e WALL BRACING

---

crossed pieces. (Examples of wall bracing are shown in fig. 4e.) Wall bracing is generally the same size as sway bracing and has the same angle specifications.

The space between two bents is called a panel, and there are some American Railway Engineering Association rules about how many panels need to be wall-braced. According to these rules, trestles higher than 15 feet and at least 100 feet in length are braced every third panel. Trestles two or more stories high should be braced every second and third panel. Of course, trestles of all heights may be braced every panel. In general, more panels are wall-braced as the structure gets higher and longer.

To connect the ends of the caps engineers occasionally erect bent-to-bent longitudinal bracing, which parallels the length of the trestle. In this method of bracing the pieces are notched 1" deep at the caps. See fig. 6a. Builders may also use another type of lateral bracing that consists of cross-braced 6" x 6" timbers. These pieces are set under the longitudinal bracing as shown in fig. 6a.

TRESTLE FLOOR SYSTEMS

The flooring system starts with stringers that are set on edge atop the bent caps, which in turn support the bridge ties. The tie part of the floor system is essentially the same as for the open deck plate and truss bridges described earlier in this series.

Wood trestles typically have a bent spacing of 12 to 18 feet. Each stringer is long enough to span at least two panels. Two-inch-thick wood packing blocks (or metal washers) are placed between the stringers, which are then bolted together. Figures 6a and 6b show the stringer system for open deck floors,

while figs. 6c, 6d, 6e, and 6f show it for ballasted deck floors. Builders may either butt the stringers end to end or lap them as shown. The size, number, spacing, and length of the stringers, as well as the bent spacing determine the load the trestle can carry. Consult the table in fig. 6.

Stringer joints may be strengthened with corbels (fig. 6g). Corbels, which are usually 10" x 10" or 12" x 12" and 36" to 48" long, are placed on the cap under the stringers. Varying the corbels' thickness enables engineers to adjust the height of the bents to compensate for irregularities and keep the floor even and level.

Harold Russell

Fig. 5. Timber trestle bents are sometimes used to support steel bridges, as in the case of this Toledo, Peoria & Western RR bridge near Le Harpe, Ill. To distribute the load between there are short crosswise timbers between the bent caps and the single cap supporting the steel beams of the floor.

Fig. 6 TRESTLE FLOORING

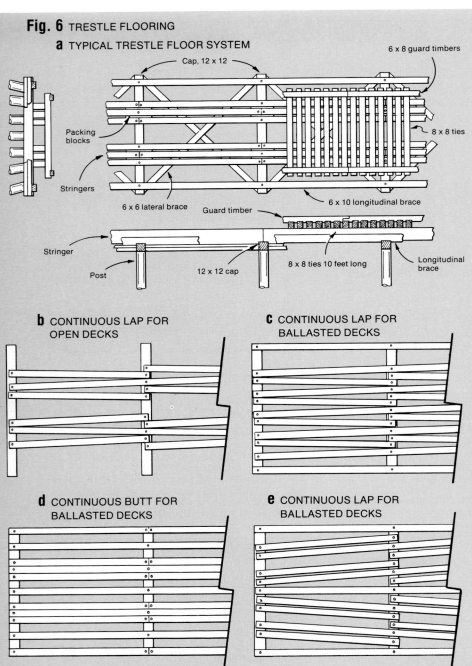

a TYPICAL TRESTLE FLOOR SYSTEM

6 x 8 guard timbers
Cap, 12 x 12
Packing blocks
8 x 8 ties
Stringers
6 x 6 lateral brace
Guard timber
6 x 10 longitudinal brace
Stringer
Post
12 x 12 cap
8 x 8 ties 10 feet long
Longitudinal brace

b CONTINUOUS LAP FOR OPEN DECKS

c CONTINUOUS LAP FOR BALLASTED DECKS

d CONTINUOUS BUTT FOR BALLASTED DECKS

e CONTINUOUS LAP FOR BALLASTED DECKS

Figure 6f shows the ballasted deck configuration, which has been used primarily since 1900. Because this system is heavier than the open deck, it requires a stronger construction. Also, a ballasted deck trestle bent of a specific E load rating will have one more post than an open deck version.

Engineers space the bridge ties on a modern open floor trestle 4″ apart. Those ties are 8″ square and, though lengths from 9 to 14 feet may be used, are usually 10 feet long. Prior to 1900, however, 6″ x 8″ ties were commonly used. Bridge ties are spiked to the stringers with ½″ x 10″-long spikes. Ties used on a ballasted deck are of standard roadbed dimension and set in ballast.

Look carefully at figs. 6a, 7, and 8a and you'll find guard timbers. These 6″ x 8″ timbers are positioned 2″ from the ends of the ties on open flooring and run the entire length of the trestle. They help maintain the spacing of the ties and retain derailed car trucks on the bridge. Guard timbers are at least two panels long, are notched to receive the ties, and are lap-jointed. Bolts or spikes fasten these timbers to the ties.

WALKWAYS AND FIRE PROTECTION

Walkways, found on one or both sides of a trestle, are supported by extended-length ties, as I mentioned in part two. They are more prevalent on longer structures. A refuge bay may be placed every 80 to 200 feet, and every fourth bay may be large enough to receive a handcar.

Some trestles had red 50-gallon wooden or metal fire barrels filled with water placed on the refuge platforms. A bucket was provided with which to dispense the water. Sand was often substituted for water, since it was found to be more effective in fighting creosoted timber fires.

Areas around the base of the bents were supposed to be kept clear of grass and foliage. Long trestles had concrete fire stops in the configuration of a bent positioned between bents at regular intervals. Sometimes sheet metal attached to the face of a bent was used to deter the spread of a fire.

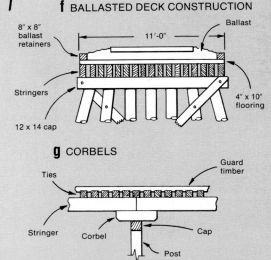

f BALLASTED DECK CONSTRUCTION

8″ x 8″ ballast retainers
Ballast
11'-0"
Stringers
4″ x 10″ flooring
12 x 14 cap

g CORBELS

Ties
Guard timber
Stringer
Corbel
Cap
Post

Type of deck	Size of stringer	10' span E45	E60	E72	12' span E45	E60	E72	14' span E45	E60	E72	16' span E45	E60	E72
Open decks	7 x 16	6	8	8	8	8	-	-	-	-	-	-	-
	8 x 16	4	6	6	6	6	8	8	8	-	-	-	-
	9 x 16	4	4	6	6	6	8	6	8	-	8	-	-
	10 x 16	4	4	4	4	4	6	6	8	8	8	-	-
	9 x 18	4	4	4	4	4	6	6	6	8	8	8	-
	10 x 18	-	-	-	-	-	4	4	6	6	6	8	-
	10 x 20	-	-	-	-	-	-	4	4	6	6	6	8

Type of deck	Size of stringer	10' span E45	E60	E72	12' span E45	E60	E72	14' span E45	E60	E72	16' span E45	E60	E72
Ballasted decks	7 x 14	-	-	-	-	12	14	-	-	-	-	-	-
	7 x 16	-	-	-	-	10	12	-	14	-	-	-	-
	8 x 16	-	-	-	-	9	12	-	11	13	-	-	-
	10 x 16	-	-	-	-	8	10	-	10	11	-	14	14
	9 x 18	-	-	-	-	8	8	-	10	11	-	11	12
	10 x 18	-	-	-	-	-	8	-	8	9	-	11	12

SIZE AND NUMBER OF STRINGERS

Courtesy National Model Railroad Association

Harold Russell

Fig. 7. An open deck timber trestle with guard timbers and guard-rails. The latter are sometimes omitted on contemporary trestles. Lateral timbers at the tie ends are used to stabilize the structure.

Fig. 8 DOUBLE-TRACK TRESTLES AND BULKHEADS

a DOUBLE-TRACK TRESTLES

c TIMBER BULKHEAD

12 x 12 timbers

d CONCRETE BULKHEAD

b PILE BULKHEAD

Pile

Slope 1½:1

16'-0" 48"

3 x 12

12" pile

Frame

Concrete

DOUBLE-TRACK AND CURVED TRESTLES

Figure 8a shows a typical double-track trestle arrangement. It looks like two single-track trestles joined together with the two adjacent posts replaced by a single post. Notice that all the center posts are straight up and down.

Three different tie systems are used for double-track trestles. In one system each track has its own 10-foot-long tie floor. Long ties span both tracks in another, while the third has 10-foot-long bridge ties for each track with every fifth tie being long enough to span both tracks. Engineers employing the first and last systems have two guard timbers embracing each track. When all the ties are long the two center timbers are replaced with a single guard timber.

On curves, real railroads may employ separate bents for each track and stagger them around the curve so the posts will not interfere with one another. Several means have been used to superelevate curved trestles, including tapered ties and corbels of unequal height. These methods tilt the floor system. Sometimes entire bents were tilted, which caused the outer posts on the curve to have more batter than the inner ones.

BULKHEADS

Around the bents built at a trestle's ends, earth must be retained in some fashion so that it doesn't fall away from the end support. This is usually done with bulkheads, which can be made of timber, metal, or concrete. Figure 8b shows a typical timber bulkhead configuration for both pile and frame bents. Figure 8c shows a low bulkhead consisting of a pair of square timbers. Engineers rarely construct timber trestle bulkheads higher than eight feet. Figure 8d shows a cross section of a typical concrete bulkhead. Note that a ledge rather than a bent supports the stringers at the ends.

CONCRETE TRESTLES

Concrete trestles are also built for railroad traffic. The first ones appeared about 1909. Figure 9 shows a concrete trestle with single- and double-bent configurations on the Seaboard Air Line RR sometime in the 1950s. Note how the configuration of this concrete structure closely follows the design of a framed timber trestle.

STEEL TRESTLES

A steel trestle such as the one in fig. 10

G. E. Rashley

Fig. 9. This 1950s-era concrete trestle has the same general design as a timber trestle. The center span is short and has single bents, while the adjacent longer spans are supported by doubled bents. Concrete trestles date back to 1909.

Fred Schneider III

Fig. 10. A Long Island RR passenger train crosses the Manhasset steel viaduct between the Manhasset and Great Neck stations in May of 1970. These spindly structures make impressive models.

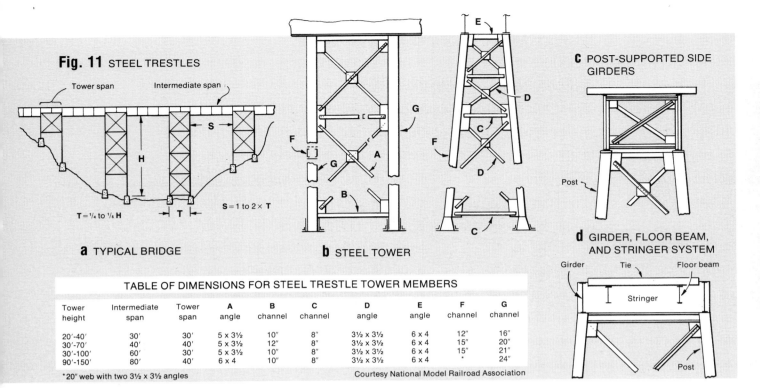

Fig. 11 STEEL TRESTLES

a TYPICAL BRIDGE

Tower span   Intermediate span

H

S

T

T = ¼ to ⅕ H   S = 1 to 2 × T

b STEEL TOWER

E, D, C, F, G, A, B

c POST-SUPPORTED SIDE GIRDERS

Post

d GIRDER, FLOOR BEAM, AND STRINGER SYSTEM

Girder   Tie   Floor beam

Stringer

Post

Tower height	Intermediate span	Tower span	A angle	B channel	C channel	D angle	E angle	F channel	G channel
20'-40'	30'	30'	5 x 3½	10"	8"	3½ x 3½	6 x 4	12"	16"
30'-70'	40'	40'	5 x 3½	12"	8"	3½ x 3½	6 x 4	15"	20"
30'-100'	60'	30'	5 x 3½	10"	8"	3½ x 3½	6 x 4	15"	21"
90'-150'	80'	40'	6 x 4	10"	8"	3½ x 3½	6 x 4	*	24"

TABLE OF DIMENSIONS FOR STEEL TRESTLE TOWER MEMBERS

*20" web with two 3½ x 3½ angles   Courtesy National Model Railroad Association

is an ideal type of trestle for a model railroad simulating the modern period. (See also figs. 11a and 11b.) The steel trestle consists of a series of deck bridges, usually plate girder types, supported by steel bents on low trestles and by towers on tall ones. With each structure designed for a specific site, these trestles become quite unique. Older steel trestle towers utilized truss rods and turnbuckle bracing.

Bridge designers like to keep the distance between bents, which is known as the tower span, equal on all towers. They generally keep it between 30 and 40 feet, depending on the height of the trestle. As a rule, they make the tower span one-fourth to one-fifth of the tower's

height. The distance between towers, which is called the intermediate span, can be equal to or even twice the tower span.

Figure 11b shows typical tower construction. You can see that the posts are made either with channels or, on older steel trestles, a channel configuration composed of plate with angles. Builders use solid plate and/or lacing to combine these pieces into posts. For further information, see the description of truss member construction in part three.

The total height of a steel trestle is divided into stories, with each story having a height approximately equal to the spacing of the tower posts. This keeps the cross bracing close to 45 degrees to the posts. The relative size of the component

pieces of the tower can be determined by following the diagram in fig. 11b and the accompanying table.

Deck plate girder or truss spans as described in part four are generally used to support the floor system. Two methods are used to attach the deck spans to the towers. In fig. 11c, the plate girder span is placed atop the tower with an open floor system. In fig. 11d, a floor beam and stringer system is used (this system is explained in part two).

Usually the same bridge type is used throughout the bridge length. In some cases, however, plate girders and trusses are intermixed. Plate girders are generally used for the tower spans, while trusses are built for the intermediate

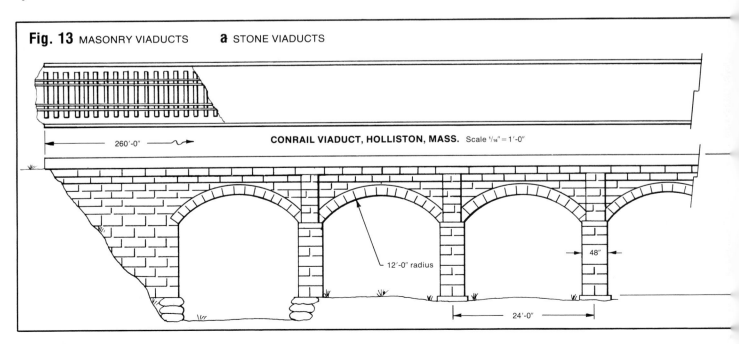

Fig. 13 MASONRY VIADUCTS   **a** STONE VIADUCTS

CONRAIL VIADUCT, HOLLISTON, MASS. Scale ¹/₁₆" = 1'-0"

260'-0"

12'-0" radius

48"

24'-0"

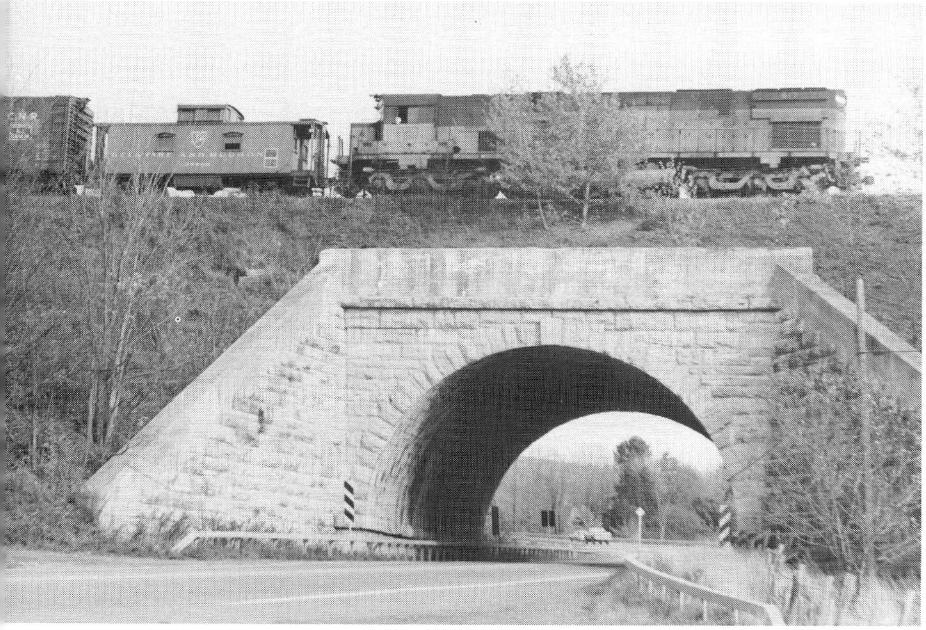

C. R. Yungkurth

Fig. 12. Built about 1860, this stone arch bridge on the Delaware & Hudson Ry. handled modern heavy equipment, as shown here, over 100 years later. Concrete is now the preferred material.

spans. Tapered concrete footings, standing 3 to 5 feet above the grade, are a common support for the tower posts.

When a steel trestle is curved, the towers and intermediate spans are made equal and the towers are tilted, with the posts on the outside of the curve having more batter than the posts on the inside.

STONE ARCH BRIDGES AND VIADUCTS

Many tall stone and concrete viaducts or arch bridges constructed in the early days of railroading are still standing. Even more impressive, many of them are still in use, which attests to the permanence of this type of construction. Stone was used until 1900, when concrete became the favored material. If a bridge has a single arch, it is called a stone (concrete) arch bridge. See fig. 12. If it has a series of arches, it is called a viaduct, as seen in figs. 2 and 13a.

The arches can be in the form of a semicircle or semiellipse, a segment of a circle, or a parabola the proportions of which are shown in fig. 13b. Engineers decide on the type they'll use after determining the relationship of the length to the desired height, with the semicircular arch being most common. For arch bridges they generally use steel in the form of a parabola.

This series will conclude in the next issue of MODEL RAILROADER. Our subjects in December will be culverts and wood bridges.

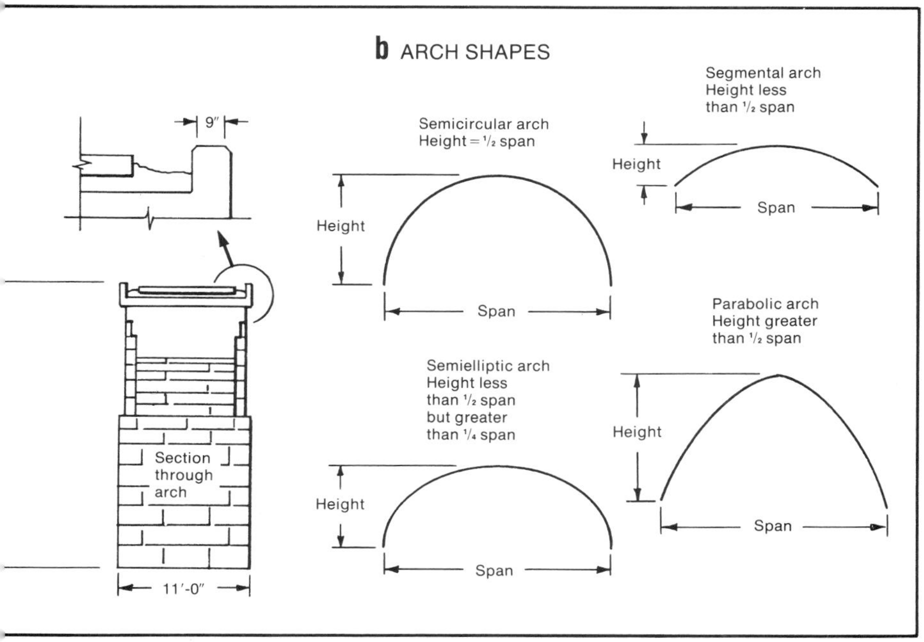
b ARCH SHAPES
9″
Section through arch
11′-0″
Semicircular arch
Height = 1/2 span
Height
Span
Segmental arch
Height less than 1/2 span
Height
Span
Semielliptic arch
Height less than 1/2 span but greater than 1/4 span
Height
Span
Parabolic arch
Height greater than 1/2 span
Height
Span

MODEL TRESTLES, ARCH BRIDGES, AND VIADUCTS

kits unless noted RTR (ready-to-run)

Type	Length (in feet)	Manufacturer	Part No.
O scale			
Timber trestle	56	Henning Rail Logic	1
Stone viaduct*	?	Mountains in Minutes	827(RTR)
Timber trestle	?	Trains of Texas	217
S scale			
Timber trestle	?	Trains of Texas	—
HO scale			
Ballasted deck timber trestle	50	Campbell	301
Timber trestle	50	Campbell	302
Timber trestle, curved	70	Campbell	303
Timber trestle, curved	110	Campbell	304
Timber trestle	216	Campbell	751
Steel trestle	80	Cannonball Car Shops	4450
Timber trestle	80	Evergreen Hill Design	504
Steel arch	103	Faller	541
Stone viaduct	51	Faller	545
Stone arch, curved	51	Faller	546
Timber trestle	131	Heljan	174
Steel arch	?	Life-Like	J8213
Concrete trestle	60	Mil-Scale	100
Concrete trestle, add on for no. 100	60	Mil-Scale	101
Concrete trestle, 2-track	60	Mil-Scale	102
Concrete trestle, add on for no. 102	60	Mil-Scale	103
Stone arch*	?	Mountains in Minutes	826(RTR)
Stone viaduct*	?	Mountains in Minutes	827(RTR)
Stone arch	102	Vollmer	2509
Timber trestle	?	Trains of Texas	215
HOn3 scale			
Timber trestle	81	Evergreen Hill Design	514
N scale			
Masonry viaduct	117	Arnold	6260
Masonry arch	117	Arnold	6270
Steel arch	117	Arnold	6280
Stone viaduct	?	Atlas	2826
Timber trestle	72	Cal-Scale (Bowser)	100
Timber trestle	146	Campbell	752
Timber trestle, curved	73	Campbell	753
Timber trestle, curved	113	Campbell	754
Stone viaduct	53	Faller	2585
Stone viaduct	100	Faller	2586
Timber trestle	178	Heljan	666
Steel arch	90	Kibri	7622
Stone viaduct	96½	Kibri	7640**
Stone viaduct, curved	101½	Kibri	7642**
Stone viaduct, curved	118	Kibri	7644
Concrete trestle	60	Mil-Scale	110
Concrete trestle, add on for no. 110	60	Mil-Scale	111
Concrete trestle, 2-track	60	Mil-Scale	112
Concrete trestle, add on for no. 112	60	Mil-Scale	113
Stone arch*	?	Mountains in Minutes	826(RTR)
Stone viaduct*	?	Mountains in Minutes	827(RTR)
Stone viaduct	115	Pola	275

*Manufacturer indicates products are suitable for any scale.
**Package contains 2 bridges

Milwaukee Road photo: Kalmbach collection

The Chicago, Milwaukee and St. Paul RR bridge across the Wisconsin River at Kilbourn (now Wisconsin Dells), Wisconsin. This photo shows the structure's Howe trusses at the time of completion in 1866.

Culverts and wood truss bridges

Culvert proportions and wood truss designs

BY HAROLD RUSSELL

THE FIVE PREVIOUS parts of this series have described an array of standard bridge configurations. But our understanding of bridges will be incomplete unless we look at culverts (openings in roadbeds through which water runs), timber bridges (in particular, the colorful covered bridge), and various details added to bridges after construction.

CULVERTS

Although seldom seen in sufficient quantity on layouts, culverts are common on prototype rights-of-way, where engineers must not allow water to dam up against the soil or gravel that makes up the base for the track structure. So they may build a culvert as a passage for streams or as a means of spreading incidental water evenly to both sides of the right-of-way.

There are three types of culverts: the pipe, the box, and the arch, as shown in fig. 1. The simplest culvert is a pipe made of metal, tile, or precast concrete (fig. 1a). Ribbed galvanized steel has now become quite popular (fig. 2). Pipe sizes range from 18 inches to 10 feet in diameter. When the clearance between

the water flow and the track is low, several adjacent culverts are used.

Small pipe culverts generally have identical ends that extend about 2 feet beyond the roadbed. Both the inlet and the outlet are protected by rocks piled against the roadbed soil. This prevents erosion and blockage of the culvert. Large culverts have funnel-shaped inlets (made of concrete, timber, or stacked stone) and plain outlets.

Box culverts have a square or rectangular opening (fig. 1b). A rectangular-shaped culvert of this type has less

chance of being blocked with debris than an assemblage of several small-diameter pipe culverts. Box culverts can be made of timber, cut or random stone, or concrete. Figure 3 shows a combination of concrete slabs with timber sidewalls to retain the ballast. Timber was commonly used in the early days of railroading, but is rare today.

Engineers don't often use box culverts, preferring pipe culverts except where an immense flow of water must be accommodated. Then they turn to the arch culvert (fig. 1c). Arch culverts can be made

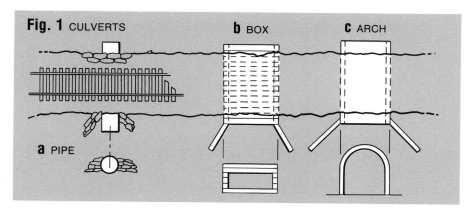

Fig. 1 CULVERTS   b BOX   c ARCH

a PIPE

Illinois Central RR photo: Kalmbach collection

Fig. 2. A common ribbed metal culvert that has been set inside an existing stone arch structure.

Harold Russell

Fig. 3. A simple rectangular culvert made of concrete slabs, with timber sidewalls to retain the ballast.

of either concrete, as shown in fig. 4, or stone, as seen in fig. 5.

TIMBER BRIDGES

Wood was readily available throughout most parts of the United States in the early days of railroading, so it's not surprising that it was the principal bridge material until the 1870s. Several early types of wood bridges are shown in fig. 6.

The simplest of these are the king post and the queen post. These designs originated in Europe, but were most widely used in North America. The first version of the king post, shown in fig. 6a, had a triangular-shaped structure under the floor stringers. As this design was vulnerable to flood damage, the support beams were moved above the stringers (fig. 6b), and an iron or steel rod was used to support the floor. Generally 20 to 40 feet long, these bridges were limited to available lumber sizes and were used for light traffic only.

An improved bridge design was the queen post (fig. 6c), which had vertical posts and short horizontal cross pieces in conjunction with iron support rods. Material specifications are given for both bridge types in the tables.

Figure 7 is a scale drawing of a straining beam pony truss used by the Southern Pacific Ry. It is derived from a variation of the king post known as the multiple king post bridge. It uses a pair of steel tie rods and inclined wood braces in place of the timber posts found on the queen post.

The remaining items in fig. 6 show a progression of bridge designs leading to the Howe truss. The Palmer, the Burr, and the Haupt relied on the arch for added strength. In the Palmer design, the roadway followed the arch curve. The Burr version, made more rigid with a series of multiple king posts, had a flat roadway. The Haupt bridge, which became popular during the Civil War, used the arch to support a truss of timber diagonals and iron or steel tension rods. Note how the angle, or tilt, of the diagonals became steeper at the bridge ends.

The need for an arch was eliminated by the design of the long-panel truss

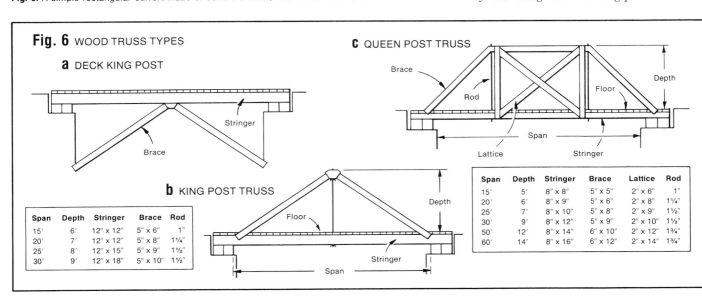

Fig. 6 WOOD TRUSS TYPES

a DECK KING POST

b KING POST TRUSS

Span	Depth	Stringer	Brace	Rod
15'	6'	12" x 12"	5" x 6"	1"
20'	7'	12" x 12"	5" x 8"	1¼"
25'	8'	12" x 15"	5" x 9"	1½"
30'	9'	12" x 18"	5" x 10"	1½"

c QUEEN POST TRUSS

Span	Depth	Stringer	Brace	Lattice	Rod
15'	5'	8" x 8"	5" x 5"	2" x 6"	1"
20'	6'	8" x 9"	5" x 6"	2" x 8"	1¼"
25'	7'	8" x 10"	5" x 8"	2" x 9"	1½"
30'	9'	8" x 12"	5" x 9"	2" x 10"	1½"
50'	12'	8" x 14"	6" x 10"	2" x 12"	1¾"
60'	14'	8" x 16"	6" x 12"	2" x 14"	1¾"

bridge, which is shown in fig. 6g. The town lattice design was composed of overlapping triangles without vertical posts and could be used for spans up to 200 feet long (fig. 6h).

Widely used during the 1830s and '40s, the long-panel and town lattice designs were eclipsed in 1847 by the Howe truss bridge, created by William Howe, whose brother Elias gained fame for inventing the sewing machine. Shown in fig. 6i, Howe's type of bridge was the predominant structure until steel bridges appeared in the 1870s.

Howe trusses were used in both deck and through configurations. Their greatest advantages were that almost any kind of wood could be used and, once sent to the proposed site, precut pieces could be assembled in a matter of days. Figure 8 shows a Howe truss on the Colorado Central RR in 1870, while fig. 9 is a scale half-plan of a Northern Pacific Ry. Howe truss 150 feet in length.

TIMBER JOINTS AND CONSTRUCTION

To make an effective model of a wood bridge, you should follow the actual construction techniques (seen in figs. 10a, 10b, 10c, 10d, and 10e) as closely as possible. The different views in fig. 10 show the joints at which timbers were notched to accept an intersecting member.

Cast-iron fittings in various socket configurations were often used in conjunction with steel rods (figs. 10f, 10g, and 10h). In addition, there were "hybrid" designs, in which a steel rod intersected a wood member at an angle (figs. 10c and 10i).

Steel rods were threaded at both ends and fastened with nuts (usually having square heads) and flat washers. The washer could be left off if an equivalent steel or cast-iron nut with a round hub (serving as a washer) was used, as seen in figs. 10d, 10e, and 10g.

When several timbers were used to make a single truss, they were usually separated by metal washers 2″ thick and 6″ in diameter. An early design had 3″ x 6″ wood spacers notched ½″ into the adjacent pieces. See fig. 10j.

Harold Russell

Fig. 4. Like most arch culverts, this concrete structure on the Nickel Plate Road has an opening designed to handle high water. Tapered wings are applied to both ends to control the flow of water.

Harold Russell

Fig. 5. Stone arch culverts are essentially identical to concrete ones, but the wing design differs. Stone culverts have stepped tops, while concrete ones have straight wings, as seen in fig. 4.

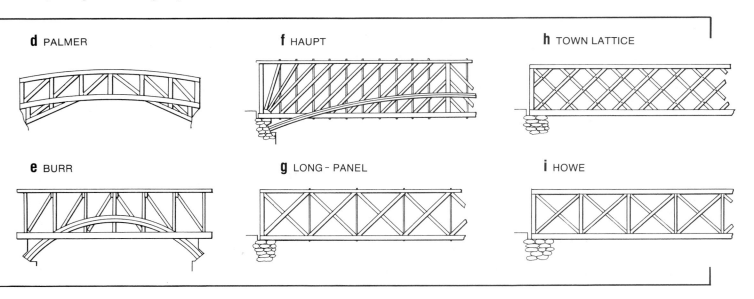

d PALMER

e BURR

f HAUPT

g LONG - PANEL

h TOWN LATTICE

i HOWE

Fig. 7 SOUTHERN PACIFIC STRAINING BEAM TRUSS

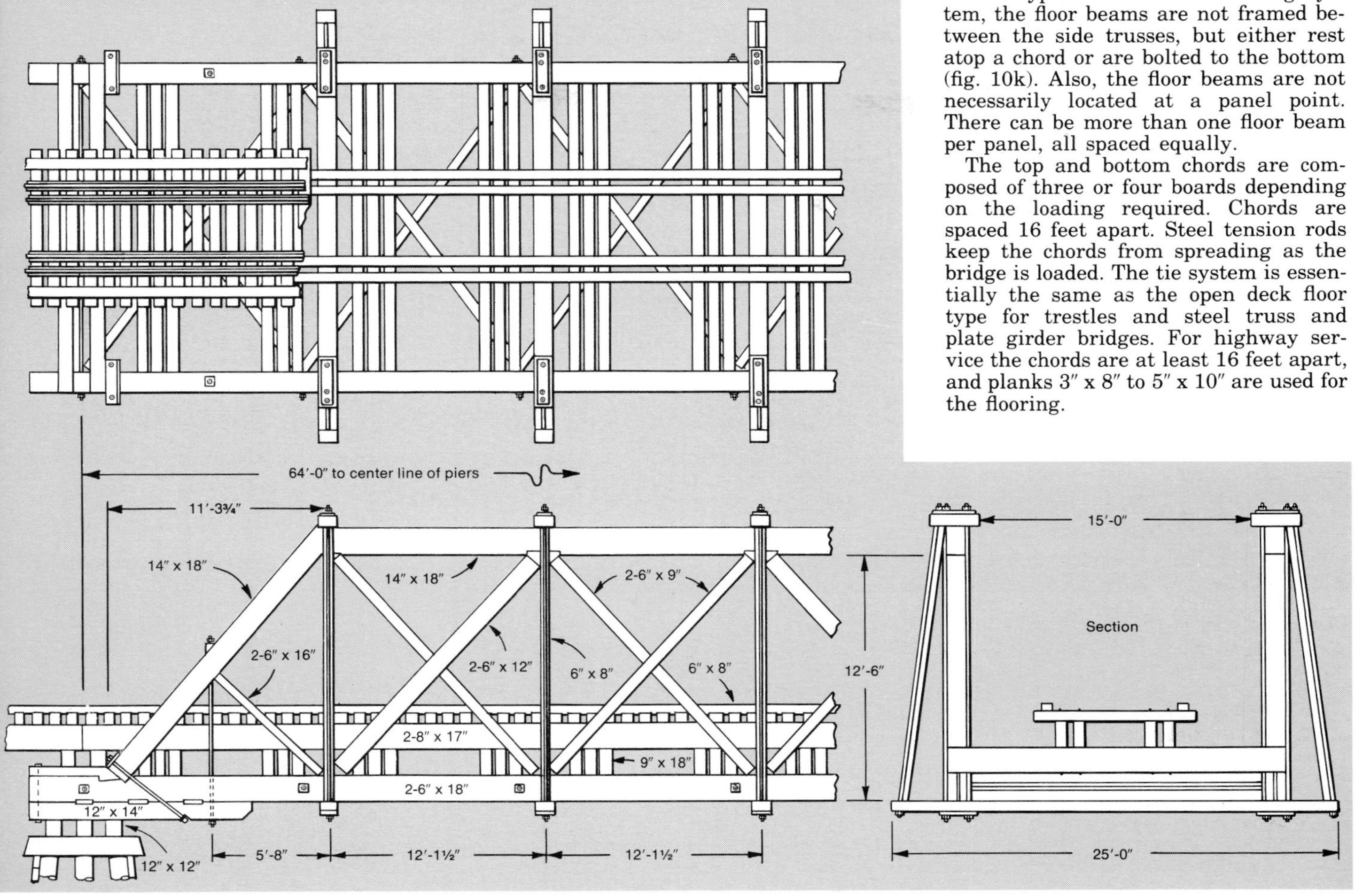

FLOORING SYSTEMS

In a typical wood truss flooring system, the floor beams are not framed between the side trusses, but either rest atop a chord or are bolted to the bottom (fig. 10k). Also, the floor beams are not necessarily located at a panel point. There can be more than one floor beam per panel, all spaced equally.

The top and bottom chords are composed of three or four boards depending on the loading required. Chords are spaced 16 feet apart. Steel tension rods keep the chords from spreading as the bridge is loaded. The tie system is essentially the same as the open deck floor type for trestles and steel truss and plate girder bridges. For highway service the chords are at least 16 feet apart, and planks 3" x 8" to 5" x 10" are used for the flooring.

64'-0" to center line of piers

11'-3¾"

14" x 18"

14" x 18"

2-6" x 9"

2-6" x 16"

2-6" x 12"

6" x 8"

6" x 8"

2-8" x 17"

9" x 18"

2-6" x 18"

12" x 14"

12" x 12"

5'-8"

12'-1½"

12'-1½"

12'-6"

15'-0"

Section

25'-0"

Fig. 8. Below: This 1870 Colorado Central RR Howe truss bridge has stone end supports. Vertical truss pieces between wood members are iron rods.

Colorado State Highway Dept.

Fig. 9 NORTHERN PACIFIC 150-FOOT HOWE TRUSS BRIDGE

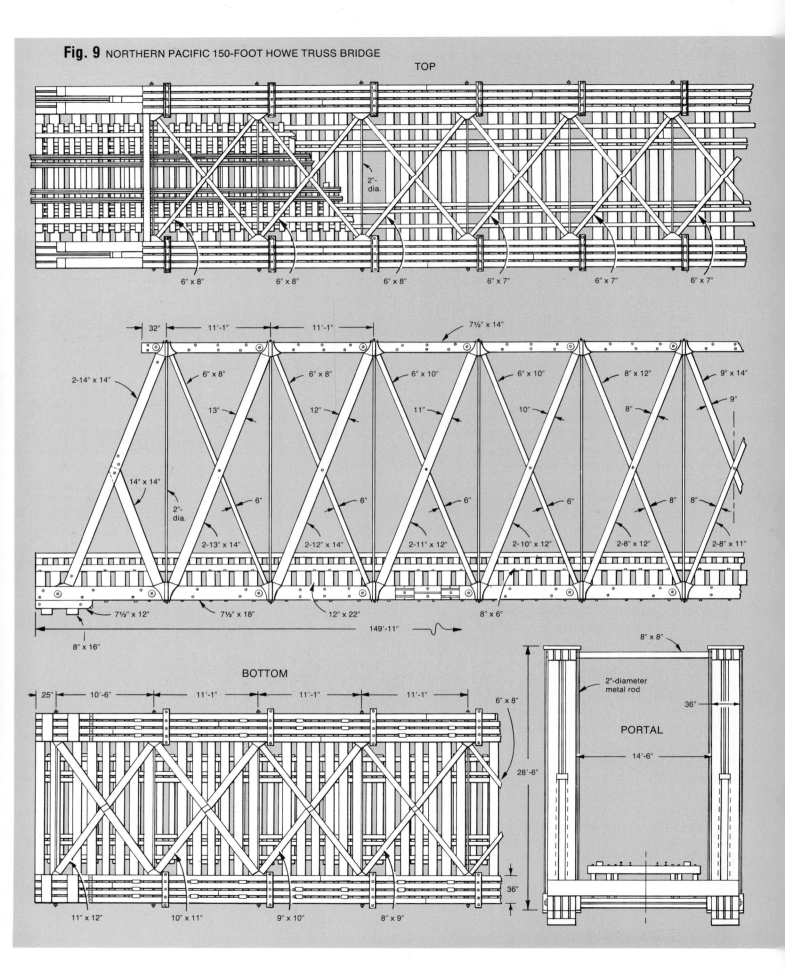

TOP

2"-dia.

6" x 8"   6" x 8"   6" x 8"   6" x 7"   6" x 7"   6" x 7"

32"   11'-1"   11'-1"   7½" x 14"

2-14" x 14"   6" x 8"   6" x 8"   6" x 10"   6" x 10"   8" x 12"   9" x 14"

13"   12"   11"   10"   8"   9"

14" x 14"

2"-dia.   6"   6"   6"   6"   8"   8"

2-13" x 14"   2-12" x 14"   2-11" x 12"   2-10" x 12"   2-8" x 12"   2-8" x 11"

7½" x 12"   7½" x 18"   12" x 22"   8" x 6"

149'-11"

8" x 16"

BOTTOM

25"   10'-6"   11'-1"   11'-1"   11'-1"   6" x 8"

8" x 8"

2"-diameter metal rod

36"

PORTAL

14'-6"

28'-6"

36"

11" x 12"   10" x 11"   9" x 10"   8" x 9"

40

Fig. 10 WOOD JOINTS AND FLOORING SYSTEMS

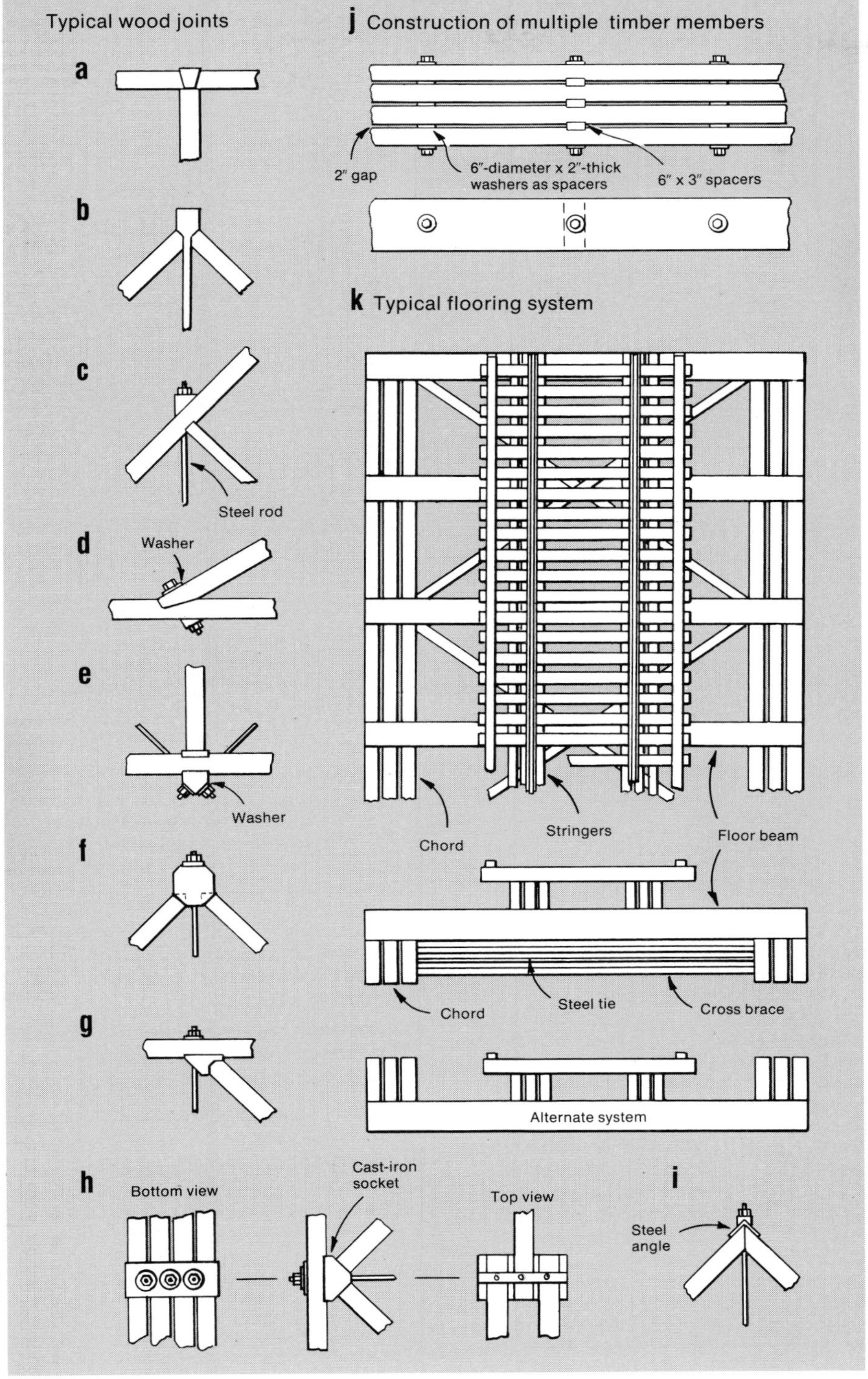

Typical wood joints

a

b

c

Steel rod

d

Washer

e

Washer

f

g

h

Bottom view

Cast-iron socket

Top view

i

Steel angle

j Construction of multiple timber members

2" gap

6"-diameter x 2"-thick washers as spacers

6" x 3" spacers

k Typical flooring system

Chord

Stringers

Floor beam

Chord

Steel tie

Cross brace

Alternate system

COVERED BRIDGES

A covered bridge consists of a wood truss (following any of the described designs) whose sides have been covered and given a roof (fig. 12). Such covering, especially the portal covering design, gives covered bridges great individuality. Various portal designs are shown in fig. 11. No particular names are assigned to the portals, but the approximate location of an example of each is indicated.

Wood bridges were covered to protect the structure from the elements. This reasoning must have been sound — after all, quite a few of these structures have survived (fig. 13). Builders used vertical as well as horizontal siding. Highway bridges often had window openings at eye level. Originally, the common roofing was wooden shingles; later, more conventional material such as asphalt shingles was used. Only a few covered bridges were ever painted, with red, white, and black being the most popular colors. In addition, some structures had their insides whitewashed.

Covered bridges might be used for railroads with relatively light loading and slow speed conditions, though their primary use was for highways. The overall dimensions of a particular structure were determined by the size of the trusses and the design of the portal, which in turn was determined by the skills of local bridge builders. Generally speaking, the height of openings was 22 feet for railroads and 15 feet for highways. Sixteen feet was the standard width for both types. Covered bridges were seldom set at anything but 90 degrees to the river or gap being crossed.

FINISHING DETAILS

Now that the bridge types, their variations and uses, the materials employed, and the approximate periods of use of each type have been covered, it's time to put this information to use and construct some bridge models. Of paramount importance to the bridge structure is the setting in which it will repose. Also important are the details on and around it.

A bridge, like a locomotive, usually has a builder's plate, typically found on the right-hand side of a truss portal or the right inside of a plate girder. Figure 14 shows a cast-metal plate. Large bridges frequently have a dedication plate, on which are inscribed the names of the engineers, builders, and local politicians responsible for their construction. The best way to model these is to make artwork and have it photoetched, though a printed or photostated sign will also work.

Fig. 11 COVERED BRIDGE PORTALS

RAILROAD BRIDGES

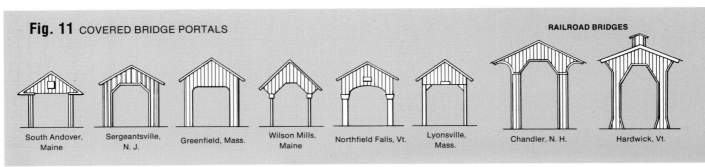

South Andover, Maine

Sergeantsville, N. J.

Greenfield, Mass.

Wilson Mills, Maine

Northfield Falls, Vt.

Lyonsville, Mass.

Chandler, N. H.

Hardwick, Vt.

Fig. 12. A covered railroad bridge still in use on the Boston & Maine RR in June 1947. An intermediate triple-trestle bent is used in conjunction stone end supports, with the stone end supports. The near approach is a standard four-post framed, open deck, timber trestle.

Glenn A. Wagner

Harold Russell

Fig. 13. A vertical plank wall covers the interior lattice trusses of this covered highway bridge. Windows were sometimes cut into the sidewalls.

Harold Russell

Fig. 14. An example of a bridge builder's plate. These are cast-metal plates attached to an end of the bridge structure. Plates on large bridges may give information about the location and the designers and politicians involved in the project.

Railroads number their bridges differently. Some assign numbers randomly, though most choose ones that correspond to the nearest milepost number. The numbers are painted on signs near the bridge or on the structure itself. The name of the river being crossed and/or the year the bridge was built will often be attached to the top of a truss portal.

Railroad signs indicating a bridge is ahead and specifying speed restrictions are placed in advance of the bridge along the right-of-way. Similar signs are used on highways. Movable bridge spans have track derails at the approaches, along with interlocking signals to control movements. As noted before, water traffic has the right of way over railroad and highway traffic.

Utility and communication lines carried on poles with cross arms along highways and railroad tracks make the crossing at the bridge in different ways. They may be carried on cross arms at several positions inside or outside the bridge structure. On wood trestles and deck bridges there may be regular cross-armed line poles attached to the structure near track level, sometimes leaning out at an angle. Occasionally the lines are cabled and then buried beneath the ground and water. With large lift bridges the lines are often carried on separate towers that hold them above the clearance of the lifted span.

Common bridge colors are black and aluminum, and sometimes a dark or a Tuscan Red will be seen. Black often fades to a dark gray. Rust streaks are not uncommon at the steel member joints and at the junction of wood and metal parts. Adding such details helps to accent an otherwise even color in modelwork.

This concludes the six-part ABCs of Bridges. I hope these articles will provide you with the information necessary to build and install a number of realistic bridges of varying types on your layout regardless of what scale you model. As you get into the modelwork, remember that most rules about bridge construction are somewhat general, and, within limits, there are variations and exceptions. ⚘

CULVERTS AND MODEL WOOD TRUSS BRIDGES
kits unless noted RTR (ready-to-run)

Type	Length (in feet)	Manufacturer	Part No.
O:			
Howe pony truss	63	Trains of Texas	210
On3:			
Howe pony truss	47	Trains of Texas	207
S:			
Howe pony truss	63	Trains of Texas	209
Sn3:			
Howe pony truss	47	Trains of Texas	206
HO:			
Howe thru truss	105¼	Campbell	305
Covered bridge	106¼	Campbell	306
Howe deck truss	101½	Campbell	761
Howe pony truss	101½	Campbell	762
Random stone arch culvert		Chooch	7033 RTR
Cut stone arch culvert		Chooch	7038 RTR
Covered bridge	65	Mil-Scale	80
Covered bridge	?	Muir Models	27
Stone culvert*		Mountains in Minutes	204
Howe pony truss	63	Trains of Texas	208
Pipe culvert		Pikestuff	2
HOn3:			
Howe pony truss	47	Trains of Texas	205
N:			
Howe pony truss	70	Campbell	260
Random stone culvert		Chooch	2
Covered bridge	65	Mil-Scale	508
Stone culvert		Mountains in Minutes	204

*Same model for both HO and N scale

Tackle a timber trestle

What other structure can match its features? It looks big, yet doesn't hide things beyond. It looks complicated, but goes together quickly. It's sure to provide an interesting focal point and increase the railroad atmosphere of any pike

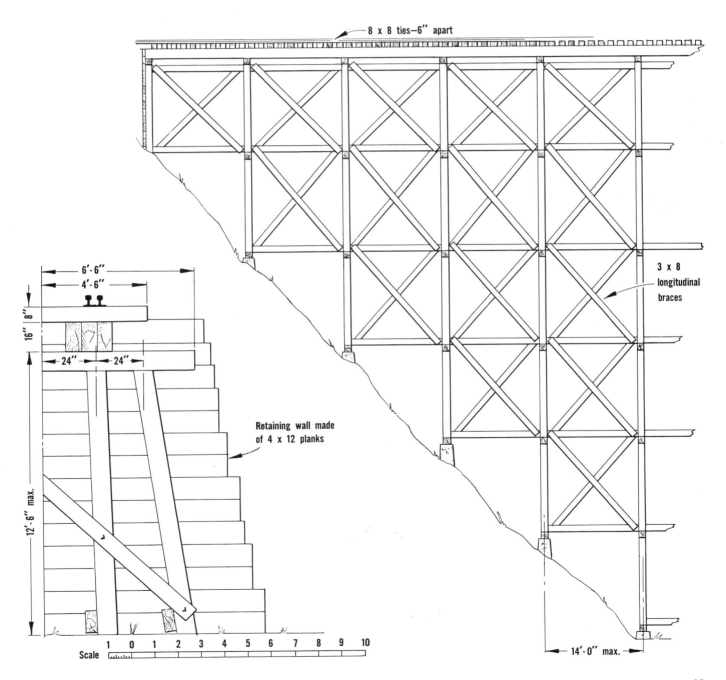

8 x 8 ties—6" apart

3 x 8 longitudinal braces

Retaining wall made of 4 x 12 planks

6'-6"

4'-6"

16" 8"

24"   24"

12'-6" max.

Scale 1 0 1 2 3 4 5 6 7 8 9 10

14'-0" max.

By John S. Corbett

ACCORDING to tradition, only a master modeler with a winter to spare is capable of scratchbuilding a really detailed timber trestle. One look at the jumble of columns, sills, and transverse and longitudinal bracing has been enough to scare many a would-be construction man into believing that a simple girder bridge was just what he had in mind in the first place!

But nothing can duplicate the thrill of seeing your own freight hog edge away from solid ground, suspended on the delicate timbered tracery of a long trestle. And fortunately, when handled correctly, the apparently complex timber trestle is actually a much easier modeling job than the simple-looking girder bridge.

If you have enough skill to cut several pieces of stripwood to the same length, you can complete a perfectly detailed trestle, several feet long, before you get your next issue of MODEL RAILROADER. All you need is a low spot between two hills and a real yen to run some trackage across it.

Are timber trestles out of place on the main line? Not on your life. Most main lines were originally built with some high, and many low, trestles. The high ones were eventually buried by running ballast cars out on the trestle and dumping dirt until the trestle was entirely covered with earth. But a few high ones and many low ones are still found on today's main lines.

Before modern earthmoving machinery changed the methods, timber trestles were used to get railroads over rough country without great cost. The filling-in with earth (or sometimes replacement with a steel trestle) took time and more money, and so was not done until the railroad was ready to make the extra investment.

Trestles are installed on main lines today for other reasons. They make economical approaches to bridge spans. They are used for shoofly tracks around a construction area. They are often used in desert country at a wash (a usually dry riverbed) or for crossing a coastal lagoon where storms might wash out any structure and a more expensive structure would be a greater loss. On the older-period main lines and on any branch line a trestle is right at home anywhere.

How to go about it

You can begin making yours by calculating the height you'll need, from the lowest spot of your terrain to the top of your future rail. Be very accurate in determining this measurement, for it's a lot easier to double-check now than it is to tear up your layout later. Determine also how long you can make your trestle. A good rule of thumb is this: The longer a trestle is, the lower it can be and still retain good semblance of reality. This is an important consideration, because most of our pikes don't have enough trackage to go very high without resorting to tinplate grades.

Turn to the plan and you will find that the short horizontal timbers are called *sills;* the vertical ones, *columns.* A single sill, with columns to hold it up, is called a *pony bent.* To achieve greater height, several pony bents can be stacked on top of each other. On the prototype the columns are usually secured to the sills by concealed steel pins. An alternative fastening would be by means of 3 x 10 scabs — short pieces of timber nailed or bolted to two abutting timbers to splice them together. However, I took the scabs off my own trestle because they didn't look right. With correctly sized lumber they appeared to be oversize, and they cluttered up the model. When scaled down to where they looked right, they tended to disappear from view.

Determine the maximum height you need to top of rail in scale feet and inches. From this figure deduct 30"; this represents the space occupied by rails, ties, and top stringers. This now leaves you with the net height from the ground to the top of the highest sills. Now determine how many rises of pony bents you want for best appearance and divide your net height by that number. Check your result to make sure it does not exceed the 30" minimum or 12'-6" maximum pony bent height noted on the plan, and you're done with figuring and ready to highball ahead with the construction. On the prototype, the available timber determined the lengths of columns and thus the number of pony bents.

A look at the sketch will show you the key to fast, accurate and easy construction of your trestle. It's a diagram of a simple jig, made up on any scrap of lumber you have handy. It will take about 15 minutes to lay this out, but it will save perhaps 15 hours while building a single trestle. It will insure perfectly aligned bents, and you'll find that all succeeding parts fall effortlessly into place.

You should know a couple of tricks before making your jig. First, when you lay it out, make sure that the sills are at right angles to the working (bottom)

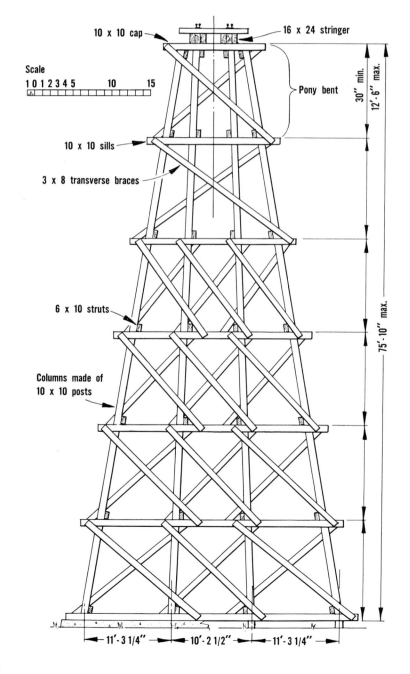

10 x 10 cap

16 x 24 stringer

Pony bent

30" min.

12'-6" max.

Scale
10 1 2 3 4 5   10   15

10 x 10 sills

3 x 8 transverse braces

75'-10" max.

6 x 10 struts

Columns made of 10 x 10 posts

← 11'-3 1/4" → ← 10'-2 1/2" → ← 11'-3 1/4" →

This photo by Paul C. Snyder; all others by the author.

The 234-foot framed trestle sports two refuges with water barrels, concrete footings over most of its length, two pile foundations protected by cribbed rubble, bank-bent abutments, dump boards.

edge of your board. That way, you can use a try square for layout and for guiding half of your cutting. Second, you can use this same jig for both high and low trestles, so after drawing a center line parallel to the working edge, draw two lines, 75 feet apart, at right angles to the center line. Then lay out column center lines each way from them. Use the 75-foot measurement *no matter what the height of your own trestle will be*. This insures that the slope, or batter, of your columns will be right. Then, just measure down from the top to lay out your sills.

Measure from sill top to sill top, using the pony bent height you determined previously.

Line up scale 12 x 12 stripwood scrap, a scale 6" away from each column center line, along the line you scribed. Check it, cement it down tight, clean off all excess cement, and let it dry. Then lay a full-length piece of your column stock against this piece, covering the center line. Cement another scale 12 x 12 on the other side of your column. Before the cement dries, make sure that your column stock has a nice, easy slip between the

guides. By sliding it you will also remove any globs of excess cement you may have squeezed out. Pin the guide to the board while the cement dries, remove the column stock, and repeat for the other columns.

When all the cement has dried, saw the horizontal notches a scale 12" wide at your sill-line levels. These are for your sills. Use your square for a saw guide and check each cut for proper fit with your sill stock. Remember, your stock has to come out of the jig easily, so make it just tight enough to hold without slippage. Your jig is now complete.

Rather than juggle 25 separate pieces of timber for each bent, with 20 chances to make sloppy joints and get bad alignment, make use of a handy bit of furniture joinery and *half-lap* the sills into the columns as shown in the sketch. This way, columns appear to be in several short lengths but actually are full length. This provides strength; yet when oriented properly the viewer sees only the side which appears to be composed of separate pieces.

You could make a miter attachment to help cut these joints. Cement some scale 6" thick hardwood stock outside your jig. These will gauge the depth of your notch cuts. However, since anyone can cut halfway through a piece of stripwood by eye, this seems like a lot of work for nothing.

To begin production, just drop four column timbers into their respective slots in the jig. Let the tops and bottoms run long. Make your first sill cuts — all the way across all four columns. Knock out the waste between saw cuts and slide a piece of scrap into the notches you created. This will keep all columns in alignment as you cut notches for the rest of the sills. After that, trim the column tops and bottoms to size. Then remove

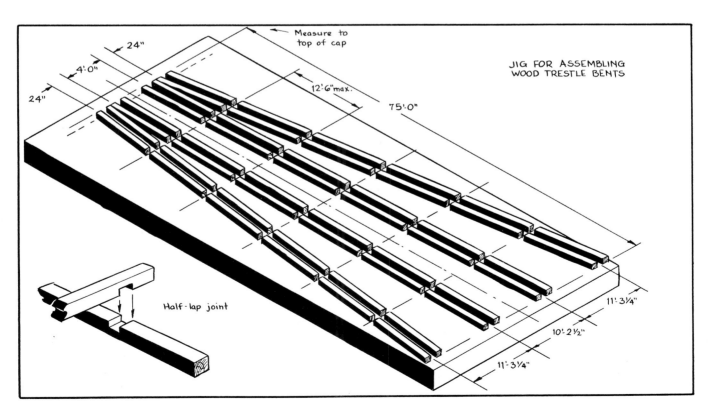

Measure to top of cap

24"

4'-0"

24"

12'-6" max.

75'-0"

JIG FOR ASSEMBLING WOOD TRESTLE BENTS

11'-3¼"

10'-2½"

11'-3¼"

Half-lap joint

all the columns and stain or paint them. (Unless you have equipment for spraying, all parts should be stained as they are made, before assembly.) Prototype timber structures are protected by a creosote stain which tastes terrible and drives a lot of insects away as well as giving protection from the weather. Walnut stain duplicates this color but should then be weathered to suit, since sun and rain bleach the creosote several shades lighter than the original color.

Be careful to lay the parts in their proper order over a sheet of paper on your bench. The inside columns are cut to a different angle from the outside ones and you don't want them to be assembled out of order.

Cut the sills to length, allowing a minimum projection of 18″ beyond the outside edge of the columns. Drop the sills into the jig and cut notches for one column. Again, wedge a full-length scrap into the notches to hold the sills in alignment, and then cut the remaining joints. When you've done that, leave the sills in the jig.

Pick up your columns, put a drop of regular-type Ambroid cement into each notch (not too much; you don't want any to squeeze out), and in reverse order from the way you took them out, drop the columns back into the jig, *over* the sills, so that the notches engage. Let the cement dry a minute or two, remove the bent from the jig, inspect it, and set it

aside. If your joints were accurately cut, it will be almost impossible to knock the bent out of square.

When you've made all the full-length bents you need, make the shorter ones that climb up the hills. Just shorten the columns or eliminate pony bents from the bottom as your trestle gets shorter.

When all bents are completed, you're ready to start the transverse bracing. Use 3 x 8 stock. Cut and fit the bracing to the first full-size bent as shown on the plan. A different length of brace will be needed for each level of pony bents. Using these braces as templates, cut enough for the whole job. Lay them in separate piles, because many of them will be so close to the same length that a mixup will be both inevitable and conducive to tantrums.

Taking your time, position and cement the bracing to one side of the bent. Lay the other bents on top of this one and run out the rest. Turn them over and do the other side. There are two things to watch for in this operation: (1) Be sure to allow room for the 6 x 12 struts which occur at the joints between sills and columns; you'll see that your transverse braces should leave a hole here for these struts to slide through. (2) Be sure to cement every brace to every timber it touches. In this way you build in the tremendous strength and rigidity of the prototype.

With bents completed and braced, you

One bent on construction board, braced plumb.

are ready to go up in the air. You'll need a base to start from; a pine board long enough and wide enough to take your trestle is what you'll pull out of the scrapbox. Scribe parallel lines to show the outside edges of the outside columns,

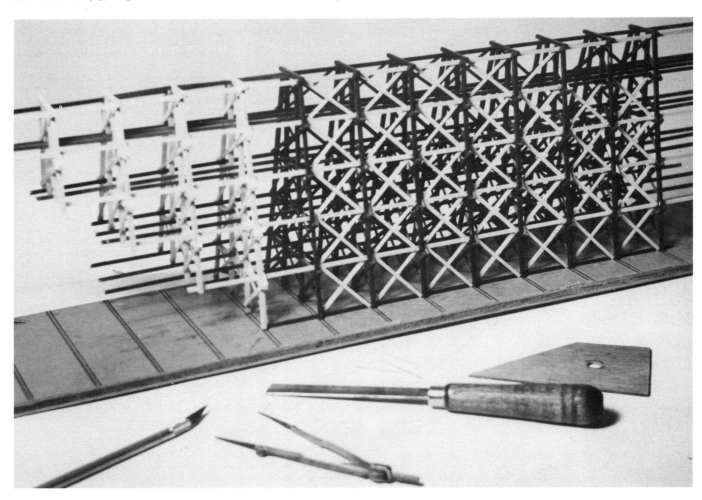

Bents are in place with struts and longitudinal bracing positioned. Additional bents are slid onto struts, showing placement method.

The trestle is now two-thirds framed, and you can see the additional diagonal bracing added to keep the whole structure aligned and plumb. At this point in construction the longitudinal braces should be added to the trestle. Only then should any of the temporary braces be removed. Then the shorter bents for the near end should be strung on the girts, each plumbed, and then cemented.

With framing completed the trestle was removed from the base and permanent wood supports were added. The trestle was elevated ¾″ from the baseboard to allow terrain variations between the footings. The wooden supports themselves will become the concrete footings for the trestle bents.

and lay out the bent spacing with your square. Then determine where the first full-length bent will come and cement one on its mark. Plumb it and brace it rigidly. See photo. Do the same with the next bent.

Slide all the inside struts into place and brace them. Leave off the struts that occur at the outside columns; it's much easier to put them on last. From here on, just slide your bents on the stringers, position them on the marks, and cement them in place. Several spacer blocks, cut to the exact distance between your columns, will be a great aid in keeping things parallel and plumb at this point. Use them as temporary gauges at the top and middle, pushing each new bent tightly to them. Cement your struts to each bent and be sure to check the bents often for plumb. When all bents are in place, add the struts at the outside col-

umns. Bobby pins make good clamps for this job.

Longitudinal bracing

Cut and fit one piece of longitudinal bracing from 3 x 8 stock. Check it in several places to make sure it fits. The same length should fit everywhere except at the top tier of bents. Fit these braces to the *outermost struts*, not to the bents. When you're satisfied with the fit, get out your razor blade and start cutting. Cut enough to do the whole job, then cement them in. Set the inside braces with tweezers. The upper end will hook under a transverse brace; the other will wedge against a column. The other brace just lies in, as you can see by the photos and drawings. You will seldom need to clamp any joints, but if you do, a bobby pin will do the job.

With the vertical assembly done, make your stringer-tie assembly. If your bents are no more than 14 feet apart you can use a 16″ stringer as shown. Cement three 8 x 16's together for each stringer. Scribe kerfs on the outside to represent standard timber lengths, and add desired bolt details. Cut and prestain enough 8 x 8 ties, 10 feet long, for the job.

Draw two parallel lines, 5 feet apart, as long as your stringers. Tack both stringers down, centered on these lines, and cement your ties in place. Either use spacer blocks or lay in a tie between each one you cement. If you do this, be sure to remove the spacing ties before the cement sets, since even a little squeezed out will stick your spacers in place. With the ties fastened down, lay down your running rails and guardrails with Goo or epoxy glue.

Add sheathing (4 x 12) and a 3 x 4 cap to your last bent to retain the ballast approach fill, and construction is done.

The subframing to hold the trestle on your train table is made easily of 1″ stock of suitable width and length. This shows clearly in the accompanying photo, and since the construction will be governed by the contours of your own hills, there is no point in my going into a lot of detail about it. Use screws and glue and the joints should never give you trouble.

You can go hog-wild in detailing your trestle. You can make boltheads at each timber connection and, by extending ties about 6 feet on center you can support a planked walkway and/or railing. By the same method of extending ties you can add platforms for water barrels and buckets. Since my own trestle is at the back of my layout, it would be impossible to see extremely small detail without field glasses; and since walkways and such would tend to obscure the sharp image of the trestle, I simply skipped them and put the effort into making the whole job a bit longer.

But whether or not you superdetail the basic trestle, you'll have a new focal point for your pike. It's easy to build, and, done even fairly well, the apparent complexity makes it look like a masterpiece. And, short of firing up a new layout for the first time, there is no thrill in railroading to compare with the one you'll get when your own heavy freight muscles out on the spidery timber miracle you have created.

A timber deck truss bridge

Fit it into a gap in your longest trestle and see how greatly the scene is improved

By Jack Work

NO doubt timber bridges are becoming scarce in this diesel-ized age, but I'd say that if a model railroad has even one steam locomotive on its roster, then wooden bridges — one or two, anyway — are in order. Instead of spanning the whole distance across a gully with a trestle, why not incorporate a timber truss into it somewhere: near the middle, or toward one of its approaches? To be sure, trestles themselves are interesting. Some are quite spectacular if built to a great height, or curved, but a timber span introduced into such a trestle is even more of a showstopper.

Naturally the span has to be justified. It can pass over another track if there is sufficient clearance below it for this, or over a stream or a roadway, or a combination of these. Any such arrangement can make the whole scene that much more picturesque.

I like timber trusses for model railroads for some special reasons. Compared with latter-day steel plate-girder bridges, the openwork of a timber-truss span and its maze of criss-cross bracing and tension rods creates an interesting pattern that is by far more engrossing in a model. I've never really understood why our ability to see through an object should arouse one's interest and curiosity more than the sight of a solid and unbroken surface; but it seems to. Perhaps this effect enhances our appreciation of the third dimension and of movement? I only know it is a truth that few of us stop to ponder.

I've made use of the view-through idea for a long time. Several years ago I was talking about it with the MR editor when he half-jokingly suggested my phrase might be changed to "peekaboo" models — a term that caught my fancy as being more fitting. Call them what you like, and whatever the true reason for their appeal, a modeler certainly can't

go wrong with a few models of lacy fabrication around. They're truly attractive!

The truss I have modeled is a deck type, meaning the road or track is above the trusswork. Before we settle down to its construction, let me point out immediately that a slight error crept into my model, but it is important to the reader only insofar as it might prove confusing if not pointed out. A comparison of the drawings with the construction photos will disclose that in the center panel of each side truss of my model, the bracing is wrong. This went unnoticed until all progress photos for the story were processed. While the finished model was easily corrected, not so the photos — that is, short of repeating all construction and photography. It wasn't worth it. The reader will have no difficulty if he disregards these few braces as shown in the photos, and instead proceeds according to the drawings, particularly fig. 3, which shows the *correct* assembly of lap-jointed cross timbers of the middle panel.

Although I had a fair supply of stripwood in a range of sizes on hand, I had to cut one or two sizes not commercially made to complete my list of requirements: see materials list. Those not fortunately equipped with a circular saw will have to make substitutions from the nearest commercial sizes available. If a little fudging takes place here or there, few will know; fewer will care; and all you have really done, anyway, is to modify the theoretical load limit of the bridge.

Some model stripwood firms supply their stock in scale dimensions for a particular scale. This is especially convenient and accurate if it is for the scale you selected for the model. If you work in another scale, or if you use stripwood dimensioned in actual fractional inches or in millimeters, you'll have to do a little calculating to arrive at the sizes for your model.

The materials list shows the linear feet needed for each size of material, but this is the bare minimum, not allowing for cutting and leftover bits from each length of stripwood. You will have more wastage where the bridge pieces are long, for instance, than for the 8 x 8 strips that are cut into many relatively short ties for the track. Some study of the drawings is necessary in determining quantities unless you provide considerable excess in each size. Be sure your stock permits cutting two unbroken lengths 75 feet long for the 16 x 18 bottom chords.

The photos and accompanying captions illustrate progressive steps in assembling the model. Precoloring all materials is recommended, since this process helps to create a naturally weathered appearance that is difficult to achieve by painting the completed model at one sitting. Besides, it's a frustrating task getting a brush into all the areas necessary to paint every bit of all the timbers.

The hanger rods can be modeled with several different materials, and in two different ways. If you cut them a little long and push them through their holes, you can then clip them off so they protrude just a little beyond the tops of the floor beams and the bottoms of the bottom struts so they will resemble the bolthead ends of the real bridge rods. Another method that is a bit more detailed-looking is to cut the rods a little short and then push bolthead-and-washer detail castings into holes at the tops and bottoms of the struts. These bolthead pieces are sold by Kemtron, and perhaps others, in both plastic and brass. The plastic variety is perfectly suitable here.

The best material for the hanger rods themselves is probably steel tool rod or welding rod (.025″ diameter for HO, other scales in proportion), because these usually come perfectly straight. However, iron wire as sold in hardware stores or garden supply houses or surplus outlets, or even copper wire with the insulation stripped away, can be used if you straighten it. This means clamping one end of a piece in a vise, gripping the other end, and pulling hard.

The rods, also the boltheads, should be painted rust color when the model is being finished.

Stripwood channel is available from some suppliers, but it's a bit heavy in appearance — understandably so. I formed my own channel by bending thin sheet aluminum over both edges of a strip of styrene that had been made the desired *inside* width of the channel. The aluminum was obtained from trays and pans in which tv dinners and other frozen foods were packaged. This material is handy for many modeling jobs, since it forms readily and yet has considerable strength after forming. Pliobond is a good adhesive when attaching such metal pieces.

1 It's advisable to select required amounts of all stripwood sizes for the whole project and to color the lot before assembly begins. Coloring can be done in a bath of wood stain, but I prefer the effect one gets from wiping thinned model paint onto the individual stripwood pieces one at a time. A cotton cloth is presaturated with thinner of a type suitable to the particular paint used. Small amounts of color are then tipped onto the cloth so the paint is diluted directly on the cloth. Wood drawn through this absorbs color, but not thick paint. The cloth is replenished with thinner and color at intervals, in varying mixtures and intensities. The result is a subtle, transparent, and weathered effect. There is a difference in the coloring of the individual pieces that is desirable. I suggest you experiment with mixtures of black and white tipped onto the cloth to achieve a silver-gray appearance typical of weathered wood. Very slight amounts of red, red-brown, maybe Floquil mud, rust, or such, will help vary the gray slightly. Keep the amounts of these latter colors to a very minimum, however. We want a subtle, faded tone — nothing garish. Rubber gloves might prevent stained fingers during this work, but first test the thinner used to see if it attacks the rubber gloves.

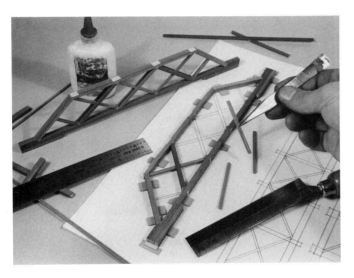

2 An accurately drawn layout of the top and bottom chords and lattice can be drawn on fairly heavy cardstock to make a work surface and jig. Small bits of scrap stripwood cemented outside the layout lines align individual model pieces as they are cemented into an assembly. This way the work can be lifted away from, and replaced on, the drawing at any stage of the assembly. Another popular method is to place this drawing over a smooth, soft-grained piece of wood and push pins through to guide each side of the timbers. In either event, use cement sparingly to avoid having excess deposits join the work to the drawing. A piece of waxed paper laid over the drawing first will prevent this, but it's hardly necessary if one is careful with the glue. Any of the "white" types of glue are suitable for this work. Note that top and bottom chords of these trusses have been recessed 2" deep to accommodate the beams and struts.

Materials list

Sizes and amounts required shown in scale inches and feet.

6 x 6	500 feet	12 x 12	300 feet
6 x 8	150 feet	12 x 14	32 feet
6 x 10	100 feet	12 x 18	600 feet
6 x 12	200 feet	14 x 18	204 feet
8 x 8	700 feet	16 x 18	150 feet
8 x 18	80 feet	12" channel	48 feet
		(16 pieces 3 feet long)	

Wire rod: 320 feet. (Use .025" or .030" for HO, other scales to proportionate size.)
Supply of bolthead-nut-washer castings (Kemtron or other).

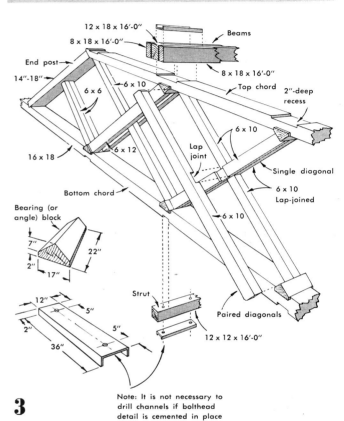

3

Note: It is not necessary to drill channels if bolthead detail is cemented in place

Reference table for nearest stripwood sizes

For fractional-dimension stripwood in inches

+ and − signs indicate whether the size is larger or smaller than exact scale. Millimeter equivalents are also given for full-size timber.

Timber dimension	Scale				
	N 160:1	TT 120:1	HO 87:1	S 64:1	O* 48:1
6"; 152 mm.	1/32 −	3/64 −	1/16 −	3/32	1/8
8"; 203 mm.	3/64 −	1/16 −	3/32 +	1/8	3/16 +
10"; 254 mm.	1/16	5/64 −	1/8 +	5/32	3/16 +
12"; 305 mm.	5/64	3/32 −	1/8	3/16	1/4
14"; 356 mm.	3/32 +	1/8 −	5/32 +	1/4 +	5/16 +
16"; 406 mm.	3/32 −	1/8 −	3/16 +	1/4	5/16 −
18"; 457 mm.	1/8 +	5/32 +	3/16 −	1/4 −	3/8

EXAMPLE: Stripwood for TT scale model of 10" timber is slightly undersize at 5/64"; 3/32" could be used almost as well, since the actual figure is between these sizes.
*The modeler will have to decide whether to make a bridge for O gauge to 48:1 proportion, the same as most American O scale equipment, or to 45:1 to be correct for the track scale. Nearest stripwood sizes will be the same in either case if commercial material is unaltered, but lengths of pieces will be greater for 45:1 models.

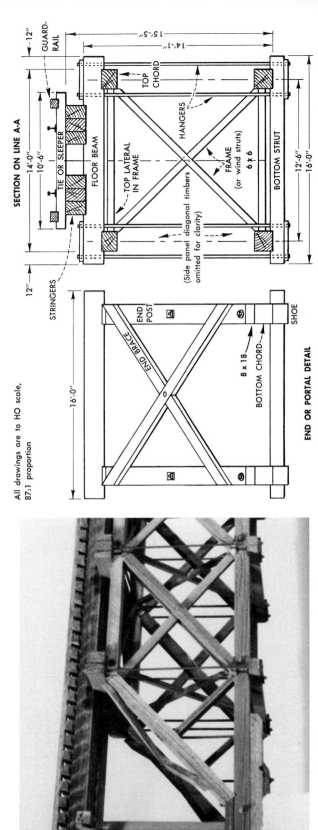

SECTION ON LINE A-A

GUARD-RAIL

12"

14'-0"

10'-6"

15'-5"

14'-1"

TOP CHORD

HANGERS

FLOOR BEAM

TIE OR SLEEPER

TOP LATERAL IN FRAME

FRAME (or wind struts)

6 x 6

BOTTOM STRUT

12'-6"

16'-0"

(Side panel diagonal timbers omitted for clarity)

12"

STRINGERS

END POST

END BRACE

16'-0"

8 x 18

BOTTOM CHORD

SHOE

END OR PORTAL DETAIL

All drawings are to HO scale, 87:1 proportion

50

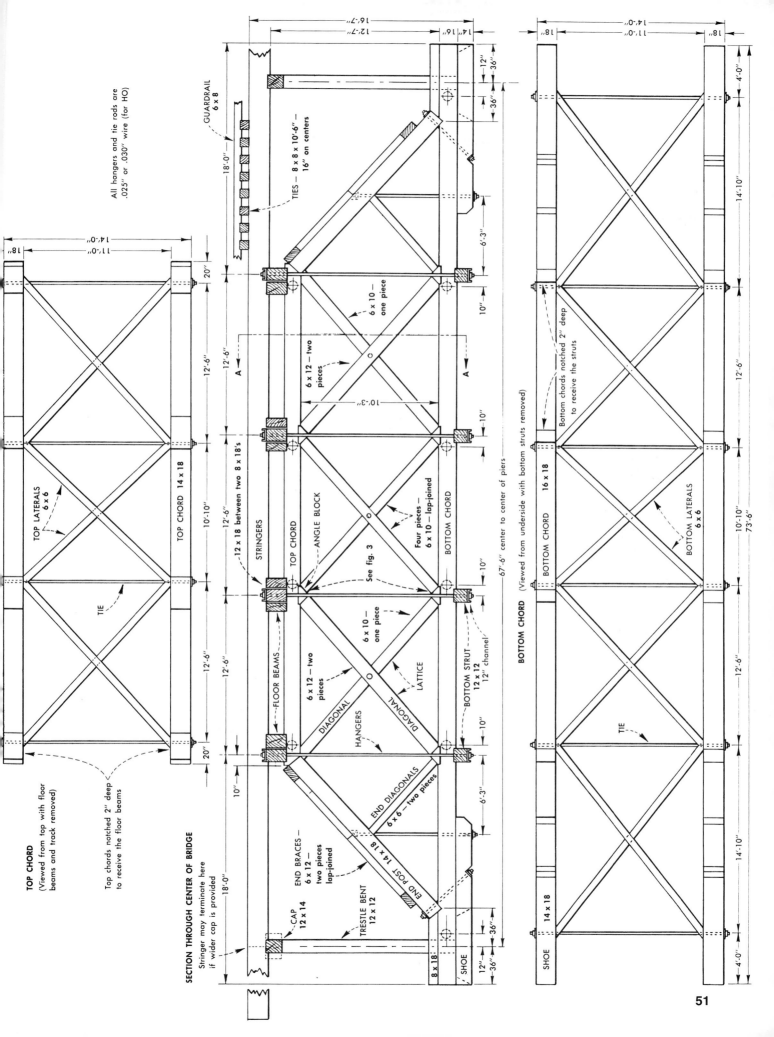

TOP CHORD
(Viewed from top with floor beams and track removed)

Top chords notched 2" deep to receive the floor beams

TOP LATERALS 6 x 6

TIE

TOP CHORD 14 x 18

SECTION THROUGH CENTER OF BRIDGE

All hangers and tie rods are .025" or .030" wire (for HO)

GUARDRAIL 6 x 8

TIES — 8 x 8 x 10'-6" on centers — 16" on centers

6 x 10 — one piece

6 x 12 — two pieces

See fig. 3

6 x 10 — one piece

6 x 12 — two pieces

Four pieces — 6 x 10 — lap-joined

BOTTOM CHORD

ANGLE BLOCK

TOP CHORD

STRINGERS

12 x 18 between two 8 x 18's

FLOOR BEAMS

DIAGONAL

DIAGONAL

LATTICE

HANGERS

BOTTOM STRUT — 12 x 12 — 12" channel

END DIAGONALS 6 x 6 — two pieces

END BRACES — 6 x 12 — two pieces lap-joined

END POST 14 x 18

TRESTLE BENT 12 x 12

CAP 12 x 14

Stringer may terminate here if wider cap is provided

SHOE

8 x 18

67'-6" center to center of piers

BOTTOM CHORD (Viewed from underside with bottom struts removed)

Bottom chords notched 2" deep to receive the struts

BOTTOM CHORD 16 x 18

BOTTOM LATERALS 6 x 6

TIE

SHOE

14 x 18

73'-6"

51

6 With trusses completed, prepare the lateral bracing. Note that each of these panels requires two laterals of 6 x 6 timbers, but of varying lengths and angles. They are notched and half-lapped where they cross. Notching, cementing, and trimming of ends can be done over the drawing as shown. If it is found easier, you can cement scraps of wood to the drawing for aligning the pieces as was done with the side trusses. Above all, make these pieces fit the drawing exactly so the bridge will go together properly.

4 Holes for tension rods should be drilled no later than this stage of construction. There is a good chance that the difficulty of drilling the various timbers of a completed bridge would result in boring holes askew. If this happens, the rods when installed will run at odd angles and look terrible. A simple jig can be fashioned in which matching timbers can be drilled in identical locations: see next figure.

7 Next, with side trusses held upside down in position over the drawing of the top chord, cement the bottom struts in position. To facilitate alignment, make several spacer bars of scrapwood like those marked A in the photo. These merely rest across the trusses like track gauges until the assembly is cemented; then they lift off. A square resting at one side can be used to check squareness of the assembly.

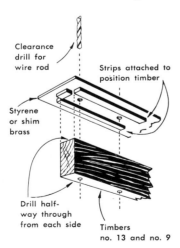

Clearance drill for wire rod

Strips attached to position timber

Styrene or shim brass

Drill half-way through from each side

Timbers no. 13 and no. 9

TIMBER DRILLING JIG

5 To use this jig it is best to drill about halfway into a timber, withdraw the drill, invert the timber and replace it in the jig, then start drilling anew from the opposite face. This assures good alignment.

8 The bridge, now right side up, allows crossbracing laterals to be installed without hindrance from the upper beam timbers. Temporary spacer bars A can be moved as necessary. Note the holes and squared-out area in the sloping end posts. These must be of a size to accommodate the bolthead-washer detail used.

9 With all bottom laterals installed, add the four wind struts of the vertical bracing frames. These pieces are all identical. It will be found that the angled ends of these wind struts will cover the holes previously drilled through the truss timbers, but it's a simple matter later to start the drill into existing holes and continue drilling through the cross braces.

10 Finally, install the top laterals in the three panels, recessing these timbers as seen in the photos. While these parts are hardly seen, the extra work seems justified, since they do help retain alignment and make for a more rigid and positive assembly.

11 Stringers are recessed a scale 2″ deep to accommodate the beam groups. Each of the two stringer sets in this model is formed of four 10 x 18 timbers laminated; thus each group has a total width of 40″ — slightly too wide, but not objectionable. A better arrangement is shown on the drawing — three 12 x 18 timbers form each stringer. There is no reason why one should not use a single piece instead if such is obtainable. After all, the fact that laminated timbers are used is barely, if at all, noticeable between the closely spaced ties. Stringer sets should extend beyond the bridge to rest on top of trestle bents and there align with the stringers of the continuing trestlework. If the bridge is to be used with abutments of stone or similar material, the stringers will rest on these and align with roadbed and ties. It seems a good idea to attach all ties to the stringers, then to attach this unit to the bridge.

12 Two bent assemblies for the approaches (see fig. 13) are assembled over a drawing as with earlier work. No matter how carefully drawing dimensions have been followed in work to this point, it is a good idea to rest stringers across the bridge and measure the actual height requirements of the end bents, then fit them properly. Be sure to allow for a scale 2″ recess in the stringers to accommodate the cap of the bent, if this practice is being followed.

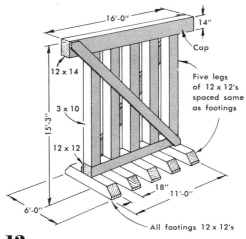

13 BENT (2 REQUIRED)

14 Using a piece of 8 x 8 tie material as a spacer, and a square checking against each tie as it was placed, I added the ties. The only consideration is that there be an equal overhang on both sides. I prepared a crude tie-placement jig of scrapwood that provided a piece across one end for placing ties square with the stringers, properly spaced, and at the same time equalized the overhang. There are numerous ways such a jig can be designed — the reader can come up with one of his own, or follow the one shown.

Girder bridge and approaches

**Complete recipe for a bridge that will take track
over another railroad, a highway, or a stream**

By Jack Work

Photos by the author

A FEW years ago the Esquimalt & Nanaimo Ry. replaced two old wooden trestles with new spans. One crossed a highway; the other, a narrow stream. Living close by, I could watch construction from beginning to end. This provided the inspiration to model a similar span for my railroad.

The two bridges are almost identical. Each has timber trestle approaches to a steel girder span supported by concrete piers. The prototype bridge crossing the stream has a bent of squared timbers to support the trestle approach where the ground appears reasonably solid. The approach on the opposite bank is supported by a bent of round piles driven into the loose earth fill. The bases of the concrete piers are shaped to points where they rest in the stream bed. This is common practice on the upstream side to deflect broken branches and other debris at floodtime; in this situation, the creek is near tidal waters, creating a flow of water in reverse following each rising tide. The other span crossing the highway naturally does not require this feature, so the bases of the piers are rectangular in shape.

One need not follow all the dimensions exactly. A longer trestle approach can be built, using extra bents, on one or both

sides. As in the case of my model, the piers and girder span can be skewed to cross another grade at an angle. The girder span was also shortened from the prototype length because the full length was not required nor desired. By the same token, the girder could be lengthened if necessary to span multiple trackage or a wide stream. If you do fudge the length, remember to keep the girder depth approximately one tenth of its length to stay somewhere within the bounds of sound engineering.

All dimensions in the story are full-size prototype measurements except as noted in the text.

Trestle bents

Begin by laying out the elevation for your bents as shown in fig. 1. First decide the bent height required for a given location, and start by drawing the top cap piece. Space off the upper ends of the leg positions against this cap as shown in fig. 1. Using the same amount of batter (or "lean") as shown for each leg,

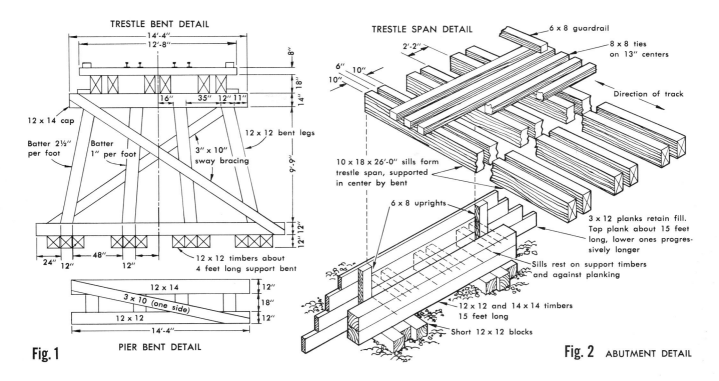

TRESTLE BENT DETAIL

14'-4"
12'-8"
8"
14' 18"
14'
16" 35" 12" 11"
9'-9"

12 x 14 cap
Batter 2½" per foot
Batter 1" per foot
3" x 10" sway bracing
12 x 12 bent legs

12' 12"

24" 12" 48" 12"
12 x 12 timbers about 4 feet long support bent

Fig. 1   PIER BENT DETAIL

12 x 14
3 x 10 (one side)
12 x 12
14'-4"
12"
18"
12"

TRESTLE SPAN DETAIL

6 x 8 guardrail
8 x 8 ties on 13" centers
2'-2"
6" 10"
10"
Direction of track

10 x 18 x 26'-0" sills form trestle span, supported in center by bent

6 x 8 uprights

3 x 12 planks retain fill. Top plank about 15 feet long, lower ones progressively longer

Sills rest on support timbers and against planking

12 x 12 and 14 x 14 timbers 15 feet long

Short 12 x 12 blocks

Fig. 2   ABUTMENT DETAIL

extend or shorten the drawing to suit. The base will spread or narrow according to height. The spacing shown at the base is correct only for the 9'-9" height of the drawing.

Place the completed elevation on a piece of soft pine board to use as a template for pinning the stripwood parts in place for cementing. Waxed paper laid over the elevation will prevent excess cement from attaching the bent to the drawing.

Prestain or prepaint all your stripwood material — all project material, for that matter. The entire project will be 95 percent painted by the time it is assembled. This is much easier than trying to work a paintbrush into the many crevices later. The prototype timbers were creosoted and appeared a blackish-brown shade when new. Creosote color gets lighter and grayer as it weathers.

Use 12" diameter wood dowels for the pile bent, and build it over the same template if you wish. Note, though, that this type of bent has no batter on the legs. The round piles stand vertically, supposedly having been driven into the earth by a pile driver. The bottom of this bent will be hidden later by plaster scenery simulating earth fill, so any method can be used to tie the bottoms of the legs together with scrap wood.

Trestle deck

A plan and template can be laid out to indicate the correct spacing of the longitudinal trestle span sills, as in fig. 2. Stripwood sills can be held in place with pins; or a tiny dab of cement will secure them until the ties have been cemented in place to complete the assembly. If the approach span is made 26 feet as in the prototype, the sills must then be this length.

A supply of trestle ties, 12'-8" long, are cut from 8 x 8 stripwood. These are ce-

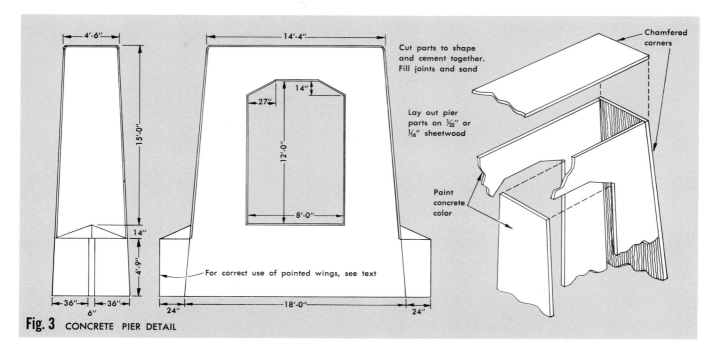

Fig. 3 CONCRETE PIER DETAIL

mented across the trestle sill pieces as shown, with equal amounts overhanging each side. They can be spaced easily and neatly by using a simply made space guide as shown in fig. 5. A piece of sheet wood or heavy cardstock is cut to a width equal to the length of the ties (12'-8" on trestle approach, 13'-4" on girder span). A spacing strip of stripwood is cemented to the bottom of this at one end. Because the tie spacing varies, as well as tie length — the trestle ties are 8 x 8 on 13" centers, thus spaced 5" apart, and the girder span ties are 10 x 14 on 14" centers, or spaced 4" apart — it is best to use two different spacer pieces. They are easy to make.

The timber abutment is simply made with a wall of 3 x 12 planks. The top one is about 15 feet in length. The others gradually lengthen, by 24" or more each, to create a spread that will match and supposedly retain the earth fill to be created later. These planks are held together with two 6 x 8 uprights as shown. In front of this wall, two 12 x 12 or 14 x 14 timbers, 15 feet long, are positioned on short footing timbers. Plaster scenery is later formed around this assembly so it will appear to actually rest in the ballast. Be certain the sill supporting timber is exactly the same distance from the top plank as the combined depth of the sill and tie on the trestle span assembly. In this case, this is 26" — the trestle span sills are 18" plus the 8" depth of the ties.

Concrete piers

The concrete piers could be made in a number of ways. The most realistic method would be to make up forms of 6" wood strips in the same manner as on the prototype. These could be made in sections that fit and lock together so that, after the pier was poured using plaster of paris, the forms could be removed and used over again. The casting resulting from such a mold should be very lifelike, complete with impressions of the individual boards in the form. The results

were surprisingly realistic, with proper handling of the color, on a concrete building foundation modeled in this manner by Muriel Vanderveen.

However, my solution was to cut various components of the pier (from 1/32" sheetwood for my HO scale model) and cement them in the form of a box. See fig. 3. The joints were filled with wood dough and sanded to create the effect of a solid concrete mass. All corners were chamfered by lightly sanding the completed pier at the places shown.

As with most other things exposed to the elements, concrete will change gradually from its freshly poured whitish tan color to a dark gray. Depending on how long the bridge is supposed to have been in service, the piers can be painted to show this weathering. Light and dark gray, as well as orange rust streaks, can be brushed downward from the pier tops to further the weathering.

Short bents atop the concrete piers support the ends of the trestles. See the lower drawing in fig. 1. To determine the correct height, you should take into account the various components that must fit together. The girder, for example, is 48" deep and its ties are 14" for a total of 62". The prototype girders appear to have been shimmed up from the piers with small steel plates totaling 3". This gives a grand total of 65". Obviously, the shimming was to compensate for a difference in height, to bring the tie levels of both girder and trestle flush. We can do the same to allow for slight discrepancies.

Girder span

Now, we have trestle ties 8" deep and sills 18" deep for a 26" total. Deducting this from the 65" total height of the girder assembly gives us the proper bent height of 39".

These short pier bents have vertical legs, and have the same spacing as that at the top of the squared timber bent of the trestle.

If your model is to be placed in such

a position that the interior detailing of a girder span will not be seen, it will save time and work to use a solid block of wood 4'-0" x 9'-6" for 42'-0" for the span. My model was close to the viewing eye, so it seemed worthwhile to build up the girder span from separate sides of sheetwood. Card strips 13" wide were cemented at top and bottom to simulate flanges, and 3" angles were cemented vertically at positions A through I as shown in fig. 4. You can use metal or wood angles.

Four crossbracing assemblies for the interior are required. On the prototype these are made of 3" angles and small steel plates riveted into a unit as in figs. 4 and 5. The thickness of the wood used for the girder sides in the model determines the width of the model crossbracing assemblies. You want to have a total outside width of 9'-6" over faces. Thus the crossbracing width is determined by subtracting the total thickness of two girder sides from 9'-6". The height of the cross bracing can also be measured from the girder sides so it fits between the upper and lower flanges of the girders. Theoretically this is 4 feet high in a "40-foot" span.

Since this inner detail is barely visible, the crossbracing assemblies could be made of stripwood (1/32" for HO, proportionate in other scales) in place of angle material. In fact, you could get by with cutting each assembly in one piece from heavy cardstock. The important thing is that light be able to pass through the bottom of the girder and be seen from the top between the ties. The diagonal bracing angles shown in fig. 4 could also be made of square stripwood.

Fig. 5 shows a general view of girder assembly construction. The tie-spacing guide described earlier is shown in use.

I painted my girder black, although various railroads paint other colors such as gray, brown, or aluminum. Whatever color is selected, it should be suitably weathered and streaked with dirt and rust stains, in varying degrees depending on the age of the bridge or the length of time it was last touched up by the bridge gang.

The most important thing in final assembly is to be sure the tie surfaces of the three separate spans will be flush at the top. This is simply a matter of determining the proper shim required under each pier and bent base. One method that works very well is to cement all components together as a complete bridge; or at least to cement the bents and piers to their various members. Then you hold all with elastic bands to the underside of a straightedge laid across the opening to be spanned. The straightedge rests on the tie tops on either side of the gap and the bridge hangs suspended in the opening. Now it is a simple matter to measure the height of shim material or supporting blocks needed at each location. These are cut and fitted individually, and when all is complete the bridge is cemented or otherwise fastened in place on the layout.

To finish the job, the running rails can be cemented or spiked (with small spikes to avoid splitting the ties) in place. Inner guardrails, placed 10" inside the running rails, go in place next. Timber guardrails, 6 x 8's, are then positioned along the outer ends of the ties on the completed span. They should be about 4" from the tie ends.

Personally I prefer mounting pedestals of appropriate height to support all bridge bents. I fasten these in place on the layout frame, then add scenery around this area up to the tops of the pedestals. Once this detailing is taken care of, the bridge is positioned and final bits of earth filling and scenic detailing completed. This makes scenerywork in cramped quarters much easier. To complete the scene, bits of growth and weeds are planted under the bridge and around the supports to create the appearance of a bridge that has been in place for some time. The model in the photo does not yet have foliage such as this, and so looks like a recently installed bridge. Which it is.

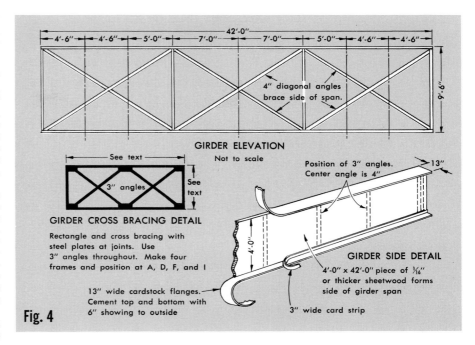

GIRDER ELEVATION
Not to scale

GIRDER CROSS BRACING DETAIL

Rectangle and cross bracing with steel plates at joints. Use 3" angles throughout. Make four frames and position at A, D, F, and I.

13" wide cardstock flanges. Cement top and bottom with 6" showing to outside.

4" diagonal angles brace side of span.

Position of 3" angles. Center angle is 4"

GIRDER SIDE DETAIL

4'-0" x 42'-0" piece of 1/16" or thicker sheetwood forms side of girder span

3" wide card strip

Fig. 4

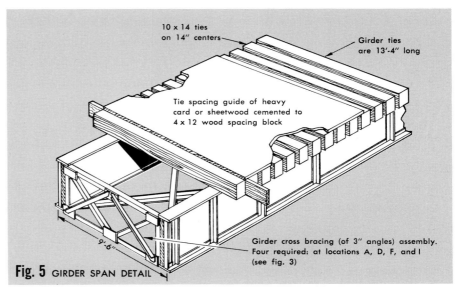

Fig. 5 GIRDER SPAN DETAIL

10 x 14 ties on 14" centers

Girder ties are 13'-4" long

Tie spacing guide of heavy card or sheetwood cemented to 4 x 12 wood spacing block

Girder cross bracing (of 3" angles) assembly. Four required: at locations A, D, F, and I (see fig. 3)

Modeling a covered railroad bridge

The prototype, built by the Chambers Logging Co.
in 1924, still stands near Cottage Grove, Ore.

BY EARL T. JOHNSON

It's possible to drive onto the other end, so the barricade at this end prevents accidents. The stick leaning against it is 5 feet tall.

COVERED railroad bridges are getting to be rare birds. There are just two of them left in my home state of Oregon, both abandoned. One is in Powers, the last of six that used to be on the old Coos Bay Lumber RR., and the other is the subject of this article.

This bridge was built by the Chambers Logging Co. about 1924 and was used until 1946. The bridge spans the Willamette River about a mile south of downtown Cottage Grove near the intersection of highway 99 and the Southern Pacific tracks. The bridge still has rail on it—even a set of switchpoints on the east end of the bridge. The probable reason for this odd arrangement was to provide for a ballon loop coming off the bridge into the mill. Space was very tight here and they needed all the room they could get.

When I first saw this bridge I knew I would have to build a model of it. It seemed to be a natural for model railroad purposes. It is tall, but not overly long; it looks massive, yet graceful; and it is a real attention getter.

Fred Smith and I spent several hours

measuring and photographing the bridge in 1975. Using these data I drew rough drawings which I used to build an HO scale model of the bridge. I worked on the model off and on over a 10-month period when I wasn't doing other projects. The model was completed in the spring of 1976, and I entered it in the NMRA Chicago Railfun Convention contest, where it took first place in the structure category.

I built my model board by board, using dimensionally correct wood throughout. I do admit taking a few minor liberties. For instance, the prototype wood was cut in the company mill to oddball sizes, and I rounded these off to more common sizes. Also, I used 2 x 12 stock for the siding instead of the 1 x 12 siding used on the prototype. I don't believe 1 x 12 stock is commercially offered in HO scale, and it is too difficult to cut wood that thin yourself.

I prestained all my wood with a dirty thinner-type mix to bring out the grain. This was followed by rag wiping-on various shades of gray. I like to use oils and turpentines for final wood coloring.

This side of Johnson's model is the opposite side of the prototype bridge shown at the left. Compare this also with the prototype end view.

I made three patterns in order to cast the many duplicate parts: one for the vertical truss fittings (I drilled these for the rods afterwards); a second pattern for the cross truss fittings (I also drilled these for the cross truss rods); and a third pattern for the upper and lower tension fittings for the vertical truss rods. The vertical truss rod pattern included nut-bolt-washer detail in the master to simulate the ends of the rods.

From these patterns I made about 100 Cerrobend castings. I selected and used about 40 of the best castings on the model. My technique is fairly crude, but it worked out satisfactorily. I glued the flat side of the master to a bit of glass. Then I carefully painted-on the rubber mold material and let this set. Then I added more rubber and a second piece of glass, parallel to the bottom one, with the mold sandwiched between. When this had set, I turned the assembly over and removed the lower glass and the master. I poured the liquid Cerrobend directly into the mold cavity and used the removed piece of glass to press it home. I made some lousy castings this way, but the procedure was fast and easy and it didn't take long to produce enough usable castings.

I used over 600 nut-bolt-washer castings in my model. They are of three sizes, as noted on the drawings. There are also about 40 truss rods.

I precolored all metal parts, using Hobby Black, and touched them up with boxcar red and/or brown to simulate rust. I found that a little rust color is okay if it is mixed with about 15 per cent black, but it is too orange straight from the bottle.

I built the main beams first. Each upper beam was made from four continuous pieces of wood, while the lower ones were spliced with tension fittings

on the sides. The four spars for each beam are 2″ apart to allow air circulation and prevent rot. Most of the spacers are from 2x6 stock as shown on the drawings. Actually, these blocks are 4x6, mortised 1″ into the sides of the adjacent spars to prevent shifting. I was too lazy to do this properly, and who's going to know except you and me?

I laminated the side tension fittings of the lower beams from styrene. There are only six of these, and they were easy to build. Note that the center fitting is to the inside of both lower beams; the side with two fittings is the one that shows.

The beams took longer to build than any other part of the model, but they

This side of the model shows the board-by-board matching of the prototype's broken sheathing.

were a great project for covert modeling at work. I spent a couple of weeks at my office with a pin vise, the beams, some glue, and lots of nut-bolt-washer castings hidden in my desk. Incidentally, I found that methy ethyl ketone works well to cement these castings into wood with minimal mess. Push the castings into holes in the wood and touch a minidrop on with a pin.

Contrary to usual model bridge construction practices, I built the cross trusses first and joined them later with the vertical trusses. Possibly it was harder this way, but it came out all right. I did get the bonus of being able to lay the trackwork directly on the lower truss without the sides' getting in the way. I cut my ties from 6 x 8 stock, using a Northwest Short Line stripwood cutting jig — an invaluable tool for this type of modeling. About every 10th tie was made from electrically gapped

printed circuit board. The rail was soldered to these p.c. ties. The p.c. ties were painted to match the wood. Surprisingly, I found that Floquil foundation color looks like silver-gray wood.

After the bridge truss was finished, I moved on to the falsework. Most of the layout is shown on the end elevation of the drawings. I cut the 8 x 10 rafter joist first, piecing it between the truss rod tension fittings of the upper beam. Apparently, this is a prototype construction error, as there was inadequate ventilation in the bridge. This must have been discovered when the first steamer went through. Parts of the lower siding were removed to correct the problem. This accounts for the random openings in the side walls. It looks like the bridge was completely sheathed at one time. This was a lucky error — the bridge is much more attractive this way.

Using the rafter joist as a basis, I erected the end framing members. Then I added the stringers along the sides that cause the siding to flare at the bottom. Then the boards and battens were added. Note that the boards are not full length, but join along the 2 x 6 stringers.

The rafters were built in a simple jig and erected on 4-foot centers. There is no ridgepole on the prototype, but I used a 6 x 6 ridgepole on my model to make the rafters line up easier. Then the roofing stringers were added.

For me, the hardest part of the model construction was making and painting the roof. I used Campbell corrugated roofing stock. The roof required 96 4 x 8-foot panels. The prototype's roof is really a weird color. It took me 2 weeks to get the paint effect so that the panels really stood out as on the prototype. It taught me to study my prototypes more carefully (and perhaps pick better ones).

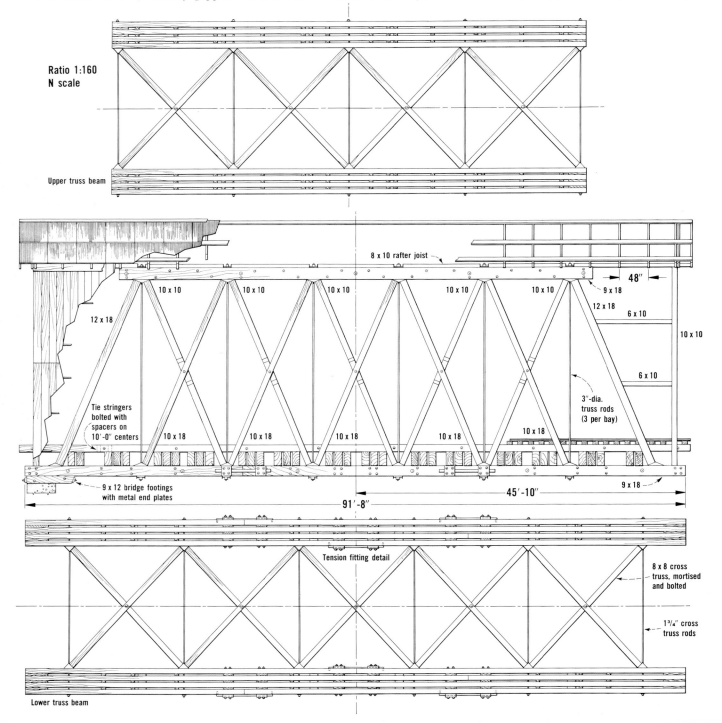

The bridge rests on cast concrete piers. They were poured in wooden forms. I duplicated this by making scale forms and pouring Hydrocal into them.

When my model was completed, I sprayed it lightly with weathered black to blend and age the finish. I also highlighted selected boards of the siding with additional light gray.

I ran across a new (to me, anyway) gimmick for reproducing scale graffiti on my model. Jean Major, wife of my hobby dealer, gave me a piece of Sarel transfer paper. This material is commonly used in a hobby called "tole painting." It is available in craft shops such as those that cater to macrame and beadwork. It comes in several colors. Whatever you mark on the Sarel paper transfers to the surface. It is really great stuff!

I got rather involved with this model, trying to build it exactly like the prototype. I did learn quite a bit about bridge construction in general and covered railroad bridges in particular. I got to wondering how many covered rail-

This photo clearly shows how the beam tension fittings were built and also shows the mortising of the crosspieces. The bolted channels are the vertical truss rod tension fittings.

road bridges still exist? In addition to the two in Oregon, I know of one in Pe Ell, Wash., and the St. Johnsbury bridge in Vermont, which is still being used. Does anyone know of others? I would be most appreciative if you'd let me know about any others (covered railroad bridges only; not highway). If you know of others, please drop me a line at 423 N.W. Van Dyke, Grants Pass, Ore. 97526. Maybe I can work up a directory of covered railroad bridges.

[Four covered railroad bridges remain in New England: between Wolcott and Hardwick, Vt., on the Vermont Northern (formerly the St. Johnsbury & Lamoille County); at Hillsboro, N. H.,

on an unused portion of a Boston & Maine branch line; and two near Kellyville, N.H., on the Claremont & Concord, a short line operating a former B&M branch. In 1976 a fifth bridge—in Goffstown, N.H., on an industrial spur of B&M—was destroyed by fire. Books recommended for railroad covered bridge fans include Edgar T. Mead Jr.'s *Through Covered Bridges to Concord*, the story of the C&C (The Stephen Greene Press, P. O. Box 1000, Brattleboro, Vt. 05301; 1970) and the series of books on covered bridges, by states or regions, written by Richard Sanders Allen and published by The Stephen Greene Press.—*J. David Ingles.*]

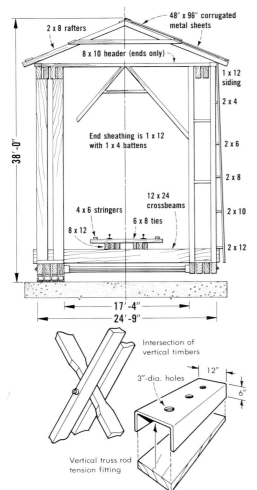

48" x 96" corrugated metal sheets
2 x 8 rafters
8 x 10 header (ends only)
38'-0"
End sheathing is 1 x 12 with 1 x 4 battens
1 x 12 siding
2 x 4
2 x 6
2 x 8
2 x 10
2 x 12
12 x 24 crossbeams
4 x 6 stringers
6 x 8 ties
8 x 12
17'-4"
24'-9"

Intersection of vertical timbers
3"-dia. holes
12"
6"
Vertical truss rod tension fitting

The unusual switchpoints on the east end of the bridge are explained in the text. Notice the graffiti: "TP-n-LB Forever" and "Tina-n-Lars." Note, too, in the left foreground, that this end of the bridge has been burned, but apparently it was a minor fire that was quickly extinguished. This view also shows the spacing of the vertical truss rods, grouped in threes.

Bash a bridge

Custom-fit a bridge to your situation

BY RICHARD L. WHITNEY

PHOTOS BY CARL LUNDQUIST

A recent editorial pointed out that trees for one scale are just as good in another. Within limits, the same applies to bridges. The sizes of members in a bridge depend much more on the loads they must carry than on the "scale" of the bridge. Thus, an HO footbridge can become an N scale mainline span, or, as author Whitney shows, an HO truss can become at least a lightweight bridge for a ¼" scale system. Whitney's assembly methods are suitable for all scales.

THE June 1971 MR provided the inspiration for my bridge. The cover of that issue showed a K-27 gently nosing its way over a lacy deck truss on Charlie Schwarm's ¼" scale 36"-gauge layout.

Charlie's bridge was made from an Atlas HO kit. I wanted to go a step farther and widen the truss, also lengthen it by one panel. What I did can be followed literally, or you may want to read the following steps for the precautionary value they may have for designing a bridge of your own. With perhaps a score of bridges available, the possibilities are great.

I used the Atlas no. 84 truss bridge. It is cleverly designed to provide either a pony truss or a deck truss.* I chose the deck truss idea, but I decided to make the bridge twice as wide as the original version intended for HO track. I also felt the bridge would look better if it were one panel longer.

*A pony truss has sidepieces extending above rail level but they are not cross-connected above the track. A through truss has the cross connections above the track. A deck truss is in an inverted position with the track entirely above the truss.

As the bridge comes, the truss pieces have three rectangular panels each plus two diagonal half panels at the ends. I wanted mine to be four panels plus two halves, but close inspection of the original showed that the center panel of each truss was slightly longer than the other two rectangular panels. Thus, to preserve symmetry, my design had to consist of two center and two end panels for each new truss side. The discarded portions are shown in fig. 1, a left and a right piece making a full truss side.

The project was a great exercise in kitbashing. Most modelers could complete such a project in two or three evenings with a minimum of skill. Civil engineers might point out some technical flaws in the design, and some persnickety individuals could probably correct them with a few more pieces of styrene. I did not bother, as I was primarily interested in having a steel bridge that would contrast interestingly with the heavy timber bridges found on most of the rest of my ¼" scale 36"-gauge Bonanza & Borrasca RR.

The parts I used included:

4 Atlas no. 84 HO deck truss bridge kits.
6 feet (2 meters) Camino 8 x 8 timber.
9 feet (2.5 meters) Camino 6 x 8 timber.
5 feet (1.8 meters) rail, spikes, ties.
2 pkgs. Grandt 1½" nut-bolt-washers C-23.
.020" (.5 mm.) sheet styrene.
Cement for styrene.

I began with the X-shaped sway-brace pieces. These fit inside the original truss. To make a wider truss, I joined them in pairs to make them twice as wide. Five pairs (from 10 pieces) are required; and the important thing is to have all of these pieces face the same way, because their sides are different. These pieces have tongues to fit into other parts of the bridge.

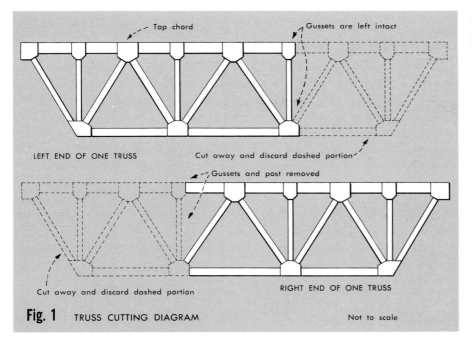

Fig. 1 TRUSS CUTTING DIAGRAM — Not to scale

LEFT END OF ONE TRUSS

RIGHT END OF ONE TRUSS

Top chord

Gussets are left intact

Cut away and discard dashed portion

Gussets and post removed

Cut away and discard dashed portion

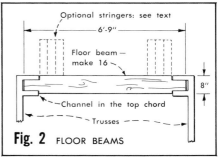

Fig. 2 FLOOR BEAMS

Optional stringers: see text

6'-9"

Floor beam — make 16

Channel in the top chord

Trusses

8"

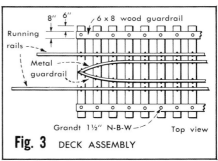

Fig. 3 DECK ASSEMBLY

8" 6"

6 x 8 wood guardrail

Running rails

Metal guardrail

Grandt 1½" N-B-W

Top view

These are still needed at the outer sides of each pair but are to be removed in the centers. Use a razor saw and swiss files to clean them off. All through this construction, flash (the ridges formed in the molding process) and sprues (the gates through which the plastic was poured) should be removed and the surfaces smoothed. Also, in some places where parts are to be butted and cemented together, you will find the so-called flat and square edges have a slight slope, making square butting impossible. This is due to the draft that is needed in the molding process. Such sloped surfaces must be squared with a file before joining the parts.

With the XX pieces now joined, you can turn to the bottom latticework. It's labeled "bottom brace" on the Atlas instruction sheet diagram. Like the sides of the bridge, one end panel should be removed from each of the four original pieces. Then they should be joined into two side-by-side pairs and finally should be joined end to end. You will have to remove some of the tongues and struts to make the parts fit. The joints won't look realistic, so cut five strips of .020" styrene scale 5" wide and 63" long. Cement these over the struts between each pair of existing gussets. Weight the assembly overnight to hold everything in position until the cement has dried.

After the plastic part of the bridge is completed you can add the floor beams. Cut these from 6 x 8 timber 6'-9" long, with the ends notched, somewhat like tenons, so they will slip into the channels on the inner sides of the top chords as in fig. 2.

Normally, the deck of a bridge consists of three layers of timber. Running lengthwise, directly under each rail, is a stringer. Typically, for a bridge this size, the stringer would be three pieces side by side, of perhaps 12 x 18 material. These are shown in phantom in fig. 2, but I did not include them in my model. The next layer consists of bridge ties. Mine are simply supported on the top chords instead of being on stringers. Finally come the rails, six of them. At the outside

are two wood guardrails. Then come the running rails, and inside of them, two metal guardrails: fig. 3.

It is important to have the ties uniform in spacing, at right angles to the trusses, and neatly aligned along their ends. To accomplish this, it helps to make a "piano key" jig. This consists of slots into which the ties fall in perfect alignment. They are held in place until the wood guardrails are attached.

I made my jig on a 15" (38-cm.) length of plywood. Pieces of 6 x 8 strip stock were attached to it permanently to form spacers and an alignment spine. Start with the spine. This is a 15"-long piece cemented along one edge of the plywood. Cement all of these pieces so the broad side is down. Now cut 34 pieces of the same material about scale 7 feet long. Attach the first at one end of the spine and be sure it is exactly at right angles to the spine. Place a tie next to it as a spacer and then attach another 7-foot "piano key." Continue, always keeping the keys at right angles to the spine, until you have formed pockets to accept all 33 ties.

With the ties held in place and in alignment, it is a simple matter to add the timber guardrails. You can also attach running rails and metal guardrails while the ties are in the jig if you wish.

Paint the nut-bolt-washer castings either a weathered black or a rusty color before installing them. Slip these into .040" (1-mm.) holes. You can drill the holes with a pin vise. Add a bit of the cement to each casting before pressing it into the hole.

Caution: The track spikes you select should not be so long that they pass all the way through your bridge ties. If they must, grind off the tip from the underside.

One's natural tendency is to end the rails on the truss opposite each other, but it will be far better to stagger them at least 5 scale feet, letting one or both rails extend onto the approach roadway before reaching the next rail joint.

If you weather your rails, the sides of the running rails and the entire surface

of the metal guardrails should be coated.

Final assembly is next. Follow steps A, B, and C on the Atlas instructions for cementing the various components of the truss assembly together. Now insert the 16 wood floor beams into the truss channels. These should be a sliding fit, as they may have to be shifted during assembly. Insert two above each end panel and three above each of the other panels. Place small pieces of masking tape over the top of each of the 16 floor beams as a painting mask. If your bridge will carry engines that are comparatively heavy, you may want to add a wood crossmember between each of the square gussets at each end of the truss in order to provide more load-bearing surface and strength. These two pieces will be triangular in cross section.

Paint the truss assembly. I used Floquil's grimy black. Spray lightly to avoid marring the fine rivet detail. Use two or three light coats if necessary, rather than one heavy one. You may also want to paint the leftover pieces from the Atlas kits for later use as detailing scraps. They make good flatcar loads and look great scattered near a line shack as if they were spare trusses being stored for use by your B&B maintenance gang at a later date. Be sure to weather these pieces with extra amounts of rust, mud, and so forth.

The deck assembly is secured to the truss superstructure by placing cement on the tops of the 16 floor beams and laying the deck over the trusses, keeping the tie overhang on each side equal. You will have to maneuver the floor beams back and forth in their slots so that each comes immediately below a track tie. I would suggest using a slow-drying cement for this because it may take some time to align everything properly. Remove any excess cement. Put a weight on the bridge and allow the joints to set overnight.

Prepare some timber cribbing or stonework abutments to support the ends of the truss and it's ready for installation and that satisfying first crossing by your favorite locomotive.

A big bridge
for your double-track main

Turn a Lionel bridge into an HO scale truss bridge

BY DEAN FREYTAG
PHOTOS BY THE AUTHOR

FROM the time I first saw the Lionel O gauge single-track bridge, there was no question in my mind that this was just what I needed to replace the double-track deck bridge over Reid Gap on my HO scale South Ridge Lines. If you have high-tonnage traffic on your double-track main, this bridge may be just the thing to carry it across a gorge.

As I modified the bridge, it is now approximately a scale 2 feet shy of having the full clearance indicated by the HO NMRA standards gauge. I can live with this discrepancy. The tracks are spaced the proper distance from the sides of the bridge. So far I have had 2-8-8-2s, 2-6-6-4s, and 0-10-2s meet on the bridge with no difficulty. If worse came to worst, I could always stop traffic on the adjoining track to avoid a meet on the bridge, but so far I've had no problems.

Your first step should be to discard the sheet-steel deck plate that comes with the bridge. A deck system that you can see through is the biggest improvement you

can make to the original structure. Cement the two top girder assemblies into position per the instructions.

When the cement has set up, your next step will be to install the two end floor beams at each end of the bridge. These first four lengths of Plastruct I-beam go in place between the angled portal sides and first pair of verticals in from each end. This will give the bridge some rigidity as you continue the project. (Note: At this point do only the *two* end floor beams at each end. You'll be doing a lot of work from the inside of the bridge and need access to it.) The way the Lionel side trusses are cast, you'll need to notch the lower flanges of the truss (on the inside) the width of the web of the I-beam to allow it to fit flush up against the truss. See fig. 1.

Each of the beams is further secured by triangular gussets snugged under the flange of the beam and against the truss, also shown in fig. 1.

Next, referring to fig. 2, turn over the bridge and cement lengths of Plastruct Ts to the underside of the entire cast bridge top, forming what represents I-beam X-bracing. Cover the point where

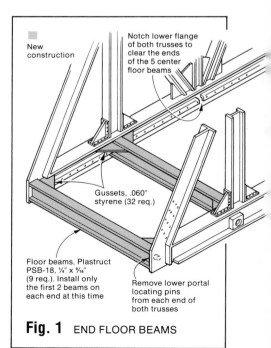

New construction

Notch lower flange of both trusses to clear the ends of the 5 center floor beams

Gussets, .060″ styrene (32 req.)

Floor beams, Plastruct PSB-18, ¼″ x ⁹⁄₁₆″ (9 req.). Install only the first 2 beams on each end at this time

Remove lower portal locating pins from each end of both trusses

Fig. 1 END FLOOR BEAMS

the girders meet with a gusset the same size as the cast-on one on the top.

Still working with the bridge upside down, as shown in fig. 3 cement Plastruct horizontal braces between corresponding verticals. (I used my NMRA standards gauge to determine the proper above-floor height. You can position yours based on the height of the end cross beam in fig. 4.) Cut triangular supporting gussets and cement them in position according to fig. 3.

Working with the same pair of verticals, your next step will be to fabricate X-bracing from Evergreen styrene, also shown in fig. 3. The ends of the braces fit inside the truss verticals as shown. Simply cut them to fit as closely as you can. As with the top X-bracing, the first cross piece is full length; the other is actually two pieces that meet in the center to form the X. Cement rectangular gussets on each side of the X. Repeat the steps in fig. 3 all the way across the inside of the bridge.

Square off the upper inside corners of each portal (fig. 4). Then use Evergreen styrene to box in the end girders as shown. Using Plastruct beams, fabricate the end cross beams and X-bracing. I cut these as closely as possible and tacked them into position flush with the outside of the portal. Then I cut the gussets and cemented them in position. Ignore the rivets for now; I'll tell you about them later on.

Now go ahead and complete the installation of the floor beams and gussets (as in fig. 1) the entire length of the bridge.

After determining the center line of the bridge, I cemented four strips of Evergreen styrene (positioned for appropriate track gauge and track spacing) the length of the bridge on top of the floor beams. See fig. 5.

I really "fudged" on the next step — the stringers between the floor beams. See fig. 6. I cut lengths of Plastruct, and with the bridge upside down, I fitted all

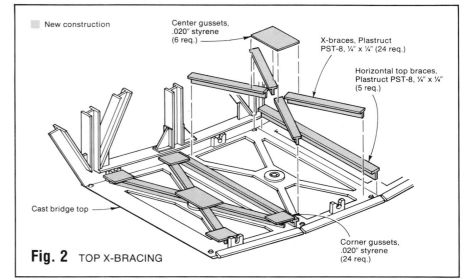

Fig. 2 TOP X-BRACING

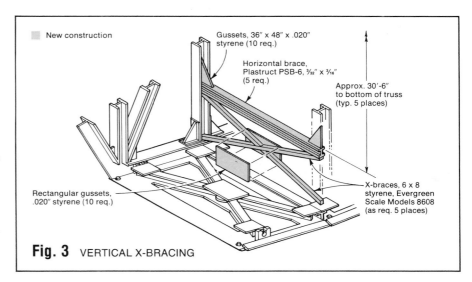

Fig. 3 VERTICAL X-BRACING

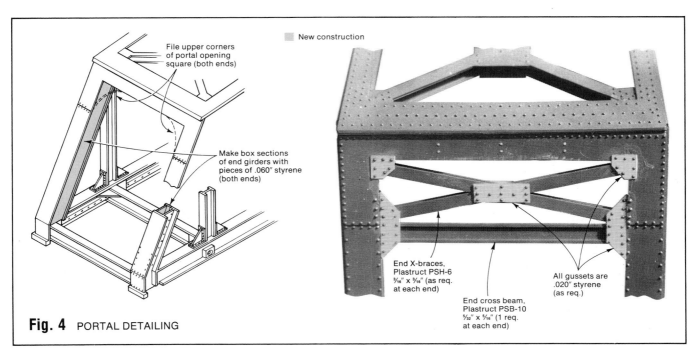

Fig. 4 PORTAL DETAILING

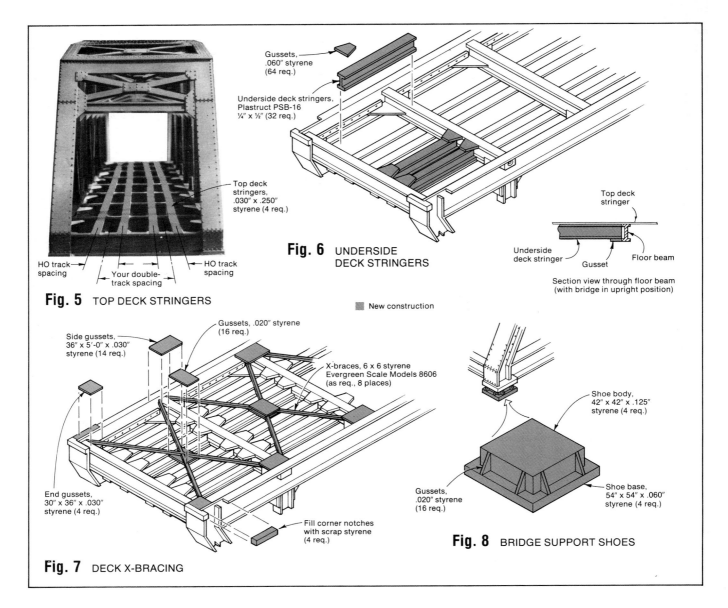

Fig. 5 TOP DECK STRINGERS

Fig. 6 UNDERSIDE DECK STRINGERS

Gussets, .060" styrene (64 req.)

Underside deck stringers, Plastruct PSB-16 ¼" x ½" (32 req.)

Top deck stringers, .030" x .250" styrene (4 req.)

HO track spacing

Your double-track spacing

HO track spacing

Top deck stringer

Underside deck stringer

Gusset

Floor beam

Section view through floor beam (with bridge in upright position)

New construction

Side gussets, 36" x 5'-0" x .030" styrene (14 req.)

Gussets, .020" styrene (16 req.)

X-braces, 6 x 6 styrene Evergreen Scale Models 8606 (as req., 8 places)

End gussets, 30" x 36" x .030" styrene (4 req.)

Fill corner notches with scrap styrene (4 req.)

Fig. 7 DECK X-BRACING

Shoe body, 42" x 42" x .125" styrene (4 req.)

Shoe base, 54" x 54" x .060" styrene (4 req.)

Gussets, .020" styrene (16 req.)

Fig. 8 BRIDGE SUPPORT SHOES

32 of them individually and cemented them to the underside of the styrene strip. The ends of the stringers butt against the top flange of the floor beams.

Next, I cut gussets and applied them to the underside of the bridge at the intersection of the stringers and floor beams. The flat portion of the gusset is cemented to the stringer, and the long edge is affixed to the beam. These hold the stringers in position. They look fine and, once the tracks are in place, the gap between the stringers and the beam flanges (see fig. 6 cross section) is not noticeable.

Still working on the underside of the deck, fabricate the X-bracing between the floor beams. As with the bracing in the top of the bridge, one piece is full length, and the other is made up of two pieces. Apply rectangular gussets to both sides of the intersection.

At the intersection of each floor beam and the Lionel truss, cement a large side gusset. Figure 7 shows the various X-braces and gussets.

This completes the basic structure — but with a bit of additional work it can be made to look even better.

For some reason the two original top sections were cast with a raised flange on just one side of each X-brace. Seeing no need for them, I used an X-acto equipped with a no. 17 blade to peel them off.

In the process of removing these I shaved off a rivet or two, but never fear, there are plenty more where they came from. On the sides of the deck girders you'll find round clusters of rivets that, to my way of thinking, have no apparent function now that the new floor has been installed. I always thought it was silly to transfer rivets, but it turned out to be easy to do, and they looked so good on the gussets that I went ahead and did it.

I simply peeled off (into the palm of one hand) enough for each new location as I went along. I gave the new location a liberal coat of liquid cement, dipped the no. 11 point in same, touched the point to a rivet in my hand, and in nothing flat the rivets were transferred to their new location. I counted the little buggers and there were 200 plus, but the job was certainly not as time-consuming and/or as tedious as one might think. They add a lot to the overall appearance of the bridge — particularly the ends.

There are a couple of other places to patch up. Where the two top panels join there is a very obvious gap in the center. I covered it with a .020" gusset and applied more rivets. On the sides where the screws are supposed to go through to the sheet metal deck, I fitted a piece of .010" styrene to hide the hole.

For the rail and ties I used sections of Atlas Snap-Track soldered together. Then I stripped the rail from other pieces and cemented the tie sections upside down to the other ties, making them look deeper, as bridge ties should be.

The final bit of detail is a single walkway on the one side. I used Evergreen styrene no. 8212 2 x 12s and built up the railing using no. 8204 2 x 4s.

With construction completed, I painted the bridge, built and put the piers in position, fabricated shoes for it to rest on (see fig. 8), added an approach section at one end, soldered the bridge rails to the approach tracks, and started running those heavy freights across Reid Gap once again. ✿

Build a straining-beam pony truss

Practical timber bridge can be adjusted in size to fit many model railroad situations

By Whit Towers

BRIDGES can provide lots of interest in the model scene, and they are fun to build. This straining-beam bridge is a pony truss on the Howe pattern that is relatively simple to construct, yet has enough detail to be attractive to the eye.

In building bridges for your model railroad you'll want to choose a type in keeping with the period you are representing and the sort of traffic your main or branch line will be handling. This particular bridge might be out of place on a permanent location on a heavily trafficked main line. My Alturas & Lone Pine is a short line with light traffic, running through country where timber is easily produced. The period is the early 1930's, when there were still plenty of timber bridges around, especially in the West.

Construction is simple. You can use any make of accurately dimensioned stripwood. I suggest building up the side trusses first. I made mine by drawing the arrangement full size for the model on paper, covering this with waxed paper so cement would not stick to the drawing; then by pushing pins into the drawing I could lay the various timbers so they would not move out of place until the cement had set. Since I made two spans, the same pins served four times over, and each truss was exactly the same size and shape as the others.

The top and bottom chords of the prototype are actually two 11 x 14 timbers side by side, and the bottom chord must be one long piece the full length of the span. This is because it is a tension member. Both tension rods and compression posts reach vertically from upper to lower chord, and the two posts at each location are slightly canted to give the spans lateral rigidity. The diagonal timbers vary in cross section depending on their position in the truss, since not all will get the same loading.

After the two trusses are built, they can be joined. This, again, is done with both timbers and rods for tension. The cross timbers are notched Chinese-puzzle fashion to seat underneath the bottom chords, and the vertical tension rods hold them there.

I use 00-90 brass threading rod for my tension rods, threading it at the ends and using 00-90 nuts to take up the tension. The nuts at the upper end can be recessed into the timber, since they are oversize, and can be covered with Kemtron bolthead castings of proper size. Some fastidious modelers may realize that 00-90 rod is 4" in diameter in HO scale, while the prototype had only 2"-diameter tension rods. You could correct this by using wire straightened and fastened into the timbers. For this the wire size should be as follows:

N, .013"; TT, .017"; HO, .022"; OO, .026"; S, .031"; O, Q, .042".

Theoretically the whole bridge can be assembled and held together with threaded truss rods if you can figure out how to hold the parts together while assembling them. In practice, cementing the timbers together and adding the rods later seems more practical. A word of caution if you do use threaded rod: tightening it too much will throw the truss out of shape.

The bridge floor is supported on groups of three timbers lying across the tops of the bottom chords. The stringers, spaced at about track gauge, run lengthwise over these. Over the stringers go the ties and rails. It is simpler to assemble all this as a unit and then place it between the trusses during bridge assembly.

Where you require two or more bridges to span the area being crossed — in my own case a river valley — the bridge will be supported on piers whose height must be adjusted to fit the actual conditions encountered. End support can be provided by piers with a trestle leading to solid ground; where the embankment is steep, a masonry abutment such as I used would be in keeping.

Normally, wood bridges are creosoted to prolong their life, but the completed bridge can be painted if you prefer. It is a good plan to paint or "creosote" the stock before building the bridge. Then, merely touch up any raw edges afterward.

Modifying bridge size

While many "impossible" bridges have been built on model layouts, this is mostly due to haste or ignorance. Actually you have much more freedom in changing bridge dimensions than you do in modeling cars or houses. A truss, doubled in height and length with somewhat heavier timbers (or steel members), may be just as credible a bridge after its enlargement as it was before. Where amateur bridge redesigners go astray is in making the timbers or other members too thin or too thick for the size of the bridge and the load the bridge is to carry, or heavier in the wrong places.

Usually the slanting members in a truss are at an angle near 45 degrees — rarely any more horizontal than this, occasionally a little more vertical. Members that slant downward toward the span ends will be heavier than members slanting downward toward the center. Whether verticals are heavy or lightweight depends on which way the other members slant.

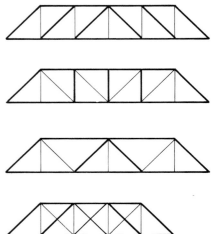

Another way a bridge can be changed in length is to add or subtract panels as Whit did in making a six-panel bridge into a nine-panel bridge. If the bridge will carry the same load, the members should be made heavier when this is done, but if — as in Whit's case — the load will be lighter, the lengthened span may not need heavier members. The limit to truss lengthening by adding panels comes when the span length becomes 8 to 10 times its height: Whit's is about the limit, being 9 times. For a still longer span, the bridge engineer would find longer, deeper panels more economical. — MR staff.

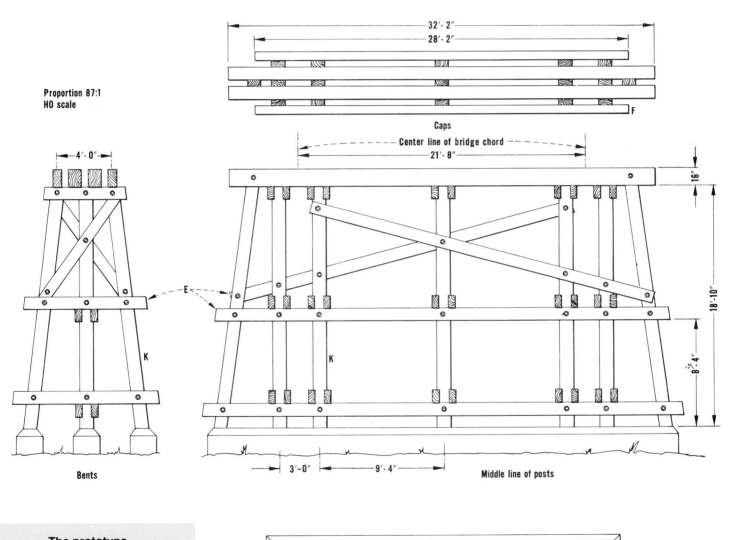

Proportion 87:1
HO scale

32'- 2"

28'- 2"

Caps

F

Center line of bridge chord

21'- 8"

16"

18'-10"

8'- 4"

4'- 0"

E

K

K

Bents

3'- 0"   9'- 4"   Middle line of posts

The prototype

These drawings are based on information used by permission of All-Nation Line of Chicago.

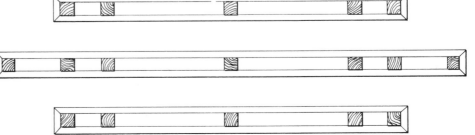

Foundation

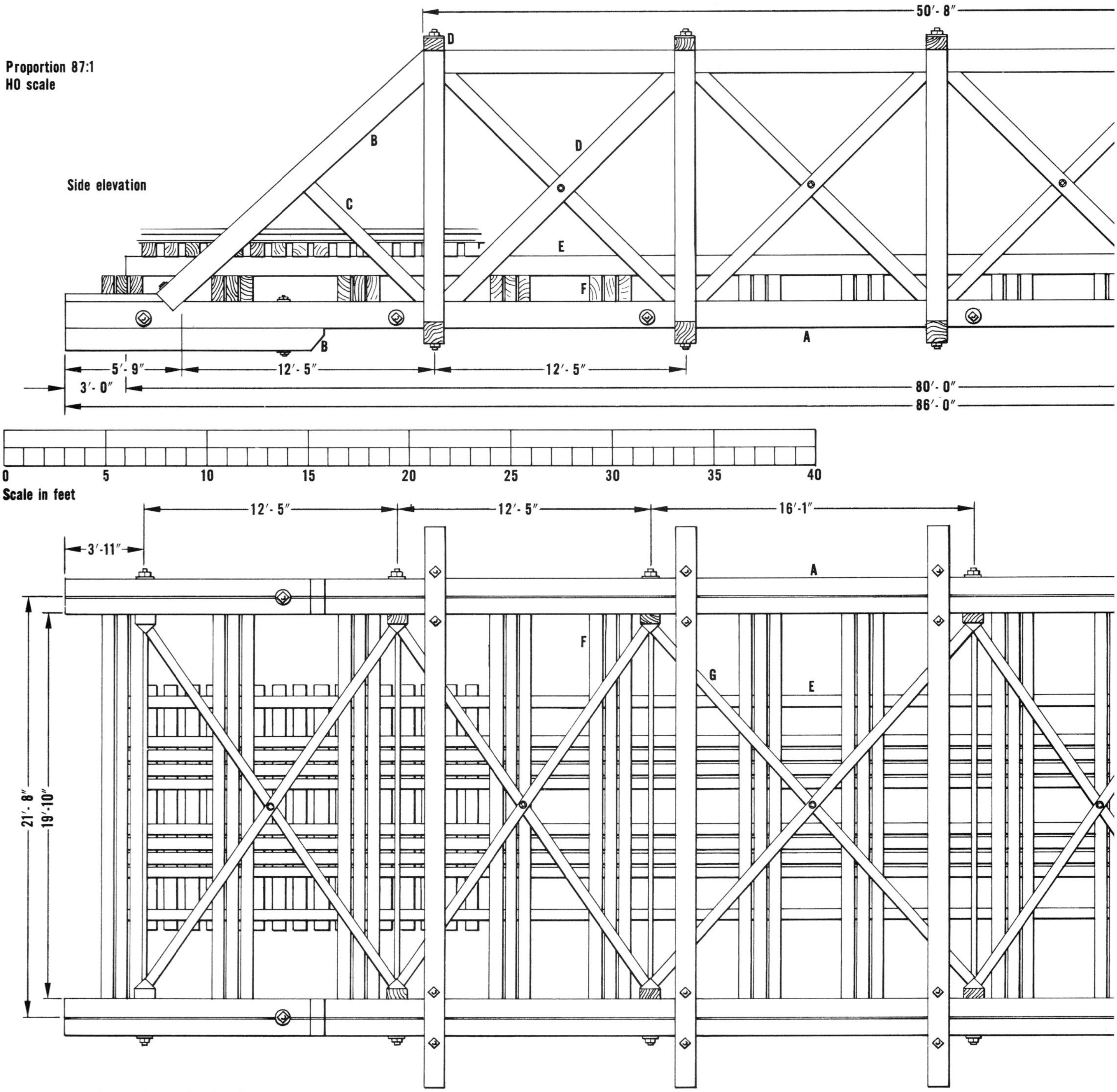
Proportion 87:1
HO scale
Side elevation
50′- 8″
D
B
C
D
E
F
A
B
5′- 9″
12′- 5″
12′- 5″
3′- 0″
80′- 0″
86′- 0″
0
5
10
15
20
25
30
35
40
Scale in feet
12′- 5″
12′- 5″
16′-1″
3′-11″
A
F
G
E
21′- 8″
19′-10″

Timber sizes in inches

A	10½ x 16	F	8 x 16
B	14 x 23	G	6 x 6
C	6 x 9	H	12 x 14
D	8 x 12	J	5 x 22
E	6 x 12	K	12 x 12

Closest fractional inch to above sizes

Proto	N	TT	HO	S	O, Q
5	1/32	3/64	1/16	3/32	1/8
6	1/32	3/64	1/16	3/32	1/8
8	3/64	1/16	5/64	1/8	5/32
9	3/64	5/64	3/32	9/64	3/16
12	1/16	3/32	9/64	3/16	1/4
14	3/32	7/64	5/32	7/32	17/64
16	3/32	9/64	3/16	1/4	21/64
23	1/8	3/16	1/4	3/8	1/2

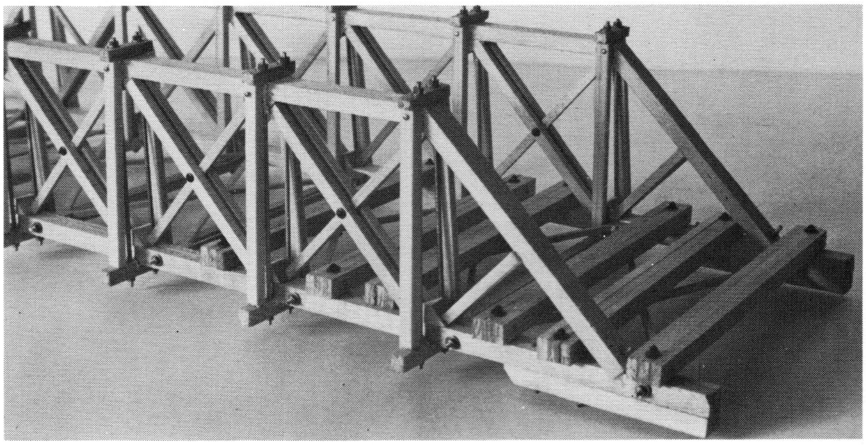

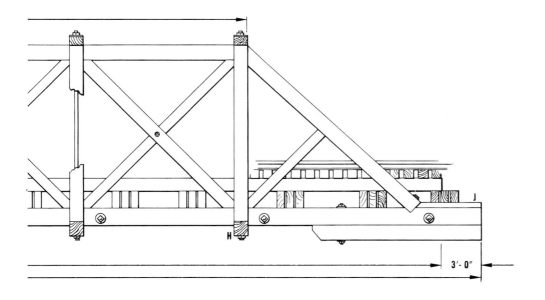

3'- 0"

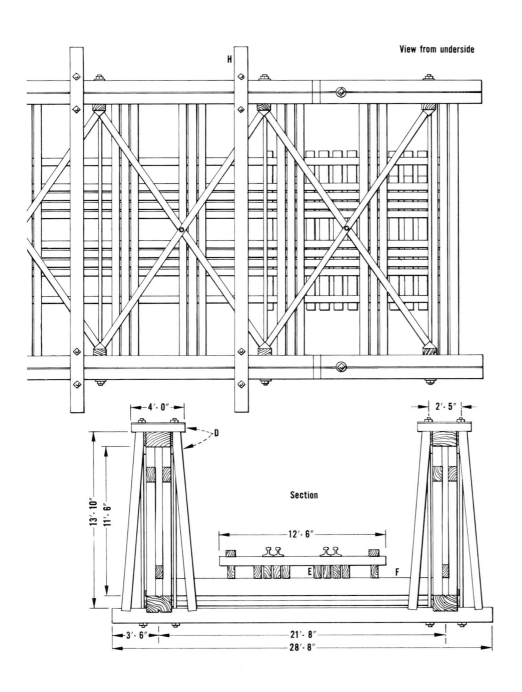

View from underside

H

Section

4'- 0"

2'- 5"

D

13'- 10"

11'- 6"

12'- 6"

E   F

3'- 6"

21'- 8"

28'- 8"

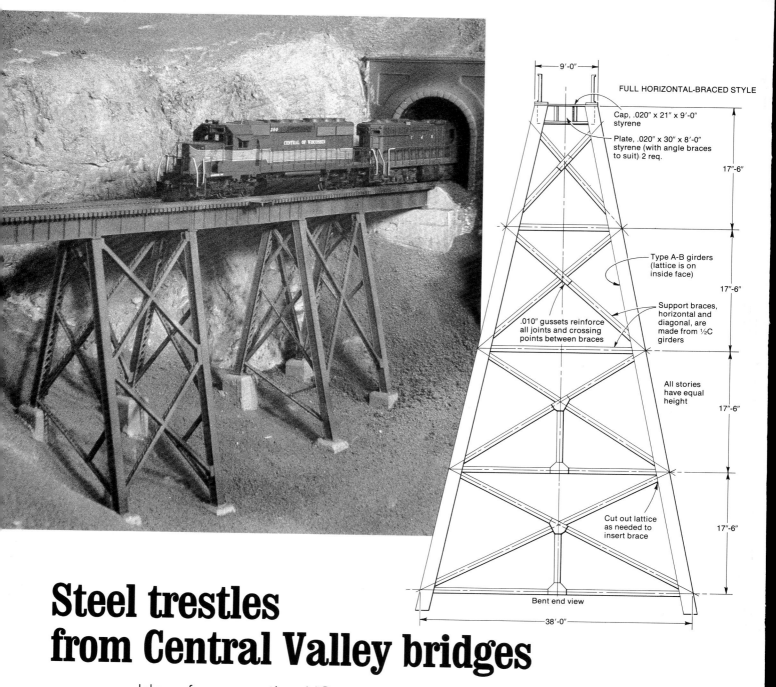

FULL HORIZONTAL-BRACED STYLE

9'-0"

Cap, .020" x 21" x 9'-0" styrene

Plate, .020" x 30" x 8'-0" styrene (with angle braces to suit) 2 req.

17"-6"

Type A-B girders (lattice is on inside face)

17"-6"

Support braces, horizontal and diagonal, are made from ½C girders

.010" gussets reinforce all joints and crossing points between braces

All stories have equal height

17"-6"

Cut out lattice as needed to insert brace

17"-6"

Bent end view

38'-0"

Steel trestles from Central Valley bridges

Ideas for converting HO scale truss bridges into steel trestles

BY STEVE KARAS

WHEN I laid out my HO scale Central of Wisconsin RR's Kingsford Division, more than 8 percent of its main line was on bridges. Since the CW is a modern iron-ore hauler, it needed steel bridges to handle heavily loaded trains. In addition, the almost constant curvature of the trackage put many of these bridges on curves.

Steel trestle construction is straightforward and not too difficult. In fact, most of the construction time is spent making the lattice-work beams needed for the trestle bent posts and bracing. A few evenings of this tedious work convinced me that there had to be a better way. Then I built a styrene Central Valley 150-foot Pratt truss bridge kit. I

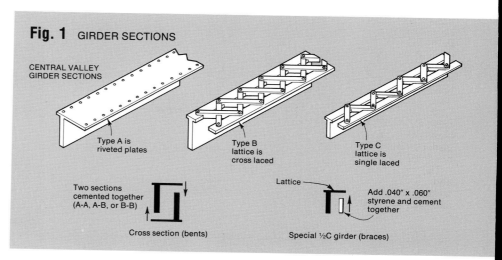

Fig. 1 GIRDER SECTIONS

CENTRAL VALLEY GIRDER SECTIONS

Type A is riveted plates

Type B lattice is cross laced

Type C lattice is single laced

Two sections cemented together (A-A, A-B, or B-B)

Cross section (bents)

Lattice

Add .040" x .060" styrene and cement together

Special ½C girder (braces)

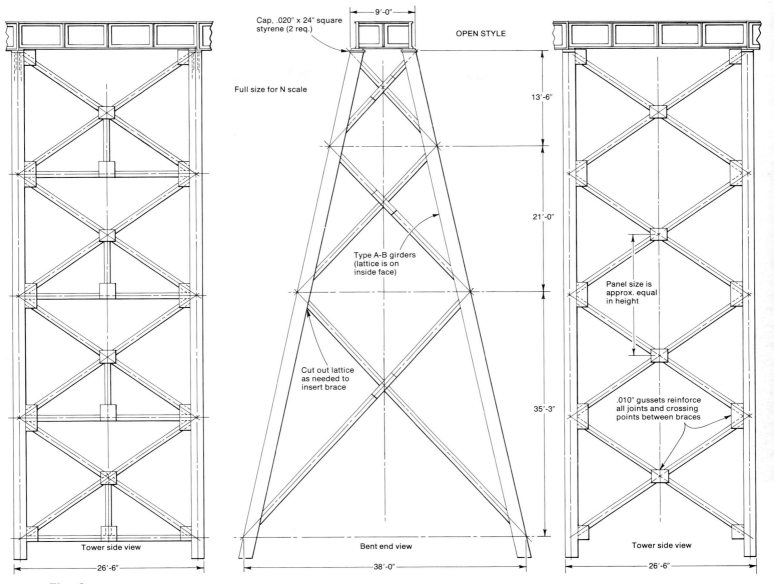

Fig. 2 FREE-LANCED BENT AND TOWER CONSTRUCTION

quickly realized that its parts would go a long way toward simplifying my trestle construction projects.

The Central Valley bridge girder sections are the key to this whole steel trestle construction method. Figure 1 shows the three basic girder types found in the Central Valley bridge kit. Each girder is cast as a pair of long L-shapes which must be cemented together to get the box beams. The type A and type B sections are interchangeable to make beams with both sides plated (A-A), one side latticed and one side plated (A-B), or both sides latticed (B-B). The type C girder sections are smaller, so they are not interchangeable.

The type C girders make good cross and sway (angle) bracing in the steel trestles. I use them to make two different beams. The first type follows the Central Valley procedure with two type C sections cemented together with lacing showing on top and bottom. I call the second version a ½C girder. In this version I cement a piece of .040″ x .060″ styrene strip to the underside of the lacing on a type C casting to create a U-shaped beam. See fig. 1. These beams are useful to help stretch the supply of castings in areas where only one side of the beam will be visible.

TRESTLE BENTS

While I found many good articles and books on bridge construction, none of them offered adequate dimensioned plans for steel trestle bents. The literature did indicate that there are two major types of bent designs: the full horizontal-braced style and the open style shown in fig. 2. In most steel trestles the full horizontal-braced bents have a constant story height, while the open style bents tend to have proportional story height that matches their increasing width.

In the full horizontal-braced style, the bent design includes vertical support struts to support the long horizontal braces. One variation in the design allows the height of each story to be either constant throughout or proportional to match the increasing width of the bent.

Figure 2 is drawn in N scale so that, with a scale rule, you can draw your own HO scale templates. These designs do not represent any particular prototype, but they are free-lanced following typical prototype practices. Just keep in mind that the overall width at the top of the bent should be between 8 and 9 feet. The supporting columns spread outward toward the base at a ratio of about 1:5.

TRESTLE TOWERS AND SPANS

Because steel is elastic, high trestle bents would bow and collapse unless properly stiffened. Thus, high bents are seldom used alone. In most cases you will find that what looks like a single bent is really two bents sandwiched close together. See the two end towers in fig. 3. High bents are usually tied together in pairs to form towers with longitudinal cross-bracing similar to that

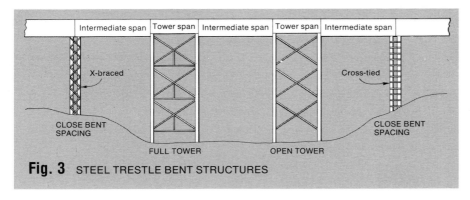

Fig. 3 STEEL TRESTLE BENT STRUCTURES

Labels in figure: Intermediate span, Tower span, Intermediate span, Tower span, Intermediate span; X-braced; Cross-tied; CLOSE BENT SPACING; CLOSE BENT SPACING; FULL TOWER; OPEN TOWER

used in the bents themselves. Such tower designs may also be either full horizontal-braced or open as shown in fig. 2. The height between longitudinal stories is usually equal, even if the bents have proportional story heights.

For the open tower type, I recommend using the same Central Valley ½C girders for the longitudinal bracing that is built into the bents. This also holds true for the full horizontal tower construction.

Central Valley provides some diagonal-lattice roof braces in the Pratt truss bridge kit that make a fine alternative for sway bracing. These braces come in male-female pairs ideally suited for horizontal and diagonal tower bracing. Unfortunately, one bridge kit does not have

sufficient roof braces to build even one medium-size steel trestle. However, if you are set on building many bridges, use the ½C girders on some bridges until you collect enough roof braces to build one bridge.

The prototype diagonal and horizontal tower braces are attached to the bent posts using steel gusset plates riveted to the posts and braces. I simulate these gussets with bits of styrene cemented to the cast girders. The exact shape of the gussets is determined by their locations and the angles of the bracing.

The tower and intermediate spans are ordinary plate girder bridges sized to fit the specific design. See fig. 3. Usually the tower spans are shorter than the intermediate spans.

For straight trestles the intermediate spans may be quite long. However, a modeler is more likely to have a curve involved, and this restricts the length of the intermediate spans. Figure 2 includes N scale drawings of my free-lanced tower designs that use the 24-foot plate girder spans provided in the Central Valley Pratt truss kit.

Now that I have described the general principles behind steel trestles, it's time to show how they may be applied to produce appropriate bridges for some actual model railroad installations.

PARTRIDGE VIADUCT

Partridge Viaduct, shown in fig. 4, spans a small river on the CW's Ontonagon Subdivision. Iron-ore traffic is very heavy on this subdivision, and the curves are sharp (Partridge Viaduct is on a 24″-radius curve). For this reason, the intermediate spans are short. I constructed this short bridge with one tower and one single bent. The tower bents have posts made of Central Valley A-B girders. The single bent simulates the narrow tower type of construction, and it has Central Valley type B-B girders for posts. I used the Central Valley bridge girders for the tower spans and Atlas N scale plate girders (bridge kit no. 2548) for the intermediate spans.

THE DECK

An accurate full-size diagram of the rails must be made where the track crosses the future bridge location. I tape a piece of tracing paper over the track (the paper must be long enough to cover the entire bridge location). Then I take a blunt dark pencil or a crayon and trace over each rail to produce an exact copy of the rail positions on the tracing paper.

Next, I mount the tracing right side up (rail markings up) on a piece of Homasote and lay out the positions of the trestle bents on the tracing. See fig. 5. To determine the bent positions I lay the intermediate and tower spans over the template just to the outside of the outer curved rail. Then I mark these locations on the template over the outer rail and draw lines transverse to these marks to position the bents on the tracing.

My deck construction takes advantage of the beautifully detailed tie strips supplied with the kit. Unless you are constructing a tangent trestle, the outer wooden guard timbers must be carefully

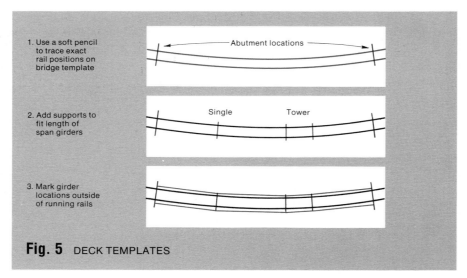

Fig. 4

1. Use a soft pencil to trace exact rail positions on bridge template

Abutment locations

2. Add supports to fit length of span girders

Single   Tower

3. Mark girder locations outside of running rails

Fig. 5 DECK TEMPLATES

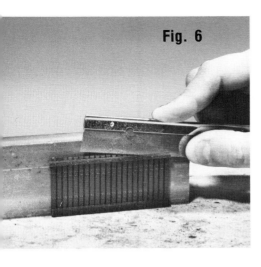

Fig. 6

Fig. 7

cut off one end of each tie strip. Use a sharp razor saw and make sure the cuts are flush with the ties as shown in fig. 6. *Save these timber sections.* Trim any remaining plastic from between the ties. This leaves the tie strips so they are easily curved, just like flexible track. I also remove the spacer/extension from one end of the remaining wooden guard timber.

Next, I position the tie sections over the tracing so the remaining wooden guard timber falls outside of the outer curved rail. I fasten the tie sections securely to the tracing with pins pushed through the tracing and into the Homasote. A pair of full-length rails, pinned into position on the tie plates, are what I use to assure proper alignment of the ties as shown in fig. 7.

With the rails in place, I cement strips of .020" x 9" styrene over the cut locations of the guard timbers on the inside of the curve and let them set hard. Then I cement the wooden guard timbers (saved earlier) over the styrene strips. I stagger the joints to assure that the ties are locked together.

I follow the Central Valley instructions to install the rails on the deck. Once the rails have been fastened to the tie plates, I affix them to the ties with a fluid ACC that easily runs between the rails and tie plates. Then I set the whole deck assembly aside to dry overnight.

BENT CONSTRUCTION

I build the bents for each bridge directly over the bent template as shown in fig. 8. Before constructing individual bents I determine the height and variations in ground contour for each bent. I sketch the appropriate ground contours on a sheet of tracing paper and tape it directly over the bent template.

On the Partridge Viaduct, I used Central Valley A-B girders for the posts of the tower and B-B girders for the posts of the single span. The bents have full-horizontal bracing made from C-C girders. The diagonal girders are ½C girders.

The special ½C diagonal girders are made from one cast section of a Central Valley C-C girder. I cement a piece of Evergreen .040" x .060" strip styrene to the open side of the casting as shown in fig. 1. This strip simulates the missing side that would ordinarily be part of the opposite casting. Once the cement sets I file the assembly so both sides of the girder match each other in height.

When the bracing is installed I position the lattice details so they are visible on top of the diagonal braces. One diagonal brace is full length. Then I trim the opposite diagonal at its intersection with the first diagonal and reinforce the joint with gussets (top and bottom) as shown in fig. 8.

FITTING THE SPAN GIRDERS

At this point the work shifts to the underside of the deck, so I turn the tracing paper over (marked side down) so its curve will be properly oriented for further construction. Then I tape the partly completed deck upside down over the rail tracing. A smooth, flat surface is necessary for these next steps to ensure good alignment.

With the deck upside down on the template, it is relatively easy to determine where the intermediate and tower spans belong. I position one span at a time, starting with the outside of the curve, and cement them in place. Each span should be centered and just outside of the rail. The idea is to keep the rail just inside the span girders everywhere on the bridge. However, the span should not be so far out that it approaches the ends of the ties.

Next, I position and cement the spans on the inside of the curve so they are also centered. These inside spans must be shortened to fit the inside curvature. I shorten them by carefully cutting material from the middle of each girder and splicing the shortened pieces together.

When I have all the spans cemented in place, I cut long strips of .020" x ½" styrene from sheet stock and cement these reinforcing strips behind the spans. These

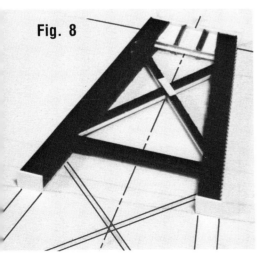

Fig. 8

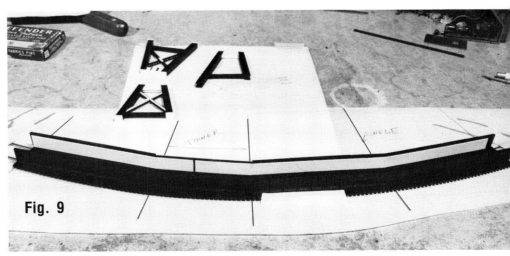

Fig. 9

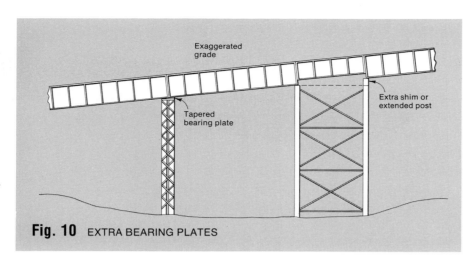

Fig. 10 EXTRA BEARING PLATES

Exaggerated grade

Tapered bearing plate

Extra shim or extended post

show as white strips in fig. 9. These strips effectively lock all the joints between spans into a single, solid piece.

My intermediate spans are slightly deeper than the tower span, so I use small pieces of styrene to level both girders at the joint. Once these have been leveled, I cement a bearing plate over each span joint for the bents to rest on. These plates are cut from .020″ styrene sheet and measure approximately a scale 12″ x 30″.

ATTACHING THE BENTS

If the bridge is going to be in a level track, I cement each bent to the deck assembly following the bent position marks on the tracing paper. Be sure to use a square to make sure each bent is perpendicular to the bridge spans. Also, take care to make sure each bent is properly centered across the bridge spans as well as between the joints of adjoining spans.

I have found it is a good idea to fasten one set of outer gussets to each tower bent before assembly. This step makes the job of bracing the towers easier and more accurate.

If the bridge is on a grade it is imperative that the bents be perpendicular to the horizon. The tower must be perpendicular to function as an engineering structure. More importantly, even a slight error will give visitors the feeling that something is wrong in the structure's final appearance. Extra bearing plates must be added to compensate for the elevation of the deck as shown in fig. 10.

Of course, if I had had the foresight, I could have made the one tower bent .030″ longer at the top. This would have avoided the shims, but it would also have taken more planning.

I finished the bracing using a template made from fig. 2, with each piece cut and fitted in the same manner I used during the bent construction. I used Central Valley C-C girders for the horizontal bracing so I did not use supports for the horizontal bracing. However, if I

had used ½C girders for this horizontal brace, I would have included the supports.

Another alternative is to use the Central Valley diagonal lattice roof braces for these horizontal supports. In this case, the appropriate vertical supports would be mandatory.

FINISHING TOUCHES

The foot of each bent post needs a bottom bearing plate as shown in fig. 11. I made these from .020″ styrene cut a scale 30″ square. The concrete footings, which show under each post in fig. 4, are made from ½″-square pine blocks that I filed and tapered to fit.

If you wish, the underside of each tower and intermediate span should have cross-bracing made from .020″ x .060″ styrene strip. Since I normally don't look at the bottoms of my bridges, I did not bother adding this detail.

My bridge abutments, shown in fig. 11, are cut from a 1″ x 6″ clear pine board on a radial-arm saw. I cut 45 degree angles at the end of the board, leaving a 1½″ flat spot in the middle. The top bearing notch in the abutments was cut into the board with a dado blade before I cut it to the final length. Then I sanded the abutments smooth and coated them with vinyl paste spackling compound to simulate concrete.

My abutments are mounted with glue and brads so the bridge ends are firmly resting on the concrete piers. Then I spike the bridge rails to the adjoining roadbed and glue all the bent posts and spans to their concrete piers with fluid ACC to complete the installation.

ROBERTS RUN TRESTLE

The CW's Roberts Run Trestle, shown in fig. 12, was built to span a larger valley that is a scale 280 feet across and 50 feet below track level at its deepest point. The track crosses this trestle on a

Fig. 11

Fig. 12

very gradual curve while rising on a 2 percent grade from south to north.

Its deck and bent construction followed the Partridge Viaduct procedures with only a few exceptions. The horizontal-bent braces are made of less sturdy Central Valley ½C girders, so the lower horizontal braces required the vertical support members to prevent sagging. In addition, the terrain sloped rather steeply on the north side of the bridge, making it necessary to use nonstandard bent bracing at the bottom story of some bents as seen in fig. 13. Note that each element of this bracing still forms a triangle with its adjoining members.

The track curvature over this trestle is so gradual that long intermediate spans could have been used between the towers. However, to maintain the illusion of a long trestle, I only lengthened the center span which actually crosses Roberts Creek. While most prototypes would have probably used a larger plate

girder to span the creek, I used an Atlas HO deck truss bridge (kit no. 84).

The Atlas truss in the center adds an interesting variation to this bridge. It rests on short vertical lengths of Central Valley C-C girders attached to the adjoining support bent as shown in fig. 14.

My full horizontal and diagonal tower bracing on this bridge also follows the dimensions of the fig. 2 drawings. For variety, I chose to make all of the tower bracing from Central Valley diagonal lattice roof braces. These braces are wide but spindly in appearance so they add to the apparent size of the structure. It took nearly all the roof bracing from four truss bridge kits to complete this bridge.

On this one I added Central Valley mounting pads at each end. I also added a pair of scale 42" x 60" personnel refuge platforms at two intermediate locations. These simple platforms, see fig. 13, are made of strip styrene and positioned equidistant from each other and the ends of

the bridge. These platforms are normally spaced at intervals of approximately 100 to 150 feet. There is no need to place water barrels on the platforms if you have an all-diesel railroad.

STILES BRANCH TRESTLE

The Stiles Branch Trestle, shown in color at the start of this article, was built to span the side of a valley near a sheer rock cliff. Building a trestle in this location was far less expensive than blasting away the cliff to provide a ledge for the CW's predecessor's right-of-way.

Since this particular line was not built by the Central of Wisconsin, the Stiles Branch Trestle is quite different from the other bridges on the railroad. In this case the trestle has the open style of bent and tower construction, and proportional-story heights were used throughout. It actually looks very much like some of the bridges found on the prototype Norfolk Southern. The only real difference between its construction and the procedures I used on the Partridge Viaduct or Roberts Run Trestle can be found in the bracing patterns.

From my experience in building the bridges in this article, I can see that the possibilities for other bridges are limited only by one's imagination. I'm sure that we'll soon be seeing bridges kitbashed from the Central Valley kits showing up on model railroads everywhere. ⚙

Fig. 13

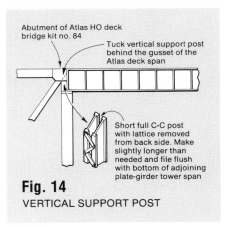

Abutment of Atlas HO deck bridge kit no. 84

Tuck vertical support post behind the gusset of the Atlas deck span

Short full C-C post with lattice removed from back side. Make slightly longer than needed and file flush with bottom of adjoining plate-girder tower span

Fig. 14
VERTICAL SUPPORT POST

Fig. 1

John Allen Memorial Bridge

A steel trestle made of two truss and two girder spans: parts from kits plus scratchbuilding are involved

BY AL KALBFLEISCH
PHOTOS BY THE AUTHOR

THE John Allen Memorial Bridge links Moffat with Salida on the mythical East Hartford Division of the D&RGW RR. Its concept came into existence after I saw a great model of the "Kiddie-Y" bridge on Glen Wagner's layout when he lived in Delmar, N. Y. The prototype Keddie Wye is located on the Western Pacific's line through the Feather River Canyon in California.

There were a couple of items I wanted to work on before the bridge was started:

• Frustration: This is a big project, encouraging procrastination. Therefore I had to be so tired of seeing a gap — see fig. 2 — that I would be driven to fill it.

• Kits: Time is so short that I planned to use anything I could find as long as it would give the look of a nice big American railroad bridge similar to the Keddie Wye. This led to the question "How much is available to cross-kit?"

• Scratch: I had to decide what was

needed and the best way to mass-produce the parts. I wasn't too crazy about making 100″ of webbed struts, piece by piece, nor also 140 gusset plates, one at a time. This problem was solved by a photographic means which I will describe later.

The actual Keddie Wye bridges are a combination of deck trusses and girder spans. Piers are open-trusswork towers. They form a beautiful, functional, American railroad structure of the 1910's period so ugly that the bridges are beauty itself!

My own John Allen Memorial Bridge is made of three spans. These rest on two trusswork towers. Between the spans is a deck truss span. A girder spans the distance between each tower and the re-

spective abutments. Two short girder spans support the track across the top of the towers. Some shortcuts which a bridge engineer would recognize were taken, but the entire trestle generally follows correct practice.

The deck carries two tracks. Much of the construction comes from readily available kit parts, but some members and gussets had to be fabricated along with the stringers under the track ties.

The model is for an HO scale line, but the construction methods could probably be used for any scale.

The first assemblywork was started by joining two Vollmer Kastenbrücke (literally, "cage bridge") kits to form the center truss 174 scale feet long (24″ or 609 mm.). A couple of changes had to be made so the truss could be used for a deck structure. One was to install all of the structural members associated with the top on the bottom, and vice versa. The lacy up-

Fig. 2

vent a locomotive from falling someday.

The approach span girders are Atlas plate girder bridges (no. 85) and Atlas girder flatcar loads. The sides were cut from the cast deck bridge and cleaned up. Their shallower extensions were cut from the flatcar loads: see fig. 3. The variation in rivet spacing and girder height is reasonably justifiable because the thinner section is only a short span supporting the deck over the tower area. Note that a crossbeam from the main truss kit is used as the first load-bearing beam in the girder bridge. This beam is cut to fit the small traveling stringer truss which should extend out from each end of the main truss assembly. This crossbeam also helps determine the proper height for the rest of the crossbeams in the girder bridges.

When your girder spans are assembled, you can begin laying stringers along the top of the truss and extending them over to the site of the girder spans. These stringers support the track ties. In all, there are 10 stringers: 2 under each inboard rail plus 3 under each outboard rail. I made mine .25″ high from strip stock.

After a few stringers have been in-

per structure is now on the bottom and in plain view. All of the plainer load-bearing beams are now on the top under the stringers and are relatively out of sight. These necessary parts are seen in fig. 3. Some crossmembers, left over from the kit modification, can be installed as sway braces inside the truss as an extra guard against twist: fig. 4.

One catwalk can be installed with the guardrail in its normal position. The pinned bridge end bearings can be installed on the bottom of each end of the truss.

A word to the wise! Don't splice the four side trusses at the same point. The joints should be staggered and backed up with styrene gusset plates. Also, if you splice the truss near a gusset plate, do not cut the beam off so you have a butt joint to make. Instead, carve material from the existing gusset plate so it will accept its mating beam with gusset plate removed. This way the cement joint is in shear, not tension: see fig. 4, upper right-hand corner. This means you will have to think out how the sides are joined ahead of time. Time spent on this task may pre-

List of materials for an HO version
of the structure
2 Vollmer Kastenbrücke no. 2506B
2 Atlas plate girder bridge no. 85
1 Atlas flatcar girder load
1 Kleiwe Brücke no. 71 (for N scale)
1 set Devcon super 2-ton glue
Elmer's Glue-All
Testors plastic cement
Testors liquid cement
1/32″ x 3/16″ basswood
10 pieces 1/4″ x 1/2″ I beam
5 pieces 1/8″ x 1/4″ I beam
HO 2 x 4's or appropriate L for webbing

Fig. 3

Fig. 4

The hollow concrete counterweight provides space for smaller concrete weights used to more exactly correct the balance. When the bridge opens, this counterweight swings down almost to rail level. The laced columns at the extreme sides of this view are not parts of the moving span; they support the racks upon which the pinion gear rolls while the bridge opens.

provision for a motor drive, but that is not used. Instead, a hand-powered chain-hoist mechanism drives the pinions along the rack to raise and lower the bridge. Apparently the slough is so seldom used that this simple arrangement suffices. There were no evidences of a bridgetender, so I presume the service must be performed by boatmen who use the waterway. I have no idea what sort of craft navigate the slough, but they must be fairly small. The lift span is only 50 feet long, and the channel didn't appear to be very deep.

From the modeler's point of view the staggering array of rivets in the bridge is likely to be a discouraging feature, especially when you realize the things are duplicated on the reverse side of each girder and plate! Nevertheless, without this impressive detail the bridge model would lose much of its appealing character, so, tedious though they are to form, rivets are a must.

For small scales — HO, TT, N — the sensible solution is to simplify the rivet pattern and widen the spacing. You can't make exactly scale-size rivets in HO anyway, so spacing them as close as they are on the model would be nearly impossible. I'd suggest making your rivets as small as you can and spacing them as closely as the material and method will allow. Nobody counts the rivets in a model, and as long as there are enough of them to create the general impression of authenticity, their purpose is accomplished. I built both O scale and HO scale versions of the span, using the same rivet-forming punch and die for both. The larger model looks better by comparison, but by itself the HO bridge is also quite impressive.

Construction notes

For those who enjoy building a model as close to the prototype as possible, we will discuss the subject in full detail with some suggestions on how to make it a working model. If you are satisfied to have the model nonworking, you will save doing some complex and exacting work:

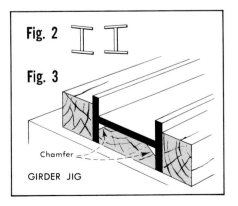

Fig. 2

Fig. 3

Chamfer

GIRDER JIG

the quadrants need not be so carefully made, and the bridge floor system—which cannot be easily seen except when the bridge is open — can be reproduced with a simple board.

You can use sheet metal such as brass, nickel silver, or iron (the so-called tin), or you can use Strathmore bristol board or styrene. I do not recommend stripwood, as this material is too thick to give the authentic "feel" of bridge girders. Much of the realism of a bridge model depends upon thin-appearing materials.

I like to work in styrene. It is easy to cut, finish, shape, and join to other pieces. It takes painting well. Bonding is very easy when using styrene. A trace of liquid solvent such as ketone, MEK, or even the liquid-type "cement for plastics" is touched to the edges of two pieces held in position. The fluid runs into the joint by capillary action and results in an almost immediate weld. It is one of the reasons styrene is considered the easiest material to use by the modelers who favor it.

I used the same thicknesses of sheet materials in both my O and HO models, but this is not as noticeable in the HO model as the relative scarcity of rivets.

It is expedient to break the modelwork into subassemblies which are completed and painted before final erection. Start with the chords, or span girders, following the assembly method of fig. 1.

It goes without saying that all parts should be cut square and true. Right here is a good place to point out a trick that will prove invaluable in making joints such as occur in girders, beams, and angles.

No matter how you cut styrene — and

this applies to other materials in varying degrees — the sheared or severed edges do not come out squared across. Any attempt to join parts not yet squared across may produce girders and other members with flanges tilted as in fig. 2. With metal you can often avoid this tendency by soldering in a jig, as in fig. 3. With cemented materials the warpage may occur after the work is removed from the assembly jig, so it is important to have the materials square across their edges *before* joining. A piece of tool steel, such as a lathe tool bit, can be ground as in fig. 4 and used for this purpose. Lay your material on a flat surface over a spacer piece (figs. 5A and 5B) and make one or two passes of the tool along the edge. The spacer prevents leaving a burr.

When you are going to cut a new piece from your large piece of stock material, first true the stock as just shown. Then, after breaking away the strip, true the newly formed edge as in figs. 5C and 5D. Here a hold-down piece has been added, and a backstop to prevent your strip from slipping.

In laying out the pieces, be especially sure that the ends of the chords are cut

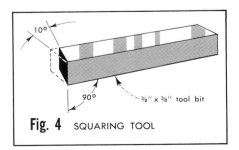

Fig. 4   SQUARING TOOL

Did the bridge painter sign his masterpiece? Name "Bob" and letters "B. B." (which might stand for Bridges & Buildings Department) have been splashed on underside of counterweight.

Attached to the sectors of the quadrants you can see castings with a central rib and side pockets, the pockets located alternately on each side of the rib. The rib rolls on a simple track at the center of the top of the quadrant-track girder across the bottom of this view. Fulcrum blocks on each side of this track engage the pockets so the moving span of the bridge will not wander out of position as it rolls along the rail. On the model, Al Armitage made the central rib proportionately deeper and provided a slot in the track girder to more firmly guide the rolling span.

90 degrees from their tops and bottoms. Otherwise the vertical columns that hold the pinion to the bridge, and the rack to the quadrant track girder, will lean. The bridge will neither look right nor operate properly.

Next, make the quadrants. If your model is to work properly these must be made and bonded to the columns with great care. It is imperative that the quadrants be *identical* in radius and in the 22-degree segment angles. Lay them out accurately as in fig. 6. Build up all flanges and add rivet strips before bonding them to their columns. The fulcrum pockets should also be applied at this time as in fig. 7. Space them equally on alternate sides of the rib, the curved rim upon which the quadrants roll. Use some means, such as a vernier caliper, to check that all pockets are identical in size. As in the prototype, these work something like gear teeth to keep the bridge from slipping out of position.

Bond the finished quadrants in position on the columns and check them carefully. Both subassemblies *must* match in profile as closely as possible. When you are satisfied that this has been achieved, add the remaining braces, gussets, and plates to stiffen the unit.

You will notice that I made a slight change in the design of the quadrants by extending their bearing ribs and adding a mating groove on the quadrant-track girder. This tongue-and-groove arrangement keeps the quadrant and girder in proper alignment during the activating cycle, a feature necessitated by the extreme light weight of the model compared to that of the prototype. While the real bridge depends entirely upon the fulcrum blocks and pocket to guide the quadrant during its travel, the model needs the added security of the groove.

Make the quadrant-track girders as before, with the groove a snug — but not tight — fit for the quadrant rib: fig. 7.

Fulcrum blocks are next. These too are

a critical job. Here's how I did it: Lay one of the quadrant assembles flat on the bench with a track girder in position against the column, and with the rib in its groove. Roll the quadrant back and forth to make sure the fulcrum pockets clear the top of the girder on both sides. With the two parts in closed position, mark the location of the first fulcrum block. Tack the block in place with a dab of ketone. Be careful not to get the ketone in the pocket. Separate the two units after a few seconds to check this. Set this assembly aside while you repeat the process on the second set of assemblies. Now go back to the first set and install the second block in the same manner. Proceed thus until all blocks are in place on both sets. As each block is applied you will find that the quadrant can be rolled back to position the next one: fig. 8. It is best to proceed alternately on both sides of the quadrant rather than finish one side first.

The finished quadrant should — nay, *must* — traverse the track smoothly without binding, lifting, or slipping in either direction. To achieve this, each block must fit the corresponding pocket fairly snugly, with no play in either direction, and must be as high as it can be without striking the flanges on the quadrant. You may have to do a bit of custom fitting on one or two.

Since it is highly improbable that the two units will be interchangeable, I suggest marking the pairs so they won't get switched around during subsequent assembly.

At this point we can assemble the floor system, comprised of floor beams, stringers, and diagonals as shown on the plan. A typical bay is shown in fig. 9.

Important: note that the stringers are short pieces that go between the floor beams. I might mention, too, that the spacing of the stringers depends on the gauge of your track. If you run narrow gauge, your stringers will be closer than

those on the standard-gauge drawing. My own bridge carries On3 track laid with code 70 rail.

I suggest using a simple cutoff fixture for trimming the crossbeams to length. A fixture to hold the major parts in position during assembly will also make the job turn out better. This fixture can be made of blocks of wood cemented to a board, or it can be just pins driven into a board upon which the floor system layout has been drawn.

After the floor system is completed you will need to add filler pieces on top of the stringers as shown in fig. 10. They should be flush with the top of the floor beams. Although not shown in fig. 9, the ties rest on these pieces.

As I mentioned earlier, the floor system

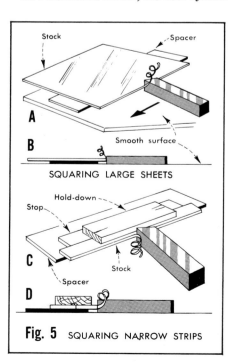

Fig. 5 SQUARING NARROW STRIPS

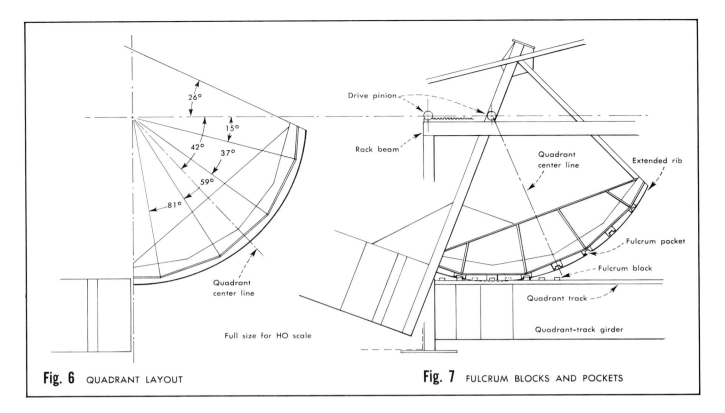

Fig. 6 QUADRANT LAYOUT

26°
15°
42°
37°
59°
81°

Quadrant center line

Full size for HO scale

Fig. 7 FULCRUM BLOCKS AND POCKETS

Drive pinion

Rack beam

Quadrant center line

Extended rib

Fulcrum pocket

Fulcrum block

Quadrant track

Quadrant-track girder

may be simplified in a nonworking model. If you prefer something just a little more sophisticated than a plain board, a method is suggested in fig. 11. This looks better with individual ties.

It is much easier to paint the floor system at this stage rather than later. I found Pactra chrome silver 'Namel to be an excellent match for the prototype aluminum paint finish. Use an airbrush or spray gun if at all possible. Set it to deliver a fairly dry first coat, to give adequate coverage without danger of sags or runs. (You have to be careful with enamel.) A second, "wetter" coat can be applied to the outer surfaces if a brighter, shinier appearance is desired. I rather like the aluminum finish as a change from the usual dull black. It shows off the rivets and other detail nicely. It would not conceal sloppy workmanship.

Allow sufficient time for the paint to dry thoroughly; then bond the girder and

quadrant units to the floor system. Be careful to see that the assembly is square and true in all respects. When it has set firmly, fit the bottom and back of the counterweight and bond them in place. Remember, the counterweight must be square and aligned. Fabricate the front and "pocket" of the weight, but leave the top open until the bridge is completed. Then the proper weight can be determined and installed.

Fabricating the crossbeam is a rather tricky proposition that will make you wish you had three hands. To assure duplication of parts and corresponding accuracy of assembly, use jigs wherever possible. Details of the chain-hoist mechanism can be seen in the prototype photos. To the best of my knowledge there are no commercially available bevel or miter gears in sizes small enough for even O scale. I believe there are small, high-precision gears of this type made for spe-

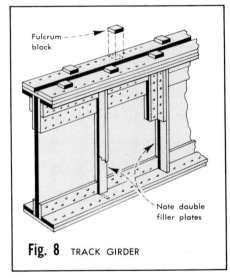

Fulcrum block

Note double filler plates

Fig. 8 TRACK GIRDER

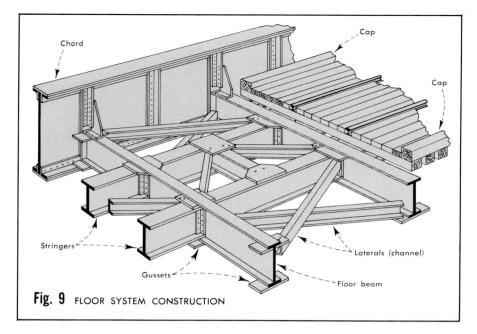

Fig. 9 FLOOR SYSTEM CONSTRUCTION

Chord

Cap

Cap

Stringers

Laterals (channel)

Gussets

Floor beam

Fixed portion

The next phase of construction covers the fixed portion of the steelwork, and starts with the track girders already fabricated. Technically the floor system for this unit is similar to that of the lift span, but since it is not visible in the model, the method shown in fig. 11 is adequate.

The important thing to remember is that both girders must be exactly parallel and level so the quadrant will track properly. Custom-fit this assembly to your span rather than to the published drawings. Test frequently during construction. Be sure to match the girders to the proper quadrants!

The completed section should now be set up on whatever you use for a base. The prototype rests on steel caissons filled with concrete. I imitated this with styrene turnings. Paint the assembly before mounting it permanently.

The columns for the rack beam are made slightly long on the lower end to allow for trimming to length to suit the height of the pinions. Fabricate the beams, install the rack, and assemble to the support columns. Add the horizontal struts and sway braces and the steelwork is done.

Paint all unfinished parts. Rig the actuating cords and test the operation of the model. It should roll back easily and smoothly when you turn the drum by hand. Less effort will be needed later, when you have added the counterweight.

Floor and track

Although the prototype structure has a solidly planked floor to suit local conditions, I prefer the more usual open floor, so I left the planking off except for a walkway along one side.

All timbers are of pine ripped on a circular saw. Cut the ties to length while you're at it, and be sure to include enough timber and tiestock for the approaches if you include them in your model. Stain all material a dark gray-brown before assembly.

Notice on the end elevation that while ordinary planks laid across the ties are used for the bridge flooring, there are two slightly higher cap strips along the ends of the ties. Cut two cap strips slightly longer than you need, and pin or tape

---

cial industrial purposes, but I'm inclined to think their cost would put them out of consideration for most modelers. I machined dummies from styrene rod with ³⁄₁₆" brass rod for shafting. Teeth can be simulated well enough with a file or razor saw. Chain with 36 links is available from ship model supply houses.

Carry the assembly, including the dummy drive mechanism, as far as you can as a separate unit. Paint it; then bond it in place and add the remaining struts and plates. Set the structure aside while we consider the drive pinions, next on the agenda.

Mechanical drive matters

A bit of discussion on these is in order for those who wish to make a working model. The easiest — and probably the most practical — way to install the pinions, even in O scale, is to make them dummy as in fig. 12. Trying to make them full working is begging for a bucketful of trouble, believe me! In the prototype, the power-driven pinion advances along the fixed track to activate the span; on a model the pinion cannot be directly driven because there is no place to mount a motor and still preserve the looks of the bridge. With any other arrangement the gear goes along just for the ride, and under such circumstances the pinion teeth set up tremendous resistance against the movement of the gear along the rack.

On my O scale model I thought to drive the pinion directly, so I installed it in mesh with the rack. I used Boston Gear pinion wire and brass rack, 64-pitch, 20-degree pressure angle. A foot of each cost in the neighborhood of 3 bucks. When the idea didn't work out in fact as well as it had in my mind, I reverted to the system which I had already employed successfully on the HO model: fig. 13. Since the big model has not been placed in service, I have not changed the pinions nor built a motor unit for it, but I can guarantee the arrangement in fig. 13 will work equally well in O scale.

In any event it is essential that the pinions, working or not, travel in an exactly horizontal line as the bridge opens. They must be located at the *exact* center of the curvature of the quadrants. If the rack is not to engage the pinion, here is where the cheating must be done. The rack must be lowered just enough that the pinion does not touch it.

This completes the assembly of the moving portion of the bridge except for floor planking and rails. We'll take these up later.

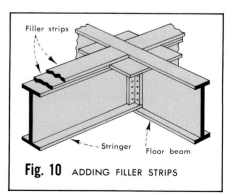

Filler strips

Stringer   Floor beam

Fig. 10 ADDING FILLER STRIPS

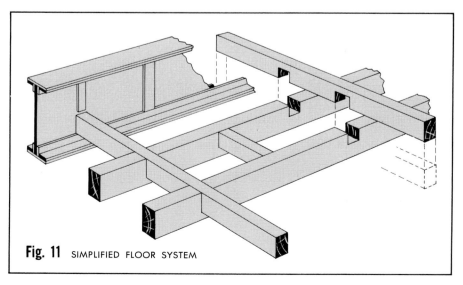

Fig. 11 SIMPLIFIED FLOOR SYSTEM

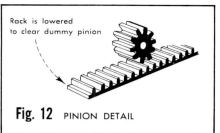

Fig. 12 PINION DETAIL

Rack is lowered to clear dummy pinion

them to a board at the correct spacing for your tie length. Using a spacer block, cement the ties across the cap strips. This is an inverted assembly at the moment. If you wish, you can add thin stripwood strips along the length of this assembly coinciding with the center lines of the stringers. Although not a necessity, these strips do stiffen the assembly during rail-laying, especially if you use spikes. Perhaps their greatest value is the fact that they absorb some of the spike length, which otherwise can become a problem in HO scale bridgework. I used Kemtron X-195 spikes, with tie plates, in O scale and still had a few poke through here and there. If this occurs, grind the protruding spike points flush so your track section will lie flat on the bridge stringer filler strips. Another beneficial service performed by the strips is to provide a larger surface for bonding the tie assembly to the stringers. I used tube-type styrene cement to fasten ties to the plastic floor system on my model.

Let the tie assembly set long enough to be firm and rigid; then flip it over and pin it to the board right side up. Lay the rails by whatever method you prefer, but be careful to get them in the proper location with respect to the bridge center line. If you paint your rails, do it now. Also do whatever touchup may be required on the timbers. When all is to your satisfaction, the section can be fastened in position permanently.

Important! I must stress the fact that track maintenance is almost impossible after the track section is installed, so be certain that the rails are accurately gauged and fastened in place. If spiked, my suggestion is to use two spikes in every third tie as a minimum.

Possibly because of the planking, this bridge does not have guardrails between the running rails. However, since it is general practice on most bridges and trestles to provide steel guardrails, I included them on my model, running them out almost to the ends of the approaches. Such guardrails look something like a narrow-gauge track centered between the regular

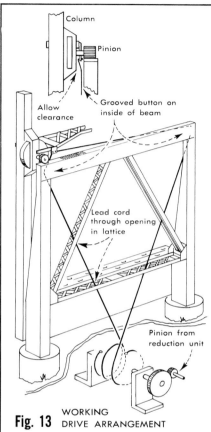

Fig. 13 WORKING DRIVE ARRANGEMENT

Column

Pinion

Allow clearance

Grooved button on inside of beam

Lead cord through opening in lattice

Pinion from reduction unit

running rails. Beyond each end of the bridgework the guardrails bend inward to a point near track center: fig. 14. The guardrails may be of the same weight as mainline rails, but are often of lighter weight: old rail from somewhere else. The spacing between guardrails is often standardized for a given road, but at any rate is such that a car cannot wander so far from track center as to sideswipe any part of the bridge framework.

The short track section over the quadrant span is made the same way as the main span; and, needless to say, its rails must be in perfect alignment with those of the lift span. And they must be at the same elevation. This may take some shifting and shimming, but it is imperative if you are to enjoy trouble-free operation. Leave as small a gap as possible between the sections. Some sort of electric contacts should be provided at each end of the lift span so that rails will be powered when the span is down: these can be simple affairs of brass shimstock wired to the running rails of each section.

This pretty well completes the bridge except for the counterweight. Now that

the track sections are in place, the amount of weight needed to balance the span section can be determined. (On the prototype, incidentally, the weight is so located that a straight line drawn from the center of gravity of the counterweight through the axis of the pinion centers would pass through the center of gravity of the rest of the movable structure, almost exactly balancing the forces of gravity at all times.) My O scale model required almost 5 ounces, but the figure will vary depending on the scale of the model and the material used in its construction. The simplest means of providing the necessary weight is to pour lead shot into the cavity of the dummy counterweight on the bridge. When the proper amount has been obtained, mix a bit of fairly thin plaster and pour it over the shot to keep it from rattling around when the model is actuated; after this dries hard, the top of the dummy weight can be added. The small removable weights in the "pocket" are little blocks of wood cemented in place. These and the counterweight are painted to represent concrete.

Any small motor can be used for power, since the load is negligible due to the counterbalancing. A 1½-volt imported motor and a few plastic gears are adequate. One photo illustrates a similar power unit used to operate a turntable: the gear train in this came from Revell's Slant-Six engine kit. A somewhat quieter arrangement can be made using a double set of worms and gears instead of the spur-gear train. A very high reduction is needed to achieve the slow motion of the real bridge — the slower the better. Remember, this is a hand-operated bridge! Wire the motor to a reversing switch on your control panel or any convenient location. Leave some means of access to the power unit for servicing.

If you like, paint the name of your road on the span girders, add a couple of NO TRESPASSING signs — perhaps warning blinker lights atop the structure as a final touch.

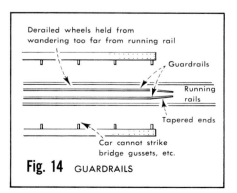

Derailed wheels held from wandering too far from running rail

Guardrails

Running rails

Tapered ends

Car cannot strike bridge gussets, etc.

Fig. 14 GUARDRAILS

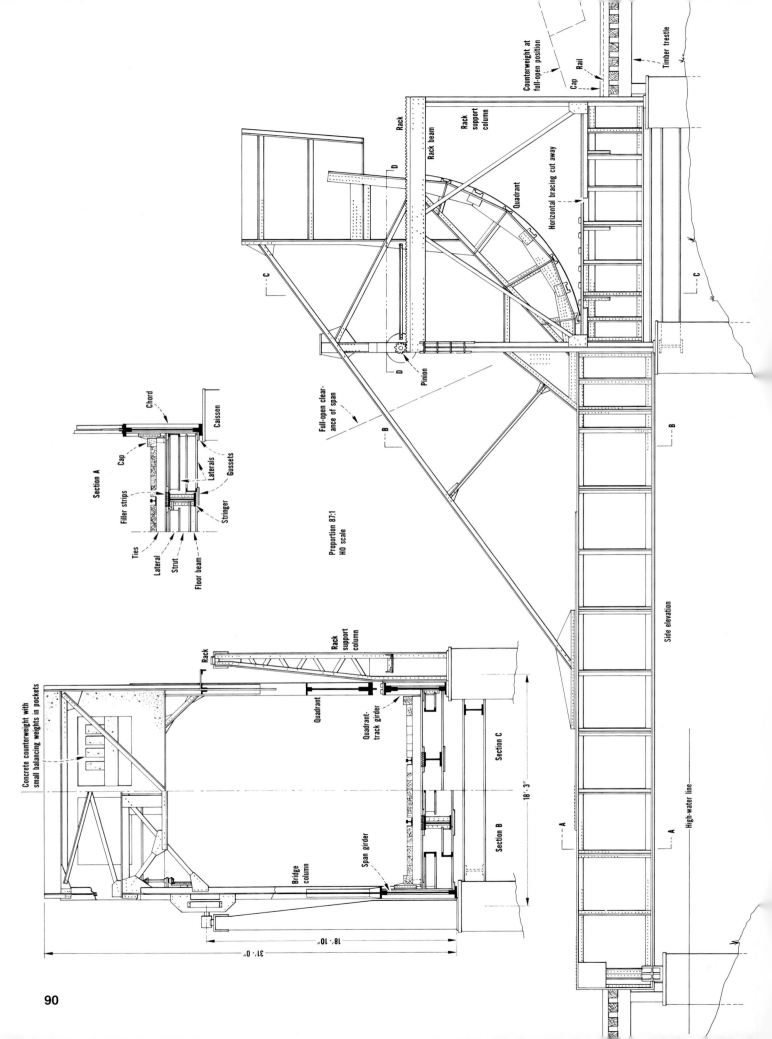

Section A

Chord

Cap

Filler strips

Ties

Lateral

Strut

Floor beam

Stringer

Gussets

Laterals

Caisson

Proportion 87:1
HO scale

Concrete counterweight with
small balancing weights in pockets

Rack

Rack support column

Quadrant

Quadrant-
track girder

Span girder

Bridge column

31' - 0"

18' - 10"

18' - 3"

Section C

Section B

Rack

Rack beam

Rack support column

Quadrant

Horizontal bracing cut away

Counterweight at
full-open position

Cap

Rail

Timber trestle

Full-open clear-
ance of span

Pinion

Side elevation

High-water line

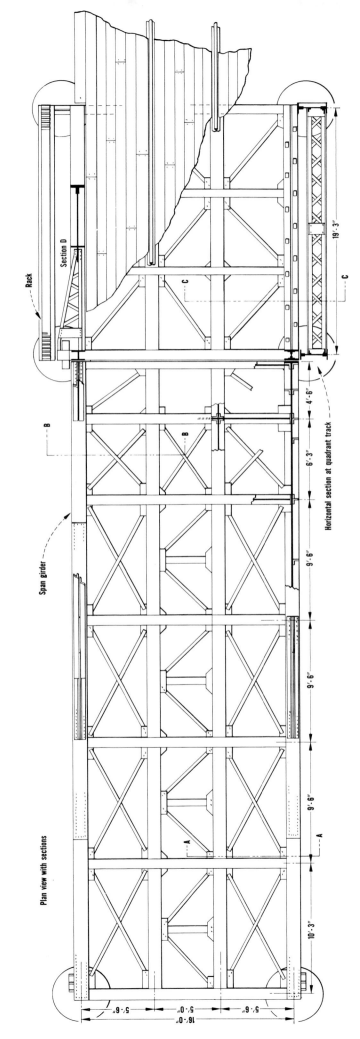

Rack

Section D

Span girder

Plan view with sections

B

C

Horizontal section at quadrant track

C

B

A

19'-3"

4'-6"

6'-3"

9'-6"

9'-6"

9'-6"

10'-3"

5'-6"

5'-0"

5'-6"

16'-0"

Scherzer rolling lift bridge

THIS type of bridge has no hinge in the manner of a trapdoor; instead, it rolls back on its quadrants in the manner of a rocking chair. This means that the span not only lifts but also recedes from the waterway. The boxlike tail high at the right holds a concrete weight at just the right position to almost exactly counterbalance the weight of the bridge. Note piles protecting the bridge abutments.

91

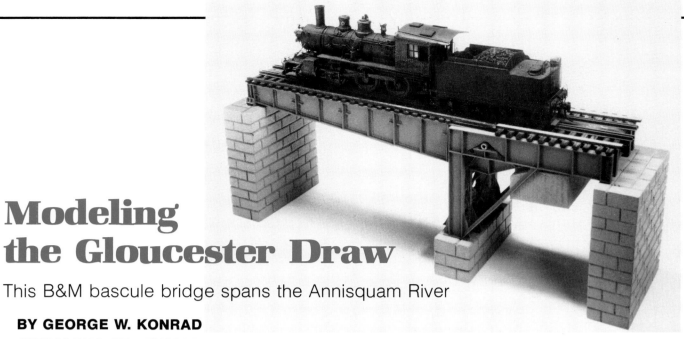

Modeling the Gloucester Draw

This B&M bascule bridge spans the Annisquam River

BY GEORGE W. KONRAD
PHOTOS BY DAVE NEWCOMB

WESTBOUND out of Gloucester, Mass., the Boston & Maine RR. crosses the Annisquam River on a short, double-track bascule bridge and a long causeway. The small size of this structure makes it an ideal subject for a model railroad. See the drawings which are part of this feature.

The construction of the bridge is such that it was easy for me to model a single-track span by eliminating one pair of support girders and removing one of the leafs. Other than that change, I followed the construction of the real thing closely, except for one or two minor deviations. This isn't a step-by-step construction story, but I hope that my notes and the photos of my model will be helpful to those of you who decide to build one for yourself.

As the structure is complicated, I relied a great deal on bridge construction information found in Paul Mallory's *Bridge and Trestle Handbook*. This book shows how bridge components are assembled and fitted together. The information most pertinent to the Annisquam bridge is found in these three chapters: Plate Girder Bridges, Steel Truss Bridges, and Movable Bridges.

MATERIALS

There are four possible materials which come to my mind for the model construction: cardstock, wood, styrene, and brass. Of these I feel styrene is best because it is easy to work with, it requires a minimum of tools, and it is easy to master the necessary fabrication techniques. Kemtron offers a booklet by Alan Armitage that provides a good insight into the use of styrene.

I used styrene sheet for the entire model except for the trunnions and pivots (which are brass tube) and the counterweight (which is wood). Evergreen Scale Models has styrene strip stock from .015" x .040" to .125" x .250", which is useful if you have trouble cutting narrow strips from sheet stock. I used .020"-thick sheet material for the main girders and cover plates, and .010" for all smaller plates, angles, and rivet strips.

The bridge has a great many rivets that are important to the finished appearance of the model. NorthWest Short Line offers a rivet-embossing tool, but I made by own. See fig. 1. It is made from a couple pieces of scrap hardwood, threaded steel rod, and a brass plate. I made the male and female dies using an electric hand tool as a rudimentary lathe. It is crude by most standards, but it proved adequate to emboss rivets in .010" styrene.

LEAF CONSTRUCTION

Begin construction by cutting two side plates for the moving leaf from .020" stock. Clamp the sides together and drill holes for the main and counterbalance trunnions. I used ⁵⁄₃₂"-outside-diameter brass tube for the main trunnions and ⅛" O.D. for the counterbalance trunnions. Add the .020"-thick cover plates to the edges of the girders, keeping them centered on the side plates. Make vertical 3½" x 3½" angles from .010" styrene and attach them to the inside and outside of both girder plates. Angles are not needed on the inside surfaces of the plates where the five cross-framing assemblies will be attached. Incidentally, all bracing on the structure has angled cross sections. There are no flat or U-shaped braces.

Cut the tube trunnion pieces as long as the girder plates are wide. Square the ends, insert them in the proper holes, and add strengthening plates around the main trunnion. Next, add six triangular braces

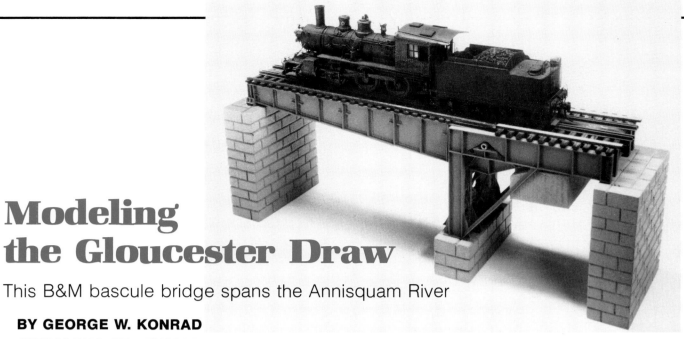
Fig. 1

around each counterweight trunnion. See fig. 2 and the drawings on page 99. None of this bracing can extend beyond the ends of the cover plates and trunnions or they will restrict the movement of the leaf when it is assembled to the support girders. I used a quick-setting ACC-type adhesive to hold the trunnions to the styrene.

Five crossbeam assemblies are required to connect the two side plates. These all have to be the same width so the leaf assembly will be square and the side girders parallel. Figure 3 shows the construction I used. The three center crossbeams are identical, except that they are of different heights to match their positions along the length of the tapering leaf. See fig. 2. If you want to build a double-track bridge you will need two of each assembly.

Assemble the two side girders and five crossbeams, keeping the sides parallel and the crosspiece square to them. Add the I-beam stringers, made from .020" styrene, between the crossbeams. Note that these stringers rest on the crossbeam nearest the trunnion, rather than butting against it.

The top and bottom angle bracing between the side girders is made from .010" styrene strips. See figs. 2, 4, and 5. The top has X-bracing while the bottom has just four diagonals. There are no cross braces at the short end of the leaf since this part fits between the support girders. Add the shoes to the bottom and front (narrow) end of the leaf, and the construction of this part is complete.

SUPPORT GIRDERS

Construction of the four horizontal support girders is similar to that of the leaf girders. Cut four identical panels from .020" styrene and attach the top and bottom cover plates. Study the photos and drawings of the girder assembly carefully as this step is quite tricky. You have to think in three dimensions to understand the interrelationship of the various parts and subassemblies. The hardest part for me was the small angle cross bracing between each pair of girders. In some places there are neither vertical nor horizontal

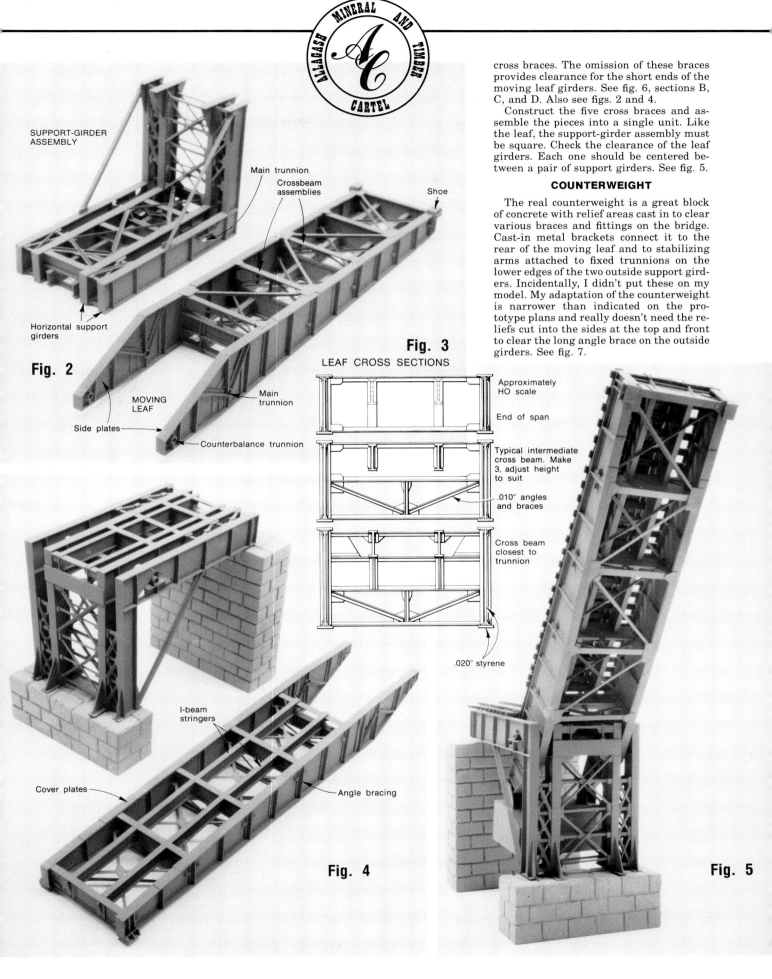

SUPPORT-GIRDER ASSEMBLY

Main trunnion

Crossbeam assemblies

Shoe

Horizontal support girders

Fig. 2

MOVING LEAF

Side plates

Main trunnion

Counterbalance trunnion

Fig. 3

LEAF CROSS SECTIONS

Approximately HO scale

End of span

Typical intermediate cross beam. Make 3, adjust height to suit

.010" angles and braces

Cross beam closest to trunnion

.020" styrene

I-beam stringers

Cover plates

Angle bracing

Fig. 4

Fig. 5

cross braces. The omission of these braces provides clearance for the short ends of the moving leaf girders. See fig. 6, sections B, C, and D. Also see figs. 2 and 4.

Construct the five cross braces and assemble the pieces into a single unit. Like the leaf, the support-girder assembly must be square. Check the clearance of the leaf girders. Each one should be centered between a pair of support girders. See fig. 5.

COUNTERWEIGHT

The real counterweight is a great block of concrete with relief areas cast in to clear various braces and fittings on the bridge. Cast-in metal brackets connect it to the rear of the moving leaf and to stabilizing arms attached to fixed trunnions on the lower edges of the two outside support girders. Incidentally, I didn't put these on my model. My adaptation of the counterweight is narrower than indicated on the prototype plans and really doesn't need the reliefs cut into the sides at the top and front to clear the long angle brace on the outside girders. See fig. 7.

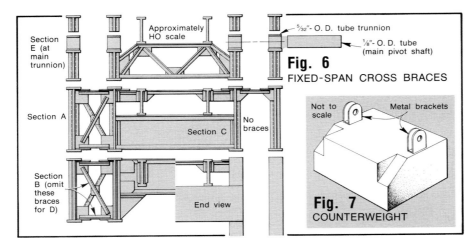

Section E (at main trunnion)

Approximately HO scale

Section A

Section C

No braces

Section B (omit these braces for D)

End view

⁵⁄₃₂″- O. D. tube trunnion

⅛″- O. D. tube (main pivot shaft)

Fig. 6
FIXED-SPAN CROSS BRACES

Not to scale

Metal brackets

Fig. 7
COUNTERWEIGHT

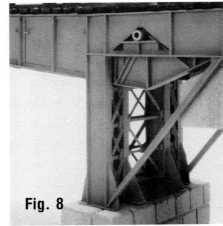

Fig. 8

I modeled the counterweight by sealing a block of balsa and painting it to a reasonable representation of concrete. Styrene can be used; however, a cast-plaster counterweight would be too heavy. The counterweight should not quite offset the weight of the long end of the leaf.

FINAL ASSEMBLY

Cut four main trunnion bearings from the same size tubing used for the leaf trunnions. See fig. 6. Cut two pivot shafts from the next smaller size of telescoping tubing. In my case this is ⅛″-O.D. tube. Two pivot-shaft assemblies are required. Slip a main trunnion tube over a pivot tube, making them flush at one end. Apply ACC to the flush end surfaces.

Position the leaf assembly into the support girder assembly, and insert the trunnion and pivot assemblies from the outside, through the triangular openings in the support girder plates. Slip the two remaining main trunnions over the pivot tube through the openings in the inside support girders. These main trunnions rest on the platforms in the girder openings. See fig. 8. Carefully align the leaf both vertically and horizontally. The top surfaces of the leaf must be level with the tops of the support girders. Adjust the height of the leaf by inserting shims between the trunnions and the platforms they rest upon.

When everything is properly aligned, cement the inside main trunnions to their respective platforms, but do not cement the outer trunnions. This makes it possible to disassemble the pieces for painting.

Attach the counterweight and move the leaf up and down to check all clearances for both the leaf and the counterweight.

Construct the other approach span, and mount the two approach spans and moving leaf into a fixed scene or on a sturdy base which can be included in your layout.

TIES AND RAILS

The ties rest on the stringers and girder top plates. See fig. 9. Real ties are attached with long bolts that go through the guard timber, tie, and top girder plate. Simulate this construction with cast plastic nut-bolt-washer castings from Kemtron.

Ties from the abutment to a point eight

The Gloucester Draw

A bascule bridge that's ideal for modeling

MOVABLE drawbridges were built as far back as the Middle Ages, but modern bascule bridge technology began in 1893 when a Scherzer rolling-lift bascule was installed over the Chicago River at Van Buren Street in Chicago, Ill. Bascule bridges have several mechanical forms, the simplest of which is the Strauss single-leaf trunnion, a pivoted type with a counterweight at the short, or rear, end of the moving leaf.

In 1910 the Boston & Maine RR. had a Strauss-type bridge designed and built by the Strauss Bascule & Concrete Bridge Co. of Chicago, Ill., to span the Annisquam River west of Gloucester, Mass. The bridge, properly called the Gloucester Draw, is still in use, although it suffers from a fractured trunnion bearing and a bent drive shaft, so movement of the draw leaf is limited to slow speed, and the leaf cannot be fully raised.

The maximum angle the bridge can be raised is 82 degrees above horizontal. The lower-chord cross bracing is a bit different from that at the top, with single diagonal braces. A single large rack gear is attached to the center girder of the leaf.

Photos by George Konrad

A model of this small structure will fit well into a layout of any size. The moving leaf is only 53 feet long spanning a 40-foot clear channel.

Originally the leaf was manually operated with one or two men turning a hand crank located on the side of the fixed support span. Bascule bridges are designed with a concrete counterbalance that almost balances the weight of the leaf forward of the main trunnion, or pivot bearing. This forward section weighs just enough more than the counterbalance to hold down the end of the span. The counterbalance, along with a 300:1 geared-reduction drive makes it possible to lift the great mass of the leaf with relatively little energy. At some point in time, an electric motor and some additional gears were added, but the hand crank has been retained for emergencies.

The original design had a pair of hand-operated locking bolts at the end of the leaf to secure it to the approach span when trains were passing over the bridge. Located at the ends of the outer girders, these locking bolts were loosened or tightened with a large Tee wrench. Presently, an electromechanical lock is used.

At a junction of rail and water routes

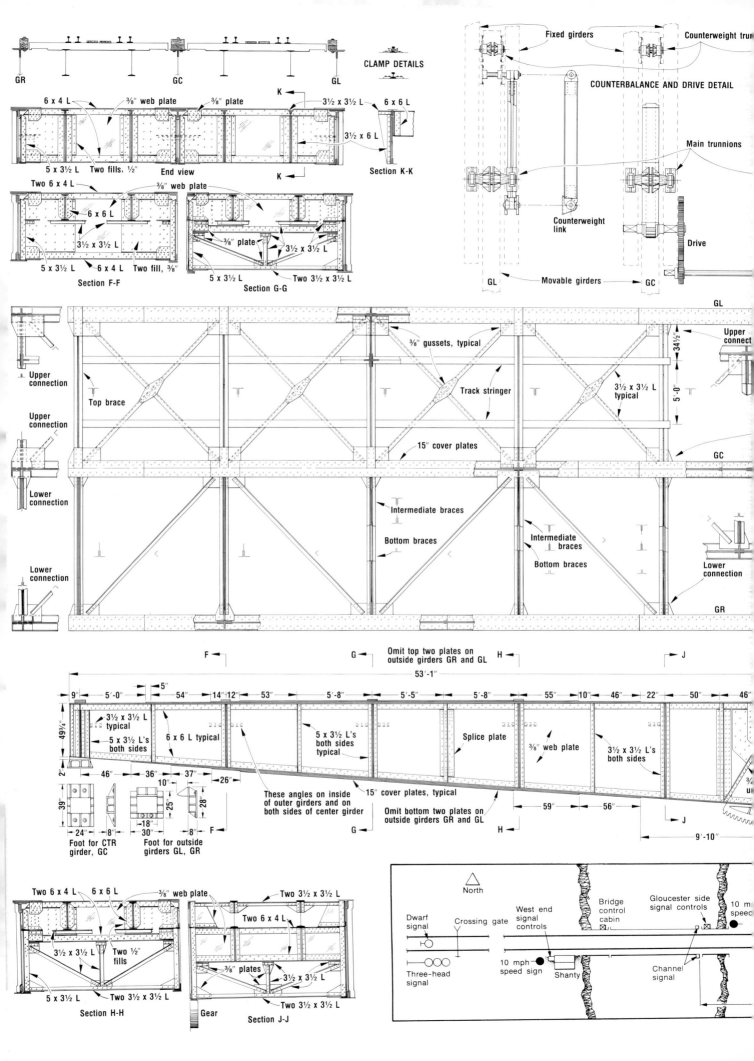

CLAMP DETAILS

GR   GC   GL

6 x 4 L   ⅜" web plate   ⅜" plate   3½ x 3½ L   6 x 6 L

K   K   3½ x 6 L

5 x 3½ L   Two fills, ½"   End view   Section K-K

Two 6 x 4 L   ⅜" web plate

6 x 6 L

3½ x 3½ L

5 x 3½ L   6 x 4 L   Two fill, ⅜"   ⅜" plate   3½ x 3½ L

Section F-F   5 x 3½ L   Two 3½ x 3½ L   Section G-G

COUNTERBALANCE AND DRIVE DETAIL

Fixed girders   Counterweight trun

Main trunnions

Counterweight link   Drive

GL   Movable girders   GC

Upper connection   ⅜" gussets, typical   Upper connect

Top brace   Track stringer   3½ x 3½ L typical   5'-0"   34½'

Upper connection   15" cover plates   GC

Lower connection   Intermediate braces

Bottom braces   Intermediate braces

Lower connection   Bottom braces   Lower connection

GR

F   G   Omit top two plates on outside girders GR and GL   H   J

53'-1"

9"   5'-0"   5"   54"   14" 12"   53"   5'-8"   5'-5"   5'-8"   55"   10"   46"   22"   50"   46"

49¾"

3½ x 3½ L typical

5 x 3½ L's both sides   6 x 6 L typical   5 x 3½ L's both sides typical   Splice plate   ⅜" web plate   3½ x 3½ L's both sides

2"

39"   46"   36"   37"   26"   These angles on inside of outer girders and on both sides of center girder   15" cover plates, typical   59"   56"

10"   25"   28"   Omit bottom two plates on outside girders GR and GL

24"   8"   18"   30"   8"   F   G   H   J

Foot for CTR girder, GC   Foot for outside girders GL, GR   9'-10"

Two 6 x 4 L   6 x 6 L   ⅜" web plate   Two 3½ x 3½ L

Two 6 x 4 L

3½ x 3½ L   Two ½" fills   ⅜" plates   3½ x 3½ L

5 x 3½ L   Two 3½ x 3½ L   Gear   Two 3½ x 3½ L

Section H-H   Section J-J

North

Dwarf signal   Crossing gate   West end signal controls   Bridge control cabin   Gloucester side signal controls   10 m speed

Three-head signal   10 mph speed sign   Shanty   Channel signal

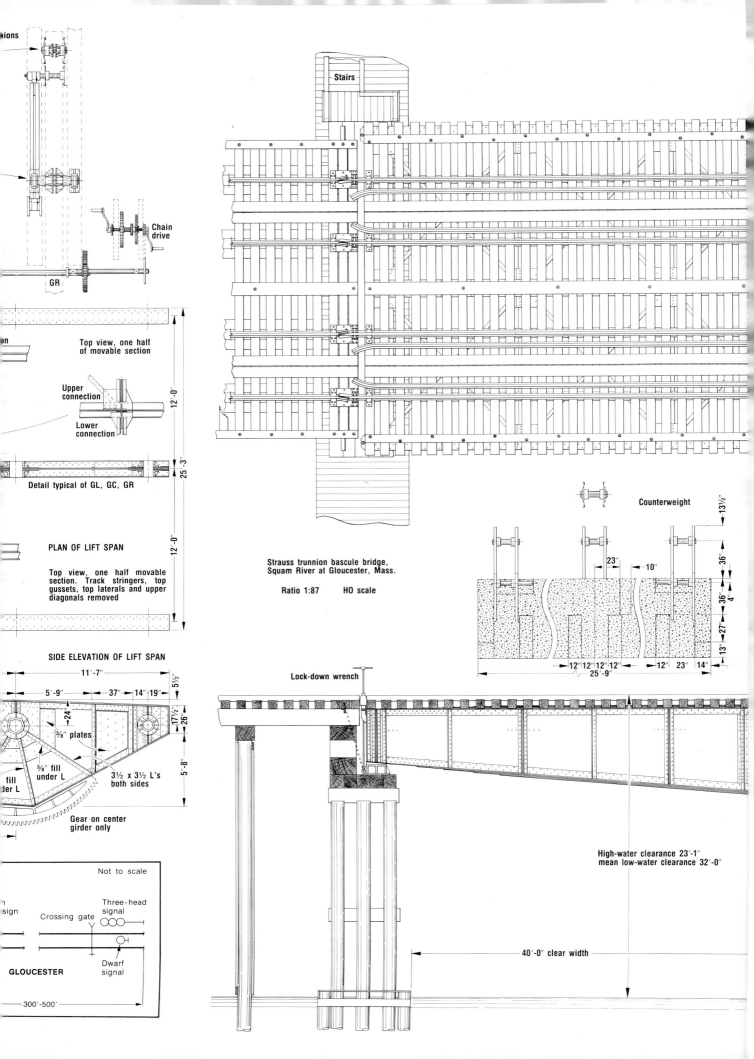

ions

Chain
drive

GR

Top view, one half
of movable section

Upper
connection

Lower
connection

Detail typical of GL, GC, GR

PLAN OF LIFT SPAN

Top view, one half movable
section. Track stringers, top
gussets, top laterals and upper
diagonals removed

SIDE ELEVATION OF LIFT SPAN

12'-0"

25'-3"

12'-0"

11'-7"

5'-9" 37" 14" 19"

5½"

24

17½"

26

⅜" plates

⅜" fill
under L

fill
der L

3½ x 3½ L's
both sides

5'-8"

Gear on center
girder only

Not to scale

sign

Three-head
signal

Crossing gate

Dwarf
signal

GLOUCESTER

300'-500'

Stairs

Strauss trunnion bascule bridge,
Squam River at Gloucester, Mass.

Ratio 1:87   HO scale

Counterweight

13½"

36"

36"

4"

27"

13"

23" 10"

12"12"12"12"   12" 23" 14"

25'-9"

Lock-down wrench

High-water clearance 23'-1"
mean low-water clearance 32'-0"

40'-0" clear width

The Railroad Gazette: June 29, 1888.

Big Warrior River Bridge

Wrought iron bridge built near Cordova, Ala., in 1887

THE FIRST completely metal railroad truss bridges were just 24 years old when the Big Warrior River Bridge was completed near Cordova, Ala., by the Kansas City, Fort Scott & Memphis RR. (now St. Louis - San Francisco Ry.) in early autumn 1887. Fashioned of wrought iron, the main 298-foot span was a curved-chord Pratt-type truss consisting of 12 panels, each of which was 24'-10" long. To complete the span across the Big Warrior River, a 150-foot parallel-chord Pratt-type truss extended from one end as shown in the engraving, which appeared in the June 29, 1888, issue of *Railroad Gazette.*

The bridge was designed to handle two 171,000-pound Consolidation locomotives and a trainload of 3000 pounds per lineal foot. The structure would have been incapable of safely carrying the type of equipment in service shortly after the turn of the century, since such equipment would have exceeded the bridge's design loading.

If you want to stay within the prototype's loading capabilities, the largest model locomotive which should be operated over this bridge is a medium-size 4-6-0 or 2-8-0, or a GE 44-ton industrial-type diesel switcher.

The cross section of the bridge members could be increased slightly on a model to provide a heavier structure suitable for rolling stock and most locomotives built in the 1920's and 1930's.

As modelers, we have the option of stretching the facts; and any model of reasonable size such as a light 2-8-2 or early diesel road switcher could be used without straining the credibility of the equipment to bridge proportions.

Bridge ties of the 1880's were usually 6" high, 8" wide, and 10 feet long. Shortly thereafter most railroads adopted a standard 8"-square tie.

Until recently guard timbers of about 6" x 8" were used running parallel to the rails and set in about 2" to 3" from the tie ends. Guardrails, no higher than the running rails and no more than 1" lower, were often set 8" to 10" inside the running rails. These ran about 50 feet from each end of the bridge, then curved in to join at the track center.

Brass, plastic, and basswood structural shapes are available in suitable sizes for building a model of this bridge in any scale. Wood will make a strong structure for scales up to HO. In the larger scales it would be advisable to have at least the lengthwise girders and floor members made of metal for strength. Also, it is difficult to represent metal with wood without a great deal of work.

The prototype affixes one end to one abutment, while the other end floats on rollers or rockers to compensate for expansion and contraction. For the same reason, one or both ends of the model bridge should float on a bearing surface. Both rails should be gapped a short distance from the ends of the bridge and joined to the adjacent rails with slip-on rail joiners to allow for rail expansion. This is especially important where the bridge will span a distance between two separate pieces of benchwork: the seasonal expansion and contraction of the walls may be considerable.

A model of the Big Warrior River Bridge would be a focal point of interest on any layout. — *Gordon Odegard.*

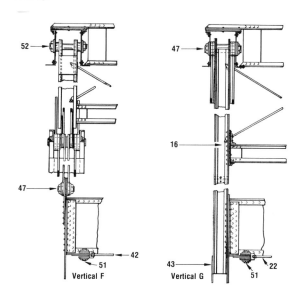

Vertical F   Vertical G

Building Black Bear Bridge

A spectacular HO model based on the CP's Stoney Creek Bridge

BY JIM MONEY
PHOTOS BY THE AUTHOR

THIS 200-foot HO bridge had its genesis in a reunion with an old friend, its inspiration in a mountain adventure by helicopter, and its culmination in four months of enjoyable planning and construction.

A visit in 1987 to the part of Ontario where I'd grown up led to an amazing reunion with my school friend Bob Ough after almost 30 years. Incredibly, our conversation and our interests in model railroading, trains, and aviation picked up almost exactly where they had left off.

A few months later, Bob and I laid the first track on my HO Athabaska RR. The following year, 1988, saw us videotaping and photographing rail operations in the Rockies by train, car, and a Hughes 500E demonstrator helicopter that Bob flies all over Canada as a marketing manager for McDonnell Douglas.

A prime target was the Canadian Pacific's Stoney Creek Bridge near Rogers Pass, accessible only by a long hike through country purportedly inhabited

by bears. Sure enough, on our first orbit looking for a landing spot, we spied a magnificent black bear just downhill from the bridge.

We clearly saw it look up and bare its fangs at the helicopter. Then it shook its glossy coat and loped into the trees — heading in the direction of the bridge! It didn't take us long to decide that a walk in the woods would probably be a hot and dusty affair anyway, so with great finesse Bob sneaked the chopper under some communications wires and set it down only a few yards from the bridge itself.

The Stoney Creek Bridge was built in 1893. The main arch structure was 336 feet long. In 1929, the Canadian Pacific reinforced the bridge to cope with increasingly heavy equipment and traffic. These strengthening measures included adding a second arch to each side as well as a series of trestle bents, and resulted in an unusual configuration with surprisingly pleasing lines and an aura of great strength. Today it carries modern SD40-2 lash-ups hauling the heavy grain, coal, and general freight trains on the CP's transcontinental main line.

I decided to build a compressed version of the Stoney Creek Bridge to fit a ready-made gap in the Athabaska benchwork and to call it Black Bear Bridge in honor of a certain bellicose bruin.

PLANNING STAGE

I began by amassing as much information as possible on the Stoney Creek Bridge and on arch bridge construction in general. John Armstrong, designer of the Athabaska, kindly sent some extremely relevant material from Paul Mallery's *Bridge & Trestle Handbook* (out of print), including some elevation drawings of the Stoney Creek Bridge itself. Harold Russell's "ABCs of bridges," a series in the July through December 1988 issues of MODEL RAILROADER, was also helpful.

Just looking at the full-scale Stoney Creek Bridge, I could see Central Valley (CV) bridge parts everywhere! Eventually it took three bridge kits and about ten girder kits to complete the bridge. I wrote to Central Valley direct, and they were very helpful.

I first drew up some working plans in HO scale of the proposed design, based on an overall main length of 208 feet. I

Left: Jim Money's HO bridge is ready to take its place in his layout. All the girders, lattice, and cross-bracing came from Central Valley bridge kits. **Above:** Our author's model is based on Stoney Creek

Bridge, high in the Canadian Rockies on the spectacular Rogers Pass route. Anyone hiking in to visit the bridge would be well-advised to wear a bell so as to not surprise any black bears living in the area.

chose this length not only because of the space available, but because I felt that the 22"-square cross section of CV's girders wouldn't realistically support a larger structure.

While many arch bridges are parabolic, Stoney Creek seems to be built on a circular curve. I laid this out using a trammel on a large sheet of paper, then

filled in the other components so they "looked right," referring to photos of Stoney Creek to check proportions.

I took a good deal of time and made several attempts to lay out the ribs and bents on paper. I wanted to be reasonably sure the bridge followed basic engineering principles and would assemble without any glitches.

ASSEMBLY BEGINS

Satisfied with the plans, I taped the arch drawing on a large cork board, pinned a sheet of waxed paper over it, and started laying in the zigzag vertical and diagonal rib braces using CV type-C-C girders, as shown in fig. 1.

I shimmed up each brace section using

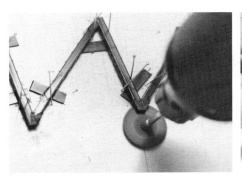

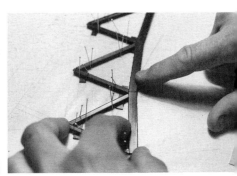

FIG. 1. BUILDING THE ARCHES
Left: Using Central Valley C-C girders, our author laid out the interior members of the arches and cemented them together. He

shaved off the flanges near the ends. **Middle:** The arch side pieces were marked with a razor saw, then cut at the author's workbench. **Right:** The B-B girders slipped neatly over the ends of the C-Cs.

107

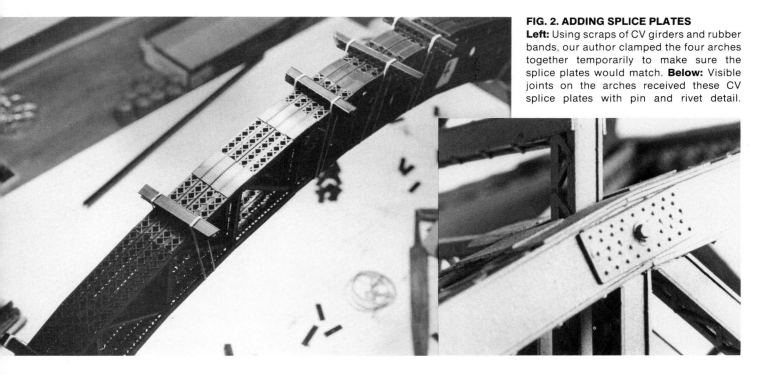

FIG. 2. ADDING SPLICE PLATES
Left: Using scraps of CV girders and rubber bands, our author clamped the four arches together temporarily to make sure the splice plates would match. **Below:** Visible joints on the arches received these CV splice plates with pin and rivet detail.

pieces of web cut from CV type-A girders to gain clearance for fitting the main girders later. Then I cemented the parts together with liquid plastic cement.

Once these braces had set, I used a cutoff wheel in a motor tool to slim the girder ends so they would slip-fit into CV type-B-B girder sections.

Next I started cutting the B-B sections and adding them. This is a vital step, and I scrapped the first arch I built after I was forced to admit that the girder joints looked terrible because the angles were off.

On the second attempt, I marked each girder section in place on the plan with a razor saw, then transferred the section to a simple stop-block cutting board to complete the cut. The lattice was then cut back at each end, and the section was cemented into place. I did this work as carefully as I could, as I wanted the four completed arches to be as identical as I could make them.

Figure 2 shows how I clamped the arches together before adding the top and bottom splice plates to areas that had been shaved free of lattice. The idea was to get the best possible match. Although the principle shown is valid, the photo is a bit misleading because later I decided these plates, made from Central Valley girder parts, were too thick. I sacrificed the rivets and remade the splice plates out of .010″ styrene.

Photos seem to indicate that Stoney Creek is a pin-connected bridge, so I used the CV splice plate/pin anchors to cover the joints in the sides of the arches. Since my bridge can be viewed from only one side, I added these details to just the faces there.

DOUBLING THE ARCHES

The next step was very satisfying. In one operation the most unique feature of the Stoney Creek Bridge, namely the paired arches, was re-created. Holding the ribs across a knee like an old master bow maker, I clamped them together in pairs with rubber bands, using short sections of B-B girder as spacers.

Then, as shown in fig. 3, I connected the truss pairs with 5′-6″-long crosstie plates made from lengths of type-A riveted plate and cemented across the gap between the braced ribs, with one at each end of every splice plate. During this operation I constantly checked that the ribs remained perfectly aligned.

Not all of these crosstie plates are identical on the prototype, so for variety I fabricated a number of them from .010″ styrene with 4″ x 4″ Plastruct angle as edge stiffeners.

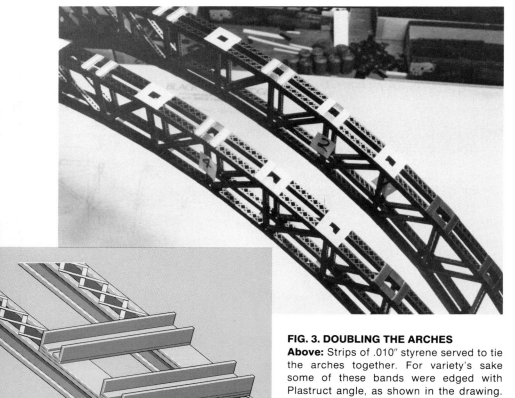

FIG. 3. DOUBLING THE ARCHES
Above: Strips of .010″ styrene served to tie the arches together. For variety's sake some of these bands were edged with Plastruct angle, as shown in the drawing.

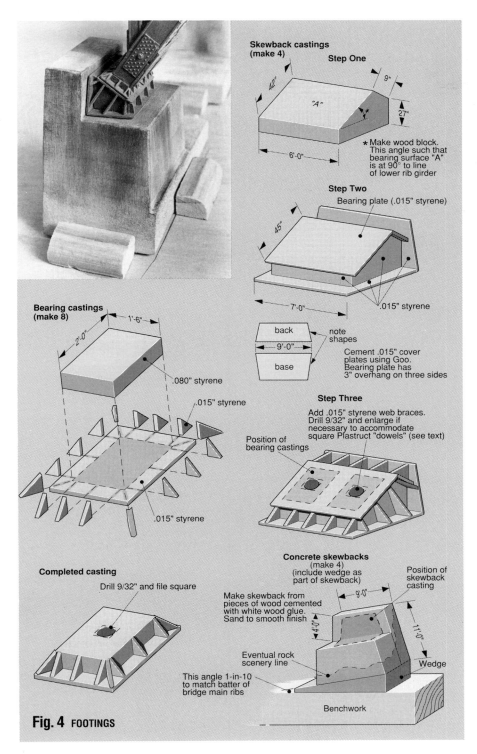

Skewback castings (make 4)

Step One

"A"

42"

9"

27"

6'-0"

★ Make wood block. This angle such that bearing surface "A" is at 90° to line of lower rib girder

Step Two

Bearing plate (.015" styrene)

45"

7'-0"

.015" styrene

back

9'-0"

base

note shapes

Cement .015" cover plates using Goo. Bearing plate has 3" overhang on three sides

Bearing castings (make 8)

1'-6"

2'-0"

.080" styrene

.015" styrene

.015" styrene

Step Three

Add .015" styrene web braces. Drill 9/32" and enlarge if necessary to accommodate square Plastruct "dowels" (see text)

Position of bearing castings

Completed casting

Drill 9/32" and file square

Concrete skewbacks (make 4) (include wedge as part of skewback)

Position of skewback casting

9'-0"

11'-0"

Make skewback from pieces of wood cemented with white wood glue. Sand to smooth finish

4'-0"

Wedge

Eventual rock scenery line

This angle 1-in-10 to match batter of bridge main ribs

Benchwork

Fig. 4 FOOTINGS

FIG. 5. ATTACHING FOOTINGS

As shown in the drawing, square pegs were installed in the ends of the arches. These were inserted into matching holes in the footings. The photo shows how two machinist's squares were used to hold the parts in alignment until the cement set.

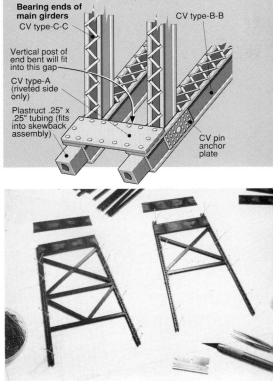

Bearing ends of main girders

CV type-C-C

CV type-B-B

Vertical post of end bent will fit into this gap

CV type-A (riveted side only)

Plastruct .25" x .25" tubing (fits into skewback assembly)

CV pin anchor plate

FIG. 6. BENT ASSEMBLY

Above: The bents were built up over templates the author covered with waxed paper. **Below:** He made gussets from .010" styrene.

GETTING YOUR BEARINGS

At this point, I turned to the bridge supports and fabricated the bearing castings, the skewback castings, and the concrete skewbacks themselves, as shown in fig. 4. I painted the skewbacks with Floquil Foundation and aged them with powdered chalks.

To fasten the arches to the footings, I cemented a length of Plastruct 9/32"-square ABS into the end of each main rib girder, drilled and filed a matching

hole in the bearing and skewback castings, and cemented the arches and footings together. See fig. 5. I used two machinist's squares to hold the arches vertical on a sheet of plate glass until the cement had set.

MAKING THE BENTS

Next I went back to the cork board and waxed paper overlays to make up the bents, working directly on the plans as I had for the braced ribs. See fig. 6. I used CV type-B girders for the

Text continues on page 93

BLACK BEAR BRIDGE

Scale = 1/2 HO

FIG. 7. IT COMES TOGETHER

Above: Wow, we've built ourselves a bridge kit! **Bottom left:** A strongback is being used to join the bents to the arches.

Right: Plates of .010″ styrene trimmed with Plastruct angle secure the bents to the arches. **Bottom right:** The shorter bents are held by bridge-width retainers.

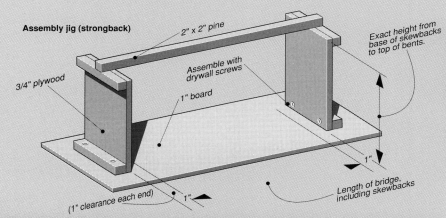

Assembly jig (strongback)

2″ x 2″ pine

3/4″ plywood

Assemble with drywall screws

1″ board

Exact height from base of skewbacks to top of bents.

1″

(1″ clearance each end)

1″

Length of bridge, including skewbacks

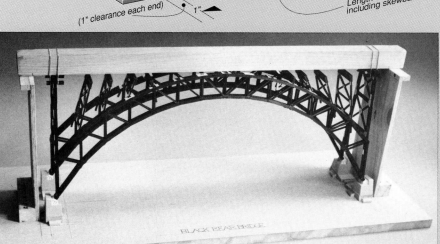

uprights and horizontals and C-C girders for the diagonal bracing.

The bearing girders spanning the top of each bent were cut from CV stringer sections and came out closely resembling the Stoney Creek originals. I made the gusset plates from .010″ styrene. The five center bents had to be ad-libbed a bit because of reduced clearances, but this variation in form gives the real Stoney Creek part of its charm. I made the bearing girders for these bents out of .020″ styrene, with Plastruct 4″ x 4″ angle edge stiffeners.

ASSEMBLY

Shown in fig. 7 is the bridge kit we've made for ourselves. To assemble it I first built an assembly jig out of ⅜″ plywood and 2 x 2 pine. Shipbuilders call this kind of jig a "strongback."

I cleated the skewbacks to the baseboard and pulled the bents up hard against the 2 x 2 top beam with rubber bands. Then I fiddled and measured and remeasured for hours until everything was square and symmetrical. This is no time for mistakes!

The bents are supported by crossstraps bridging the twin arches, also shown in fig. 7. Installing these is another satisfying operation, as it transforms in one hit a collection of discrete parts into a cohesive structure definitely resembling a bridge. I made the crossstraps of .010″ styrene with Plastruct angle edge stiffeners.

To install them I scraped back the lattice as needed and cemented them in place. Note that the cross-straps toward the center of the arch are more massive affairs spanning the whole width of the bridge. These add considerable strength and stiffness, as well as visual interest, to the structure.

DETAILS

The Stoney Creek Bridge has a distinct fascia lattice connecting the tops of the bents. I found this pleasantly simple to fabricate, using lattice from CV type-B girders (having removed the web with a razor saw) and Plastruct 6″ x 6″ angle as top and bottom stiffeners. See fig. 8. When this fascia is cemented in place the bridge really starts to look good. The structure can now be removed from the strongback.

The main load-bearing girders across the tops of the bents now had gussets and top plating installed, which I fabricated from .010″ styrene.

The Central Valley kit has some delicate lattice pieces to be used as diagonal braces in the top. I cut these slightly shorter and used them as cross-braces between the tops of the bents. Because of tight clearances I ad-libbed again at the center of the arch, but everything still looks plausible, at least to me.

Micro Engineering's 30-foot deck girder

kit provided side girders just the right length for the deck portion of my bridge. Another lucky break! Rather than build all those bridge kits, however, I tried something different.

TURNING UP THE VOLUME

Many model railroaders go to great lengths to silence their roadbed and rolling stock. Not me. Trains in real life are deafeningly noisy. You can hear 'em miles away, especially when they rumble across a bridge.

I decided to amplify the natural rattle and roar of my Athabaska grain cars by building a sound box into the

top of the bridge, with holes for the sound to escape, as shown in fig. 9. Plate girders were cemented onto the viewing side. There is nothing particularly scientific about the design of this "Iron Stradivarius," but it certainly is "live" when wheels roll across the bridge. The normal viewing angle precludes examination of the underside of the deck girders, so lack of detail up there in the shadows doesn't bother me.

INTERNAL BRACING

I turned the bridge upside down at this point and got to work on all that juicy detailed bracing between the braced

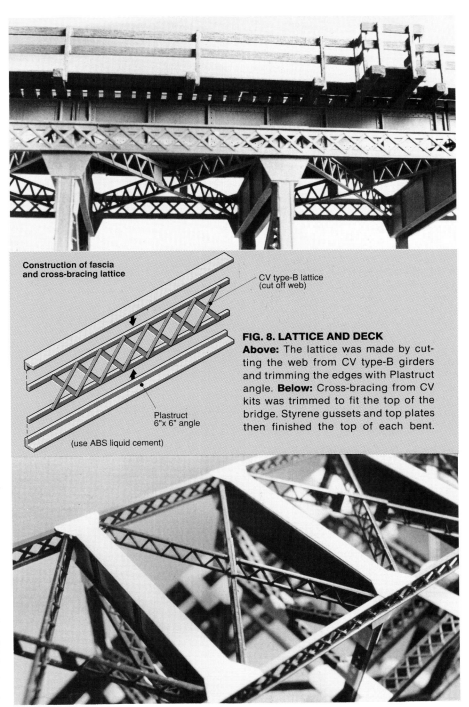

Construction of fascia and cross-bracing lattice

CV type-B lattice (cut off web)

Plastruct 6″x 6″ angle

(use ABS liquid cement)

FIG. 8. LATTICE AND DECK
Above: The lattice was made by cutting the web from CV type-B girders and trimming the edges with Plastruct angle. **Below:** Cross-bracing from CV kits was trimmed to fit the top of the bridge. Styrene gussets and top plates then finished the top of each bent.

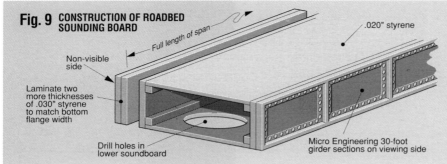

Fig. 9 CONSTRUCTION OF ROADBED SOUNDING BOARD

Full length of span

.020" styrene

Non-visible side

Laminate two more thicknesses of .030" styrene to match bottom flange width

Drill holes in lower soundboard

Micro Engineering 30-foot girder sections on viewing side

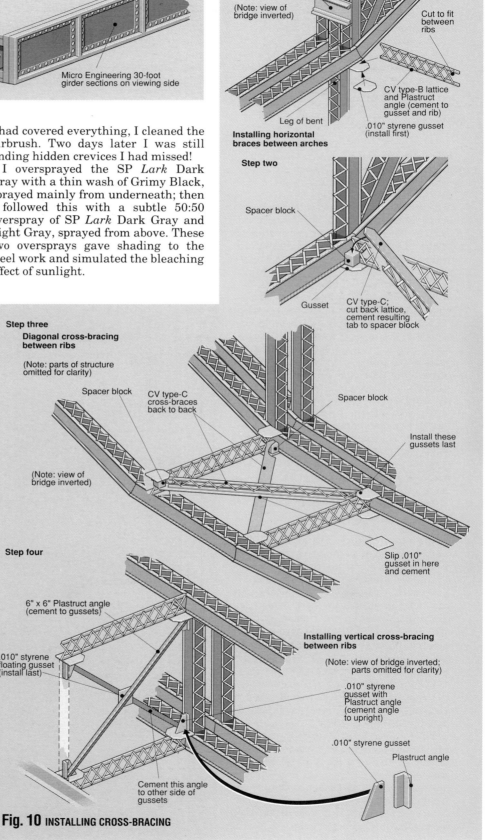

Step One

Cross-strap bent support

(Note: view of bridge inverted)

Cut to fit between ribs

CV type-B lattice and Plastruct angle (cement to gusset and rib)

Leg of bent

.010" styrene gusset (install first)

Installing horizontal braces between arches

Step two

Spacer block

Gusset

CV type-C; cut back lattice, cement resulting tab to spacer block

Step three

Diagonal cross-bracing between ribs

(Note: parts of structure omitted for clarity)

Spacer block

CV type-C cross-braces back to back

Spacer block

Install these gussets last

(Note: view of bridge inverted)

Slip .010" gusset in here and cement

Step four

6" x 6" Plastruct angle (cement to gussets)

.010" styrene floating gusset (install last)

Cement this angle to other side of gussets

Installing vertical cross-bracing between ribs

(Note: view of bridge inverted; parts omitted for clarity)

.010" styrene gusset with Plastruct angle (cement angle to upright)

.010" styrene gusset

Plastruct angle

Fig. 10 INSTALLING CROSS-BRACING

ribs. Basically, the trick in this situation is to install any bits deep inside the structure first, then work your way out layer by layer to the surface. See fig. 10.

When the last of the braces was in place about two weeks later, I certainly felt relieved. Standing back to have a look, I knew it had been worth the effort.

TRACK AND WALKWAY

I made up the roadbed on another crude strongback by connecting the Micro Engineering track sections and pinning them upside down to a length of 2 x 4. Then I removed every eighth tie and replaced it with a 15-foot-long switch tie, stained dark brown and secured directly to the rails with epoxy. After flipping the track rightside up, I pinned it again to the 2 x 4 and soldered all the rail joints.

The guardrails were fabricated from code 55 rail and secured with cyanoacrylate adhesive. I made fishplates for the visible outside rail joints from rivet-bearing slivers of CV splice plate.

I built the catwalk and safety rail, using 2" x 12" planking, 4" x 4" vertical posts, and 2" x 8" guardrails. See fig. 11. Since I wanted the catwalk to have the "railroad rustic" flavor of the Stoney Creek prototype, I built the structure by eye, without checking square or level. It looks just about right, I think.

PAINTING

I airbrushed the entire bridge with Floquil's SP *Lark* Dark Gray, using a mixture of 50 percent color, 30 percent Dio-Sol, and 20 percent Crystal-Cote. Nature gives a fine patina to almost everything under the sun so I rarely prepare a color for airbrushing without throwing in a noticeable percentage of Glaze, Crystal-Cote, or Hi-Gloss. Certainly weathered steel has too fine a finish to be represented by straight flat paint.

Airbrushing a structure of this complexity is time-consuming. I sprayed all the internal intersections and gusset joints first, turning the bridge frequently to attack from every angle. I finished with the straight-run girders, working my way from inside out to the surface again. When I had thoroughly inspected the bridge and was convinced

I had covered everything, I cleaned the airbrush. Two days later I was still finding hidden crevices I had missed!

I oversprayed the SP *Lark* Dark Gray with a thin wash of Grimy Black, sprayed mainly from underneath; then I followed this with a subtle 50:50 overspray of SP *Lark* Dark Gray and Light Gray, sprayed from above. These two oversprays gave shading to the steel work and simulated the bleaching effect of sunlight.

FIG. 11. FINAL DETAILS
Above: The guardrails were made with Rail Craft code 55. **Right:** Our author eyeballed in the wood railings and stand-off platforms so they wouldn't come out too perfect.

To finish the track and catwalk I sprayed on my own Old Creosote mixture. This isn't a cough syrup, but rather a blend of 40 percent Engine Black, 20 percent SP *Lark* Light Gray, 20 percent Dio-Sol, 10 percent Tuscan Red, and 10 percent Hi-Gloss. I followed this with an overspray of SP *Lark* Dark Gray mixed with 20 percent Hi-Gloss to suggest age.

The track center I sprayed with a 50:50 mix of Engine Black and Hi-Gloss to represent the dark, greasy film that the prototype picks up due to flange oilers on both approach curves. I brush-painted the outside edges of the running rails a dirty rust color.

When all the paint had dried for 24 hours, I coated the top of the "sound box" with epoxy and carefully positioned the complete track/catwalk assembly, weighting it down overnight while the epoxy set.

Finally, I weathered the whole structure with powdered chalks and a small, stiff brush, using light gray, black, raw umber, and raw sienna for bleaching, grimy dirt, rust, and mud spray respectively. This mud spray sifts down through the ties of the prototype and coats the entire steel structure below the track with a soft yellow-brown mist.

With the 50-foot and 30-foot Micro Engineering approach spans in place, resting on their weathered concrete abutments, Black Bear Bridge is complete. All I have to do now is drop it into the gap in the benchwork, scenic the gorge with rocks and pine trees, and whip up an epoxy whitewater Black Bear Creek rushing below. Oh, and I don't want to forget that glossy-coated black bear glowering up at the first Athabaska SD40-2 to make the crossing. ◘

Our author's bridge is especially dramatic when seen from a black bear's point of view.

115

Short girder-type overpass

Original supported both traction and steam roads; drawing is modified for a single track

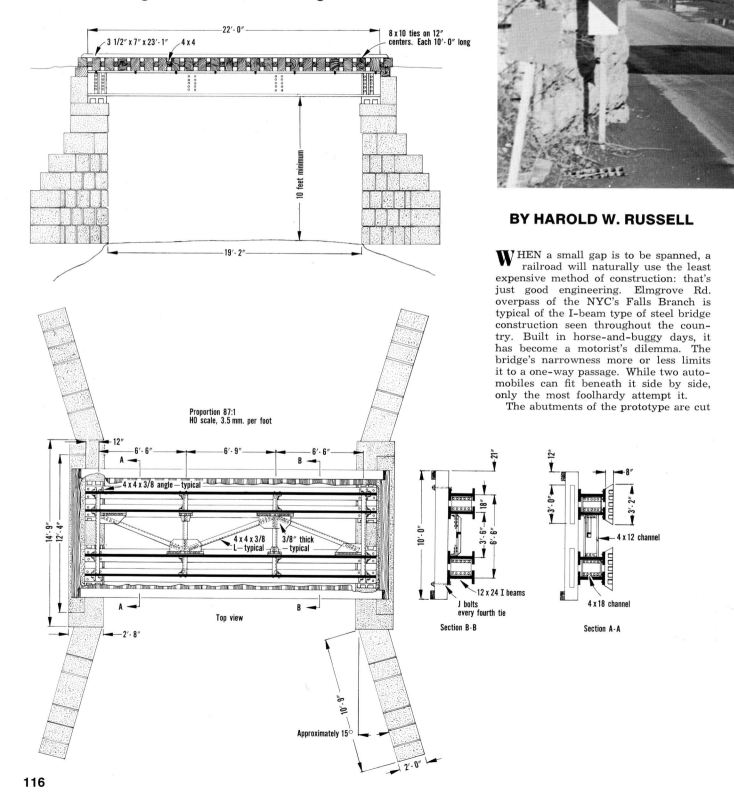

22'- 0"

3 1/2" x 7" x 23'-1"   4 x 4

8 x 10 ties on 12" centers. Each 10'- 0" long

10 feet minimum

19'- 2"

Proportion 87:1
HO scale, 3.5 mm. per foot

12"

6'- 6"   6'- 9"   6'- 6"

A   B

4 x 4 x 3/8 angle – typical

14'- 9"   12'- 4"

4 x 4 x 3/8 L – typical   3/8" thick – typical

A   B

Top view

2'- 8"

Approximately 15°

10'- 9"

2'- 0"

21"   12"

8"

3'- 0"   3'- 2"

10'- 0"   18"

3'- 6"   6'- 6"

4 x 12 channel

12 x 24 I beams

J bolts every fourth tie

4 x 18 channel

Section B-B   Section A-A

BY HAROLD W. RUSSELL

WHEN a small gap is to be spanned, a railroad will naturally use the least expensive method of construction: that's just good engineering. Elmgrove Rd. overpass of the NYC's Falls Branch is typical of the I-beam type of steel bridge construction seen throughout the country. Built in horse-and-buggy days, it has become a motorist's dilemma. The bridge's narrowness more or less limits it to a one-way passage. While two automobiles can fit beneath it side by side, only the most foolhardy attempt it.

The abutments of the prototype are cut

116

Harold W. Russell.

stone. Poured concrete could also be used, and would be on a more modern installation. The prototype has an overhead clearance of only 10 feet, which, again, would not be made so low today. The drawing shows 11 feet but 14 or more would be more typical today.

The drawings show vertical walls. More often retaining walls and bridge abutments are built with a slight batter — the wall slopes inward from the base at an angle of perhaps 1 in 20. A long girder would have a roller or rocker pedestal between it and the stone at one end to prevent the expanding and contracting metal from dislodging the stone or causing other trouble. On this short span the pedestals are simple blocks of cast metal on which the girder rests.

The exposed bottom flanges of the steel bridge girders are bent and scarred from occasional collisions with the tops of trucks. The abutment stones show a multiplicity of automobile paint colors where cars have scraped them.

The lower stones are likely to be stained by mosses and dirt spatter, while streaks of rust may show draining downward from the metal parts. However, weathering is different in each part of the country.

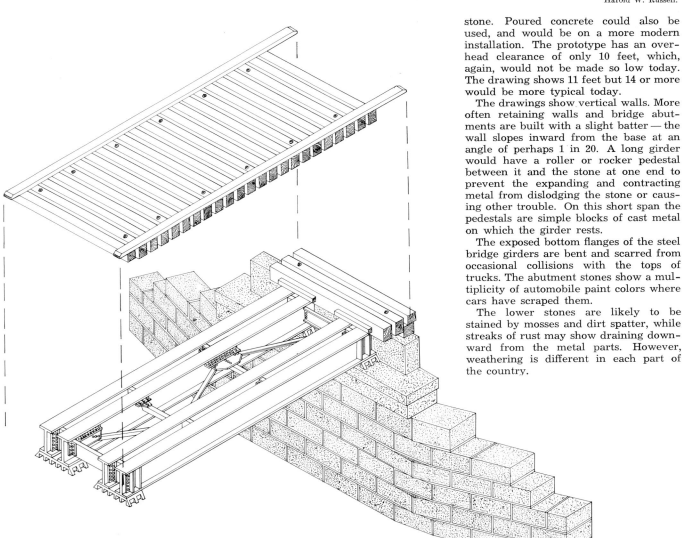

A short through plate-girder bridge

THIS short bridge carries railroad tracks over a road leading to a cemetery in Lancaster, N.H.

The outside steel girders are composed of three separate steel plates that are spliced together and reinforced with angles. The deck is composed of smaller girders also reinforced with angles. The three X-braces at the bottom give rigidity to the structure. The ties are bolted to the steel deck. The bridge does not have guard rails. The abutments are made of granite blocks.

A model of the bridge could be easily built from basswood, cardboard, styrene, or brass. Taking the time to add the rivets would give the model a distinctive appearance. — *Harold Russell.* Ō

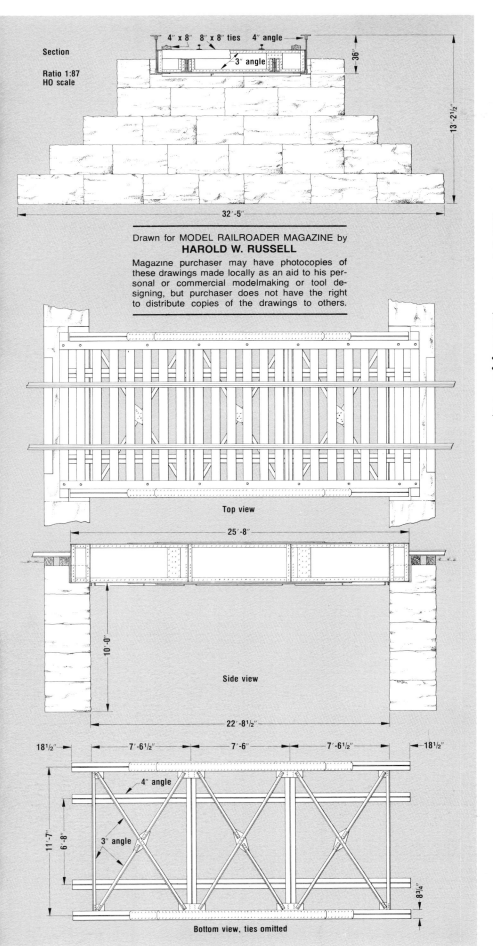

Section

Ratio 1:87
HO scale

4" x 8"   8" x 8" ties   4" angle

3" angle

36"

13'-2½"

32'-5"

Drawn for MODEL RAILROADER MAGAZINE by
HAROLD W. RUSSELL

Top view

25'-8"

10'-0"

Side view

22'-8½"

18½"   7'-6½"   7'-6"   7'-6½"   18½"

4" angle

11'-7"

8'-6"

3" angle

8¾"

Bottom view, ties omitted

Bruce W. Giles.

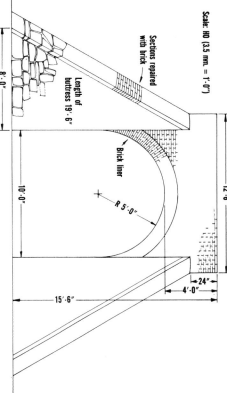

Scale: HO (3.5 mm. = 1'-0")

Sections repaired with brick

Length of buttress 19'-6"

8'-0"

10'-0"

Brick liner

R 5'-0"

12'-6"

15'-6"

24"

4'-0"

Masonry arch underpass

THIS underpass, obviously built in horse-and-buggy days, allows road traffic to pass under the Long Island RR. three quarters of a mile east of Yaphank station. It is of field-stone and brick construction, and could be the prototype for an outstanding model.

119

B&O short girder bridge

WYOMING, N. Y., is on the Baltimore & Ohio freight-only line that connects East Salamanca and Rochester. Here the railroad crosses a small stream, making use of a short two-span deck girder bridge. Draftsman Harold W. Russell calls it a lunchtime project for modelers.

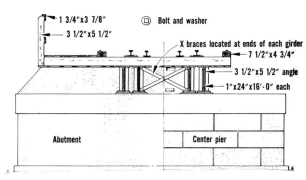

1 3/4"x3 7/8"
3 1/2"x5 1/2"
Bolt and washer
X braces located at ends of each girder
7 1/2"x4 3/4"
3 1/2"x5 1/2" angle
1"x24"x16'-0" each

Abutment   Center pier

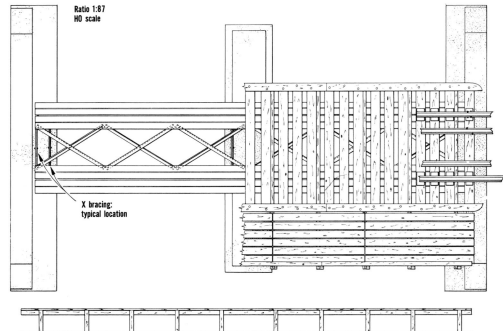

Ratio 1:87
HO scale

X bracing:
typical location

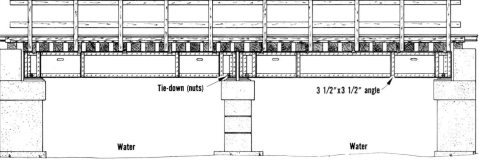

Tie-down (nuts)   3 1/2"x3 1/2" angle

Water   Water

SP excursion train on trestle at Wilder, Calif., in 1948. Fred Matthews Jr.

Common standard trestles

Timber trestlework as built for Southern Pacific and other roads

DATA FROM SOUTHERN PACIFIC RECORDS BY COURTESY OF BRIAN B. HAGEN

THE word "trestle" is believed to have come from "transom": a horizontal beam above an opening. In railroad use it means an elevated roadway directly supported on a number of posts or bents. This is different from a bridge in that the spans between supports consist simply of the stringers or deck material under the track:

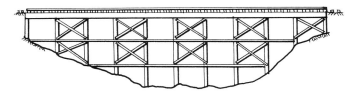

However, the word trestle is also applied to a series of similar girder or trusswork spans on bents, posts, or towers:

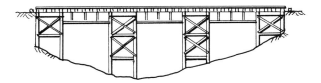

Trestles are made of timber, steel, concrete, and combinations of these. The trestles illustrated here, Southern Pacific designs, are very similar to many timber trestles used by other roads in North America and other parts of the world.

Wooden trestles are particularly common in North America because timber reserves have not yet been depleted. They were attractive to early railroad builders because they used locally available materials, could be built at a moderate cost for labor, and could be assembled fairly quickly. This was important. It took months to build a large earth fill using horse-drawn scoops and mine-size dump cars working from the ends toward the center. The railroad could be opened months — even 2 or 3 years — sooner if trestles were built first, then the fill dumped around them after the railroad was opened.

Trestle economics have changed. Using large machines, fills can be built quickly without resorting to the trestle method. Steel, concrete, and especially prestressed reinforced concrete not only save maintenance costs as compared to timber but also simplify erection.

Shoofly trackage uses timber trestlework where an earth fill would obstruct a highway or damage a dwelling; or where earth is not at hand. Timber trestles are also used in new work where the timber is directly at hand, such as some of the extensions of Canadian railroads in the Northwest. Usually such installations, today, are limited to small structures and to places where washouts might occur.

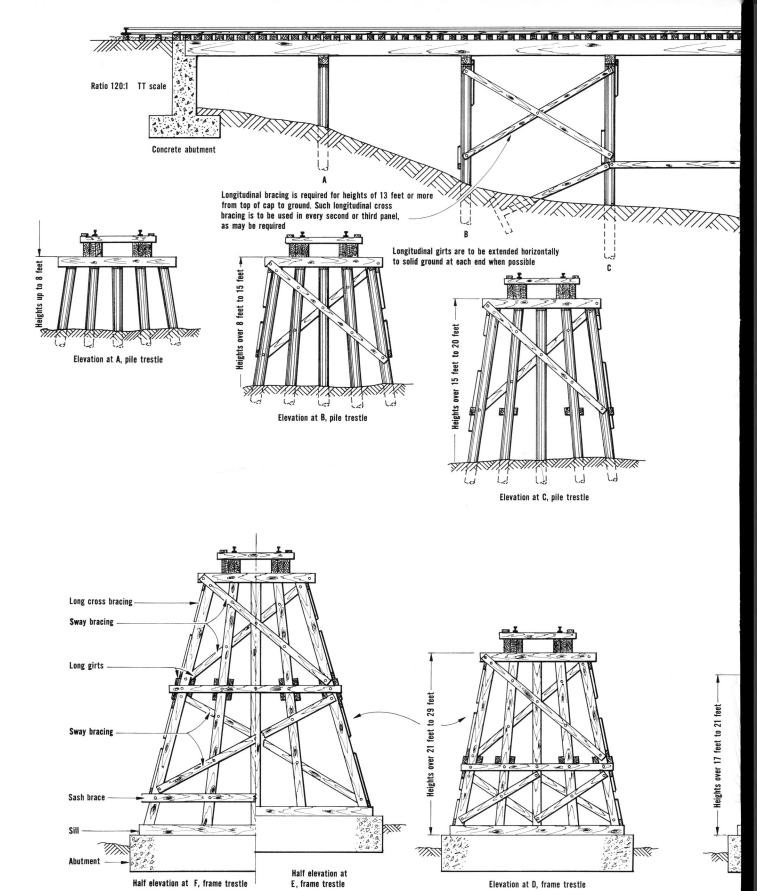

Ratio 120:1 TT scale

Concrete abutment

A

Longitudinal bracing is required for heights of 13 feet or more from top of cap to ground. Such longitudinal cross bracing is to be used in every second or third panel, as may be required

B

Longitudinal girts are to be extended horizontally to solid ground at each end when possible

C

Heights up to 8 feet

Elevation at A, pile trestle

Heights over 8 feet to 15 feet

Elevation at B, pile trestle

Heights over 15 feet to 20 feet

Elevation at C, pile trestle

Long cross bracing

Sway bracing

Long girts

Sway bracing

Sash brace

Sill

Abutment

Half elevation at F, frame trestle

Half elevation at E, frame trestle

Heights over 21 feet to 29 feet

Elevation at D, frame trestle

Heights over 17 feet to 21 feet

"Common standard" trestles: pile and frame

When Edward H. Harriman administered Union Pacific, Southern Pacific, and other "Harriman lines" as one system, common standards were developed for track, signaling, bridges, buildings, locomotives, and many other components. Eventually the empire was forced to dissolve, but the term "common standard" has been used since then for the systemwide standards of the individual railroads. These trestles are the common standard used by Southern Pacific since 1916, corrected to 1958 detailing.

Two general types are shown. In the first, 14"-diameter piles are driven five to a bent — four are permitted in light-duty ex-

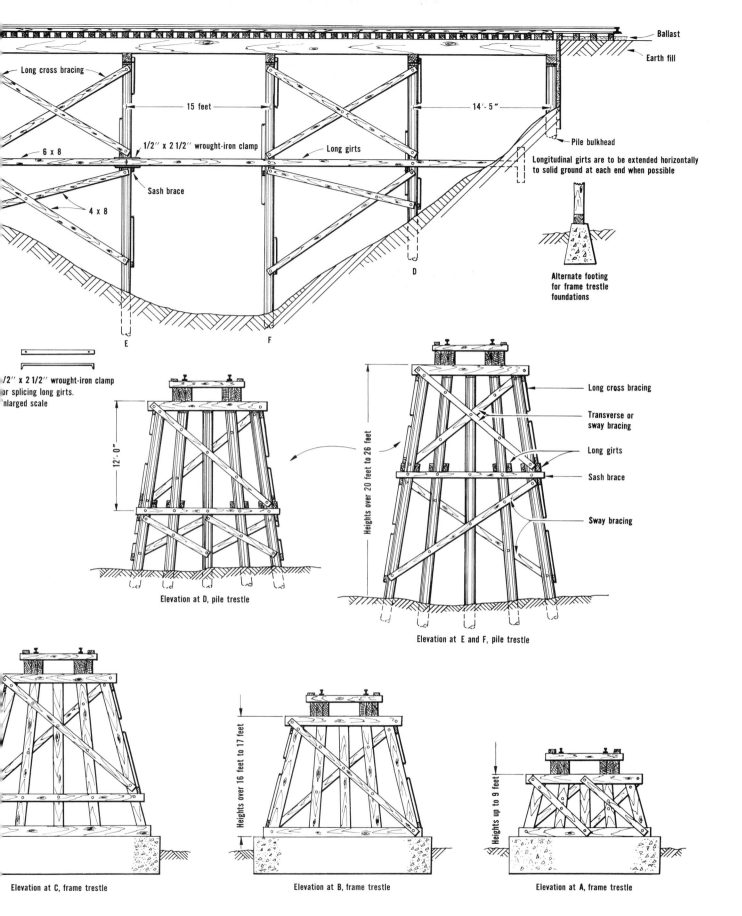

Long cross bracing

15 feet

14'- 5"

6 x 8

1/2" x 2 1/2" wrought-iron clamp

Long girts

4 x 8

Sash brace

Ballast

Earth fill

Pile bulkhead

Longitudinal girts are to be extended horizontally to solid ground at each end when possible

D

E

F

Alternate footing for frame trestle foundations

1/2" x 2 1/2" wrought-iron clamp for splicing long girts. Enlarged scale

12'- 0"

Elevation at D, pile trestle

Heights over 20 feet to 26 feet

Long cross bracing

Transverse or sway bracing

Long girts

Sash brace

Sway bracing

Elevation at E and F, pile trestle

Elevation at C, frame trestle

Heights over 16 feet to 17 feet

Elevation at B, frame trestle

Heights up to 9 feet

Elevation at A, frame trestle

ceptions — directly into soft soil or riverbeds. These are "pile" trestles. "Frame" trestles are made of frames resting upon foundations. Two foundation styles are shown: One is a sill laid across the tops of five buried piles. The other is a cast concrete footing of prismoidal section. This can be laid on rock or in soil to below the frost line. If the soil is loose, the concrete footing will have a broader base.

All drawings except one show parts and dimensions for E-50-loading trestles suitable for most uses. The E-60 variations indicated by one special drawing are for heavy mainline use.

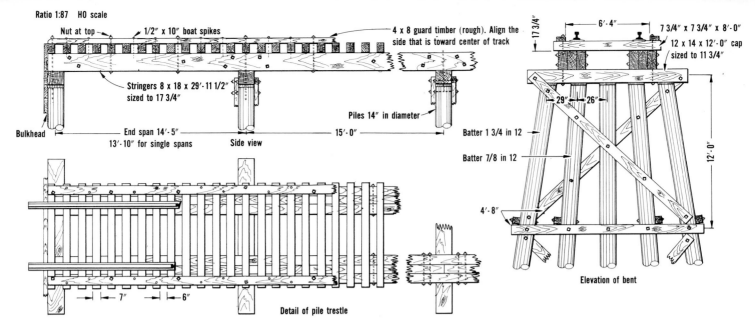

Nut at top   1/2 x 10" boat spikes

4 x 8 guard timber (rough). Align the side that is toward center of track

Stringers 8 x 18 x 29'-11 1/2" sized to 17 3/4"

Piles 14" in diameter

Bulkhead

End span 14'-5"
13'-10" for single spans

15'-0"

Side view

17 3/4"

6'-4"

7 3/4" x 7 3/4" x 8'-0"

12 x 14 x 12'-0" cap sized to 11 3/4"

29"   26"

Batter 1 3/4 in 12

Batter 7/8 in 12

12'-0"

4'-8"

Elevation of bent

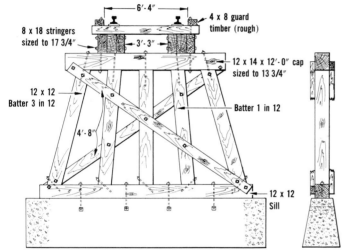

7"   6"

Detail of pile trestle

In one respect these trestles are not typical of most others. Here the stringers supporting the ties are bolted tightly together side by side. On many railroads the stringers are either run separately one to several inches apart, or are spread a fraction of an inch by using metal washers at the bolting points. This is to prevent rot from moisture accumulating in the cracks.

6'-4"

8 x 18 stringers sized to 17 3/4"

4 x 8 guard timber (rough)

3'-3"

12 x 14 x 12'-0" cap sized to 13 3/4"

12 x 12 Batter 3 in 12

Batter 1 in 12

4'-8"

12 x 12 Sill

Frame bent on concrete footing

4 x 8 guard timber (rough)

3'-3"

12 x 14 x 12'-0" cap sized to 13 3/4"

Sway brace

Frame bent on piles

Details of pile trestles

Piles are driven into the ground or mud at spacings and batters indicated. Piles actually vary slightly from their 14" nominal size. If the top surface of any pile is exposed (not covered by a cap), this part is adzed at a 45-degree angle downward to drain the surface. The toothed-ring timber connectors indicated in the drawings are crown-shaped rings of metal that are entirely hidden once the trestle bolts have been drawn home. These details show a trestle for E-50 loading. See the separate diagram on page 43 for alteration to convert this to E-60 loading.

Bents for double track

On tangent (straight) track, this double-width bent can be used. It provides for 14-foot track-center spacing. On curves, two separate trestles should be built. Their bent sites should be staggered sufficiently so that the slanting bents of one trestle do not interfere with those of the other. Where heavy water currents can be expected, the two trestles should be separated sufficiently so that staggering is not necessary, thus giving freer flow of water from one trestle through the next.

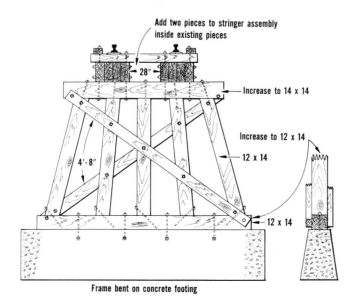

Add two pieces to stringer assembly inside existing pieces

28"

Increase to 14 x 14

Increase to 12 x 14

12 x 14

4'-8"

12 x 14

Frame bent on concrete footing

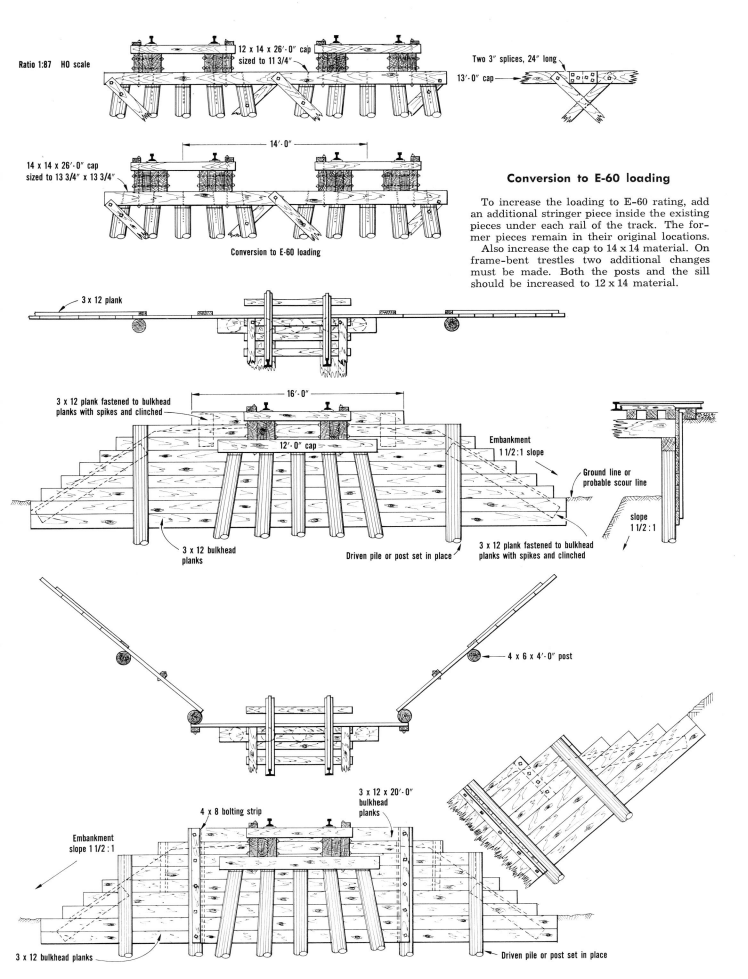

Ratio 1:87   HO scale

12 x 14 x 26'-0" cap
sized to 11 3/4"

Two 3" splices, 24" long

13'-0" cap

14 x 14 x 26'-0" cap
sized to 13 3/4" x 13 3/4"

14'-0"

Conversion to E-60 loading

Conversion to E-60 loading

To increase the loading to E-60 rating, add an additional stringer piece inside the existing pieces under each rail of the track. The former pieces remain in their original locations.

Also increase the cap to 14 x 14 material. On frame-bent trestles two additional changes must be made. Both the posts and the sill should be increased to 12 x 14 material.

3 x 12 plank

3 x 12 plank fastened to bulkhead
planks with spikes and clinched

16'-0"

12'-0" cap

Embankment
1 1/2 : 1 slope

Ground line or
probable scour line

slope
1 1/2 : 1

3 x 12 bulkhead
planks

Driven pile or post set in place

3 x 12 plank fastened to bulkhead
planks with spikes and clinched

4 x 6 x 4'-0" post

4 x 8 bolting strip

3 x 12 x 20'-0"
bulkhead
planks

Embankment
slope 1 1/2 : 1

3 x 12 bulkhead planks

Driven pile or post set in place

125

Carriso Gorge on the San Diego & Arizona Eastern (SP). Dick Steinheim

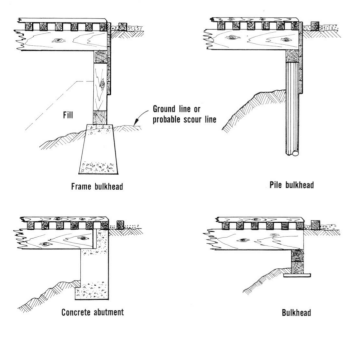

Frame bulkhead

Pile bulkhead

Ground line or probable scour line

Fill

Concrete abutment

Bulkhead

Carriso Gorge. Collection of Ernest Sevde.

Bulkheads

Loose earth must be prevented from spilling from the approaches to the trestle into the stream or road below. Bulkheads for this purpose can be of timber, masonry, metal piles, or concrete.

The timber bulkhead with a straight face is shown with dimensions suited to a standard 22-foot-wide roadbed over the top. (The roadbed is the surface to which the ballast is added.) For less important track a roadbed 18 feet wide may be used; in this case the center details and the 16-foot bulkhead plank are unchanged. All of the lower planks are shortened 2 feet at each end and each of the two vertical side piles is moved in 2 feet.

All material "shall be precut and creosoted before delivery to the site." No material may be sawed at the site except to trim the tops of piles. This is to avoid exposing untreated wood. Bulkhead planks are limited to 24 feet long. All those shown longer than this are actually two planks butted at track center line.

Timber bulkheads are limited to 8 feet in height — except with the approval of the engineering office — and must extend 2 feet below the earth surface. If the surface might be scoured by a stream, the bulkhead must extend 2 feet below the scour line that might be expected.

Rural road overpass

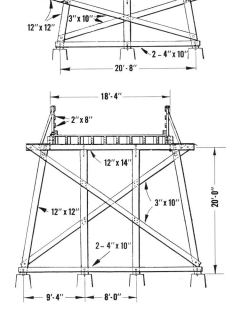

Bents No. 2 and No. 5

12" x 12"
3" x 10"
2 - 4" x 10"
20'-8"

18'-4"
2" x 8"
12" x 14"
12" x 12"
3" x 10"
2 - 4" x 10"
20'-0"
9'-4"
8'-0"

You've seen many a kingpost timber overpass, but this one is unusual — slightly on the skew and slightly on a grade

ARTICLES on the extensive improvements to the Louisville & Nashville RR., published in 1913 and 1914 in *Engineering News*, brought our attention to this plan of a timber highway bridge. The plan was L&N's standard design for bridges used to eliminate grade crossings.

The bridges were simply constructed, utilizing a bent on each side to carry the 38-foot triangular truss span over the tracks. Intermediate bents supported the approaches to the bridge. All timbers were protected by creosote.

At the apex of the truss was an iron block with a pin for the hanger rod which carried the ends of the transverse beam in a casting.

Notice the unusual way in which the vertical member of the truss is attached at an angle to the base member to allow the hanger rod to be perpendicular to the base member.

Since this was a standard design, the bridge could easily be modified for highways on other grades, on level roads or different degrees of skewing.

Galvanized iron sheeting was laid over the caps and vertically between the ends of the stringers at the middle and ends of the main span, so that sparks could not lodge on the caps.

CONSTRUCTION NOTES

Scale lumber in all of the necessary sizes is available for O and HO scales from Camino Scale Models. S scale modelers can use the familiar Northeastern Scale Models dimension stripwood. Make certain to allow sufficient clearances for the trains. NMRA vertical clearances are: TT, $2\frac{1}{8}$"; HO, 3"; S, $4\frac{1}{8}$"; O, $5\frac{1}{2}$", measuring from rail top to underside of bridge.

Bents No. 3 and No. 4

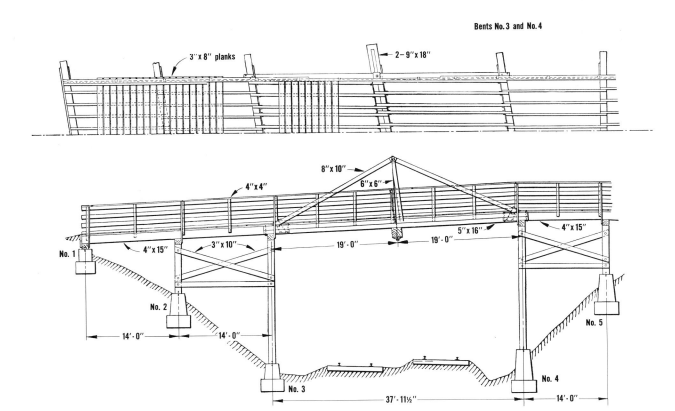

3" x 8" planks
2 - 9" x 18"

8" x 10"
6" x 6"
4" x 4"
No. 1
4" x 15"
3" x 10"
19'-0"
19'-0"
5" x 16"
4" x 15"
No. 2
14'-0"
14'-0"
No. 5
No. 3
37'-11½"
No. 4
14'-0"

Half-size for HO scale

Wood king-post truss highway bridge

This quaint old wooden king-post truss bridge spans a double-track section of Conrail (old Nickel Plate Road) trackage in western New York State. Harold Russell photos

Bridges of this type have been in use for over a hundred years

ONE of the best scenic effects on a model railroad is a bridge with either a railroad track crossing a highway, or vice-versa. This old wooden highway bridge is located south of Silver Creek, N. Y., where it spans the old Nickel Plate Road (now Conrail). The name "king post" defines the construction of the center span. The vertical center member points upward from the deck framing, as opposed to the "queen post" bridge, where the vertical center post points down. The king post is an iron bar and is in tension, whereas the queen post is in compression, and may be either iron or wood.

The bridge is typical of a type built prior to the beginning of the twentieth century. In this installation the highway runs along the top of a cut paralleling the track, then it crosses to the other side with two nearly right-angle turns, where it continues to parallel the track. The bridge is skewed about 10 degrees, but on a model railroad it can be set at most any angle, or be a straight crossing.

For building a model I suggest scale basswood materials, although strip styrene could also be used. Wood has a natural texture, while styrene must be distressed with a brush to simulate wood. Sand the wood materials to remove any roughness, then stain all the parts a creosote color before you assemble the model. Grandt Line offers suitable scale nut-bolt-washer castings.

The measurements of the bridge can be adjusted to fit specific model situations. The center span can be shorter, or slightly longer as necessary. The supporting bents can be made taller, but not too much shorter. Even in modelwork the clearance above the track shouldn't be less than a scale 20 feet.

Supplementary modeling would include fences and guard posts. There should be road signs to warn drivers about the sharp turns and the fact that the bridge has one-way traffic. There also should be a tonnage-restriction sign. Normally, the roadway adjacent to a bridge like this would be a secondary dirt, or at best gravel, road. — *Gordon Odegard*

The framed supporting bents have six square posts. Square posts are never driven into the ground. There is a square horizontal sill at the bottom of each bent which rests upon, and is pinned to, round piles driven into the ground.

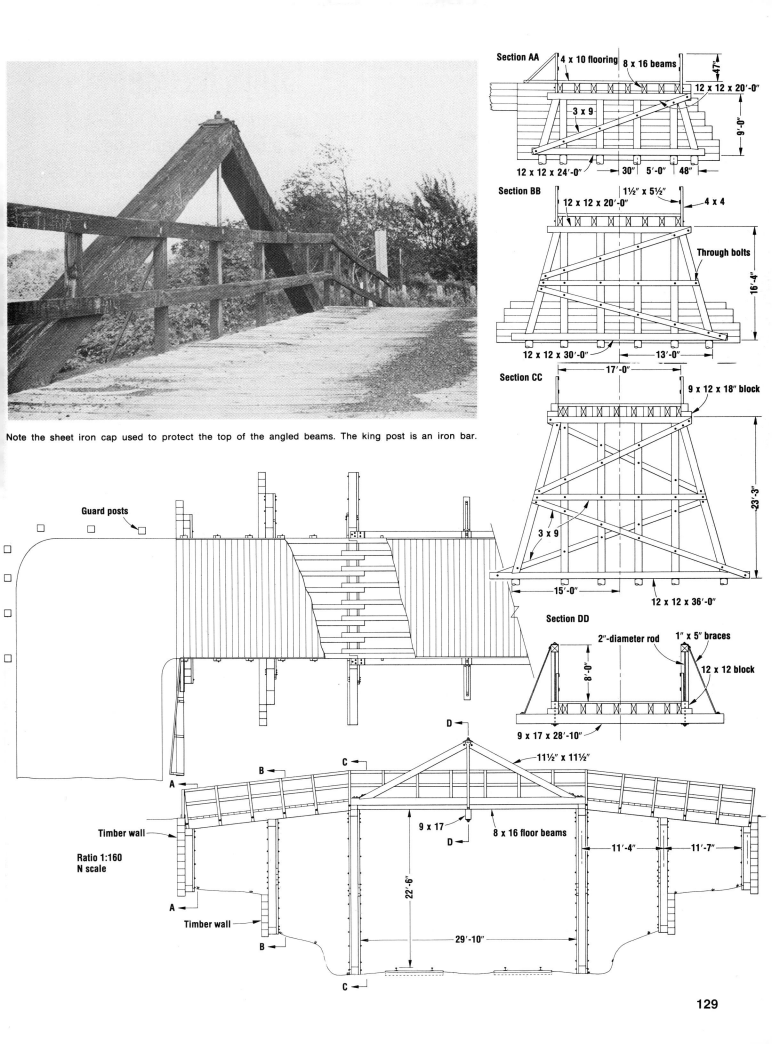

Note the sheet iron cap used to protect the top of the angled beams. The king post is an iron bar.

Section AA
4 x 10 flooring
8 x 16 beams
12 x 12 x 20'-0"
3 x 9
47"
9'-0"
12 x 12 x 24'-0"
30"
5'-0"
48"

Section BB
1½" x 5½"
12 x 12 x 20'-0"
4 x 4
Through bolts
16'-4"
12 x 12 x 30'-0"
13'-0"

Section CC
17'-0"
9 x 12 x 18" block
3 x 9
23'-3"
15'-0"
12 x 12 x 36'-0"

Section DD
2"-diameter rod
1" x 5" braces
8'-0"
12 x 12 block
9 x 17 x 28'-10"

Guard posts

D
11½" x 11½"
B
C
A
9 x 17
D
8 x 16 floor beams
11'-4"
11'-7"
Timber wall
22'-6"
Ratio 1:160
N scale
A
Timber wall
B
29'-10"
C

129

Forest Park overpass

Steel and concrete are combined in this ornamental bridge

IN Saint Louis, Mo., one can find a number of good modeling ideas along the tracks of the Wabash RR. Delmar station is one of them. This classic gem was built in 1929 so that nearby residents need not go into the center of the city to board the Banner Blue and other name trains of Wabash's past. Track planners might find an inspiration in the curious way in which these Wabash trains left the city for points east and northeast. They started from Union Station pointed south but immediately rounded the wye to head toward the Rocky Mountains. After passing Forest Park and through Delmar station, trains turned north, paralleling the western city limits.

Now they have made a half circle of turning, but more is to come: in fact, the exit from Saint Louis takes the shape, on a map, of a great question mark lying on its face. Two more turns to the right almost complete a circle and almost bring the trains to their starting point before the first left turn is made to cross the Mississippi and continue into Illinois and beyond.

W. A. Akin.

An engineer approaching Delmar station inbound passes under a highway bridge somewhat similar in construction to the Forest Park bridge but built later. It features a simplified balustrade.

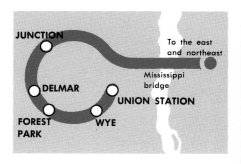

The chief subject of this feature, however, is a double-track bridge that was built in Forest Park in 1904.

A part of the immense park was the site of the Louisiana Purchase Exposition,

Al Rung.

A passenger looking back from a vista dome of the Banner Blue used to see Delmar station this way. An escalator was installed a few years after the original construction, but eventually the station was closed. Wabash is now part of the Norfolk & Western system. Modeled literally, even this small station would be too large for most model layouts, but motifs taken from these photos and those on page 54 could easily be developed into usable free-lance passenger station designs.

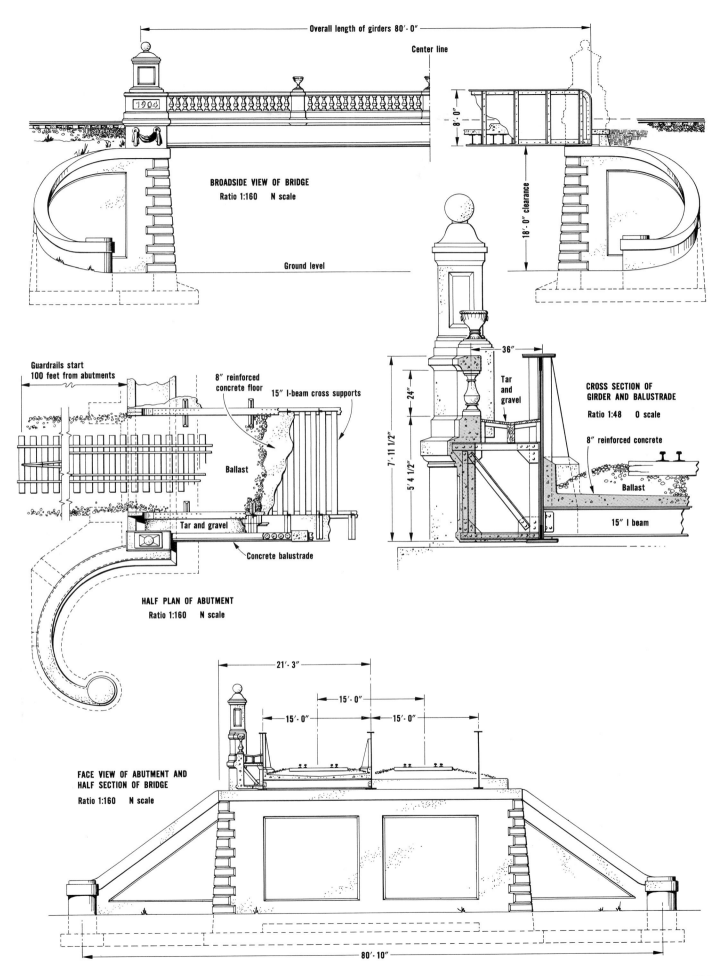

Overall length of girders 80'-0"

Center line

8'-0"

18'-0" clearance

Ground level

BROADSIDE VIEW OF BRIDGE
Ratio 1:160   N scale

1904

Guardrails start
100 feet from abutments

8" reinforced
concrete floor

15" I-beam cross supports

Ballast

Tar and gravel

Concrete balustrade

HALF PLAN OF ABUTMENT
Ratio 1:160   N scale

36"

Tar
and
gravel

24"

7'-11 1/2"

5'-4 1/2"

**CROSS SECTION OF
GIRDER AND BALUSTRADE**

Ratio 1:48   O scale

8" reinforced concrete

Ballast

15" I beam

21'-3"

15'-0"

15'-0"

15'-0"

**FACE VIEW OF ABUTMENT AND
HALF SECTION OF BRIDGE**

Ratio 1:160   N scale

80'-10"

Through most of its years the Wabash was a "railroad," but at the time Delmar station was built, the corporate name used the word "railway"

the world's fair of that day. It was necessary to widen a park entrance road, and this involved the Wabash RR. It crossed the road on a steel girder bridge of 40-foot clear span. A new overpass was needed with a 70-foot clear span. The work was done rather cleverly both in its appearance and in its engineering.

In those times it was stylish to use masonry arch bridges in city parks, but this was not feasible in this case because there was only 22 feet of grade separation between roadtop and rail base — too little for constructing an arch. The new bridge could be supported by girders somewhat like the old bridge, by making them 80 feet long and 8 feet deep. An objection to this was that steel girders were considered too utilitarian to be decorative.

The problem was solved by hiding the girders of the bridge behind a balustrade of reinforced concrete. The wing walls of the bridge abutments were given a new sweeping curve, adding to the monumental effect in a rather graceful manner. The city's Board of Public Improvements accepted the railroad's design and paid $15,000 of the cost of the bridge, as had been agreed previously. The railroad paid the rest, about $10,000.

The bridge was unique for its time. In those days girder and truss bridges were always built with open floors, with the ties resting on stringers as they do in many bridges today. However, A. O. Cunningham, the railroad's civil engineer, had tried a new idea on a more modest bridge near Carpenter, Ill., earlier in the year. Now he was ready to use it on this larger structure.

A concrete floor 6″ thick was cast over 15″ I beams. Above the floor the track was laid in the normal manner in 14″ of loose ballast. This ballast deck construction, now commonly used, reduced noise and simplified track and bridge maintenance. [Later in that same year the Santa Fe completed a ballast-deck truss bridge at Pueblo, Colo. In that instance the objective was to provide greater clearance under the bridge for high water.]

Cunningham devised a clever way to install the new bridge with a minimum of delay to traffic. Wabash had a number of early-morning suburban trains at the time plus some through trains throughout the day. The Rock Island also ran all of its freight and passenger trains into the city over this line. In all, about 300 trains a weekday used these tracks. Thus the new concrete bridge was constructed in a temporary position to the south of the old bridge, supported over the park roadway on timber falsework. The reinforced concrete floor was laid and then allowed to harden 2 weeks before the next step was accomplished. Meanwhile the earth fill at the old bridge's approaches was excavated and replaced with additional falsework.

The old bridge was supported on three girders, one of them between the tracks in much the same way as the new bridge, except that it was shorter, had no decorative features, and had an open floor.

At 9 a.m. on a Sunday, when traffic had become light, the inbound track on the south side of the old bridge was taken up and the side girder of the bridge was also removed. All traffic now used the north track. This done, the new bridge was shifted halfway to its future position, to the point where its north track aligned with the south track of the main line. As soon as these tracks were connected, traffic was diverted to the south main track and the remaining half of the old bridge was dismantled. This began early in the afternoon.

Late in the afternoon the old bridge was completely removed and all traffic was stopped for a short time. Both tracks were severed and the new bridge was shifted a final 15 feet to its permanent position. Nine hours after the beginning of the entire operation tracks were reconnected and traffic could use both main lines normally. The period of complete traffic interruption was brief.

The photos on this page show Delmar station as it appeared in June 1970.

Bridge for a country road

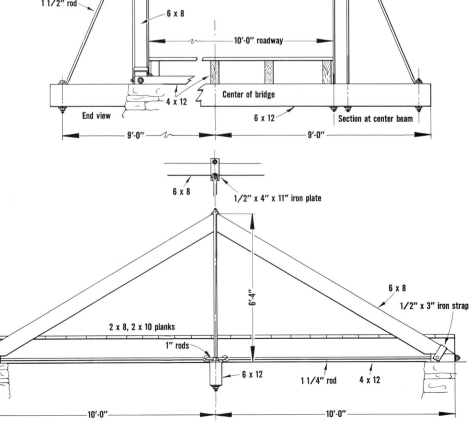

WOOD bridges of the kingposts truss type were common years ago in rural areas but are rapidly becoming scarce because of age, fires, floods, and ice jams. Certainly the example pictured on this page could not have stood a very severe ice-out, because of its loosely stacked dry wall foundations. This bridge, located somewhere in Ohio, was spotted by John Klages, who photographed it with the idea that it would add a bit of charm to any model railroad off-tracks scene.

Scale: 0 (1/4" = 1'-0")

This view of the east side of the original bridge, photographed in 1972, includes a square sheet metal Santa Fe emblem on the railing. This sign was bolted in place with wood blocks serving as spacers around the cast post.

The west side of the bridge has a plain 24″ I beam showing instead of the concrete facade. Since this view was taken in 1972, Santa Fe maintenance forces have painted the girder light blue to make it more visible to drivers.

The Witherby St. underpass

A unique Santa Fe structure with different construction techniques on each side

BY DONALD L. POPE

IN 1924 the San Diego Electric Ry. decided to build a new line into the Mission Beach area of San Diego, Calif. To do this, they planned to use existing Point Loma RR. tracks for part of the route. However, the Point Loma RR. crossed the Santa Fe Ry. at grade where the electric line's right-of-way ran down Barnett Ave. Traffic density made this level crossing intolerable, so a plan was developed to raise the electric railway to cross the Santa Fe with an overpass. In the process, the Barnett Ave. crossing would be lost, so an underpass was proposed for nearby Witherby St. The short bridge that eventually crossed Witherby St. is the subject of this article.

The bridge is a deck girder design, but it uses a number of closely spaced shallow girders instead of the usual two large girders. Railroads generally prefer the deck type of bridge because they do not restrict side or vertical clearances like through structures. The original bridge was built in 1924 as a single-track structure with a concrete facade and railing on both sides. When the line was double-tracked in 1942, the bridge was widened. However, the new side was built without the concrete facade and with a more conventional railing. Also, the two outside girders were made with rolled I beams instead of built-up girders like the rest of the bridge.

The main girders were built up by using a heavy steel plate for the web and riveting 6″ steel angles to both sides at the top and bottom to form flanges. Flange plates were then riveted to the top and bottom of each girder, except for a 6-foot space at each end.

All of the girders have diaphragm plates between them for horizontal stability and to prevent twisting. The diaphragms are positioned just below the top flange. Each diaphragm was formed by riveting angles to the top and bottom of steel plates, forming wide channels. They are positioned at the center and ends of the old girders and at the quarter points and ends of the new girders. The diaphragms used with the old girders are 24″ high, while the new ones are 30″ high at the quarter points and 20″ high at the ends. There are no diaphragms between the old and new girders. The two rolled I beams have four 21″ steel plates evenly spaced and welded between them. Plates 16″ deep are used to attach these girders to the first girder.

The prototype tracks across the bridge are slightly curved. However, I drew the plans with straight track because most model curves are very sharp by prototype standards, and a straight bridge on a sharp curve looks awkward. The prototype curve is so gentle that it makes only a couple of inches of difference in position as it crosses the bridge.

Only one end of each guardrail set is pointed. This is common on double-track bridges where traffic travels the same direction all the time on each track. The pointed end faces oncoming trains. Before someone gets all excited, the drawing is done correctly for this location. The double track is operated with trains using the left-hand track in both directions.

The bridge could be modeled as is, with both sides the same, or in single- or double-track versions. It could be done in the same manner as the prototype with 16 girders underneath, or it could be simplified by cementing a girder to each side of the road-bed board. A modeler could also build the original bridge and then set up a construction scene showing the bridge being widened. ⍉

In this view, looking south, the only hint of a bridge is the railings that show at the edges of the ballasted deck. Note that the guardrails are pointed only at the end which faces oncoming traffic. The old streetcar bridge went over the right-of-way about where the spur track is at the left rear.

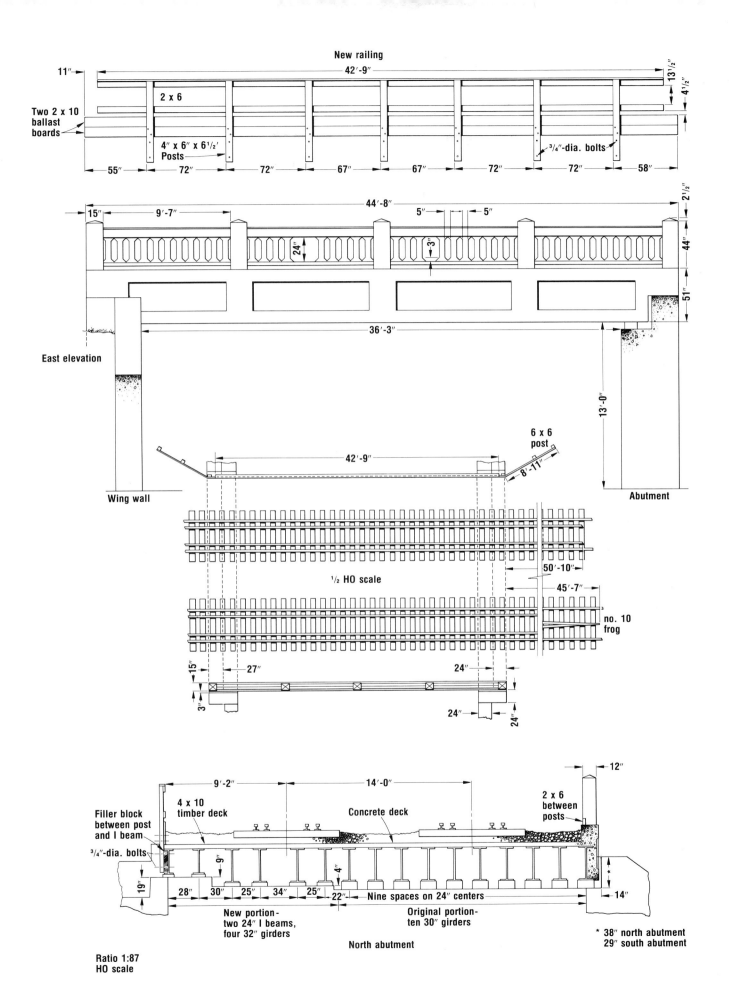

New railing

42'-9"

11"

13 1/2"

2 x 6

4 1/2"

Two 2 x 10
ballast
boards

4" x 6" x 6 1/2'
Posts

3/4"-dia. bolts

55"   72"   72"   67"   67"   72"   72"   58"

44'-8"

2 1/2"

15"   9'-7"   5"   5"

24"   3"   44"

51"

East elevation

36'-3"

13'-0"

Wing wall

6 x 6
post

42'-9"

8'-11"

Abutment

1/2 HO scale

50'-10"

45'-7"

no. 10
frog

15"   27"   24"

3"   24"   24"

12"

9'-2"   14'-0"

4 x 10
timber deck

Concrete deck

2 x 6
between
posts

Filler block
between post
and I beam

9"

4"

3/4"-dia. bolts

19"

28"   30"   25"   34"   25"   22"   Nine spaces on 24" centers

14"

New portion-
two 24" I beams,
four 32" girders

Original portion-
ten 30" girders

North abutment

* 38" north abutment
29" south abutment

Ratio 1:87
HO scale

Lattice truss bridge

These were common from the 1890s through the 1930s

IT has always seemed to me that model railroad layouts are made scenically more interesting by bridges. Among bridges, the through truss type with its spindly members, seems to be the most eye-catching.

Modern truss designs are the Pratt, Howe, and Warren configurations. Personally, I like the lattice designs that were prevalent around 1900. The drawings show a typical lattice through truss bridge of that period. I measured two nearly identical structures on the now defunct Wellsville, Addison & Galeton RR. at Westfield and Galeton, Pa. The Westfield bridge is skewed at both ends, while the Galeton bridge has one squared end and one skewed.

Both bridges were built during a reconstruction period in 1899 (when the railroad was know as the Susquehanna & New York) and used until the line was abandoned in 1979. The lightweight construction limited the railroad's motive power to small locomotives.

Around 1900 large structural shapes were uncommon in bridge work, and for many years, were not even available. Large bridge members were fabricated using small angles, channels, and tees that were laced together with small flat bars or plates. The main members of the Westfield and Galeton bridges have a pair of channels made from angles and plates, and the bracing members are made from angles with bars positioned in a zig-zag arrangement. Structures of the period were riveted together. Welding was not common until about 50 years later.

Both WAG bridges are of identical construction except for the ends. Each end has a channel that connects the undersides of the lower chords, but the angles connecting the end posts are mounted differently. The squared end has an angle running between the first and second bridge ties. On the skewed end the angle is run diagonally through notches in the bottoms of the first few ties.

One end of each bridge span is firmly attached to an abutment, and the other is mounted on rollers to allow the structure to expand and contract with changes in temperature. A bridge this size will have a length variation of several inches between the extreme temperatures of summer and winter.

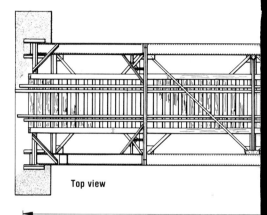

Top view

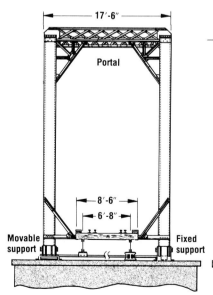

17'-6"

Portal

8'-6"

6'-8"

Movable support

Fixed support

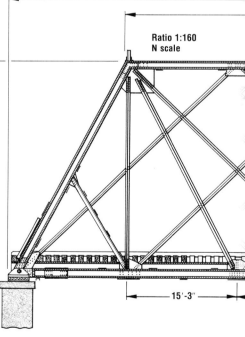

Ratio 1:160
N scale

15'-3"

Bottom sway bracing

Rollers of movable support omitted

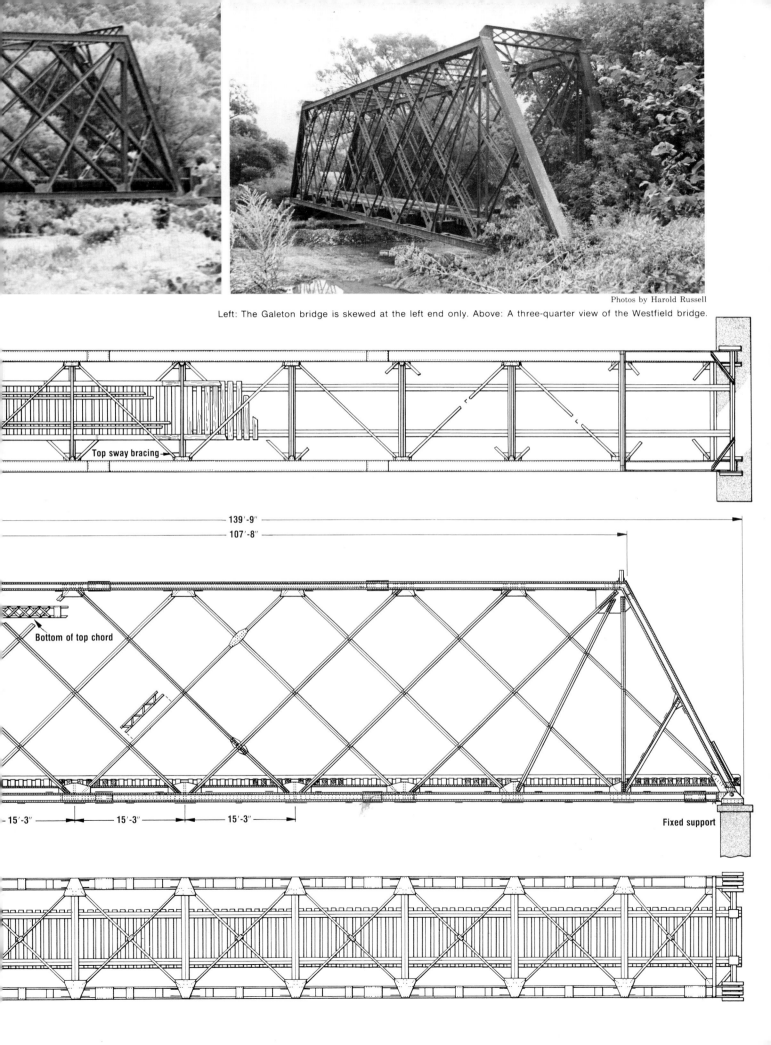

Photos by Harold Russell

Left: The Galeton bridge is skewed at the left end only. Above: A three-quarter view of the Westfield bridge.

Top sway bracing

139'-9"

107'-8"

Bottom of top chord

15'-3" — 15'-3" — 15'-3"

Fixed support

Left: On a squared-end span the end posts are tied together with an angle running between the first couple ties. Middle: On a skewed span extra support plates hold an unequal leg angle that is run diagonally through the first few bridge ties. Right: Typical gusset joint at lower chord.

A wide variety of wood, plastic, and brass shapes is available for constructing a model. To simulate the delicate look of the prototype, I suggest you use milled brass shapes from Special Shapes or Milled Shapes, or make your own sections from thin styrene strips (Evergreen Scale Models offers a selection of styrene strip materials). I also suggest you make some assembly jigs for making the laced components. Both brass and styrene are easily embossed to produce rivets.

If you work with brass shapes be extremely careful of the expansion of the metal from heat when it is soldered. Attach one or two pieces at a time and allow the assembly to cool before you proceed. If you work too fast the bridge assembly will twist and warp when it cools.

The easiest way to paint a truss bridge is to use an airbrush. Some modelers prefer to paint individual assemblies as they are built and before the model is completely assembled. — *Harold Russell*

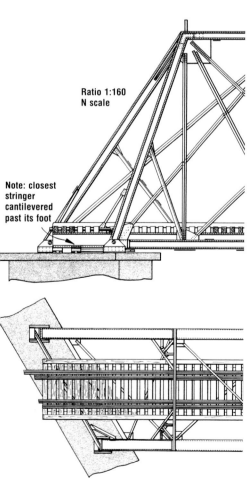

Ratio 1:160
N scale

Note: closest stringer cantilevered past its foot

Ratio 1:87
HO scale

Top chord

6" x 6" angle

3" x 3" angle

End post

18½"

6" x 6" angles

Movable feet this end

6" x 3" channel
Stringer foot

Rigid feet (shown here) on opposite end

Gusset

Tie plate

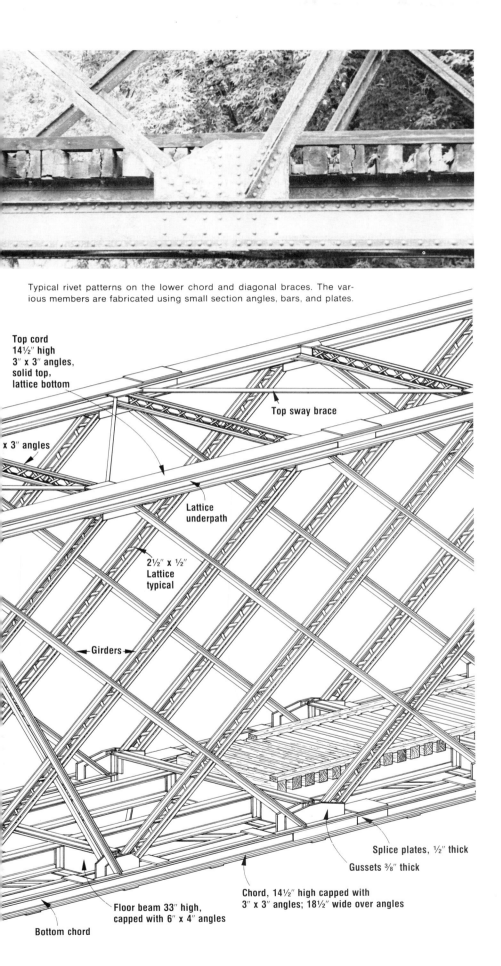

Typical rivet patterns on the lower chord and diagonal braces. The various members are fabricated using small section angles, bars, and plates.

Top cord 14½″ high 3″ x 3″ angles, solid top, lattice bottom

Top sway brace

x 3″ angles

Lattice underpath

2½″ x ½″ Lattice typical

Girders

Splice plates, ½″ thick

Gussets ⅜″ thick

Chord, 14½″ high capped with 3″ x 3″ angles; 18½″ wide over angles

Floor beam 33″ high, capped with 6″ x 4″ angles

Bottom chord

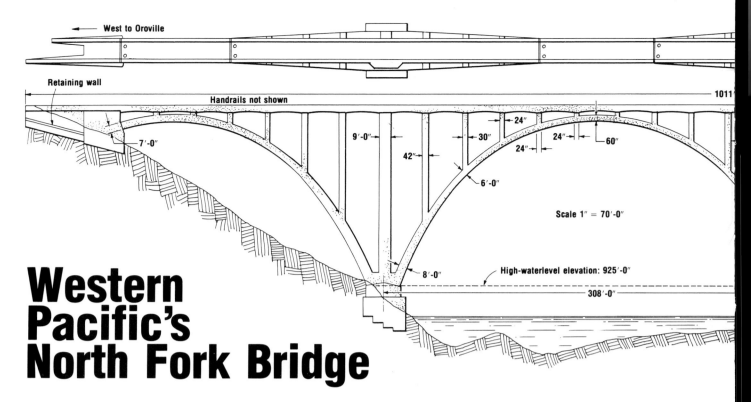

West to Oroville →

Retaining wall

Handrails not shown

1011

7'-0"

9'-0"

42"

30"

24"

24"

24"

60"

6'-0"

Scale 1" = 70'-0"

8'-0"

High-waterlevel elevation: 925'-0"

308'-0"

Western Pacific's North Fork Bridge

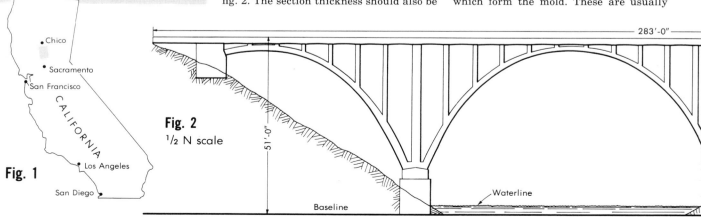

NORTH FORK BRIDGE

Tunnel No. 7

Tunnel No. 6

Tunnel No. 8

Tunnel No. 5

Tunnel No. 4

West Branch Bridge

Former Western Pacific route

Relocated Western Pacific route

Reservoir

Feather River Bridge

Diversion Dam

OROVILLE

Oroville Dam

Chico

Sacramento

San Francisco

CALIFORNIA

Los Angeles

San Diego

Fig. 1

Fig. 2

½ N scale

283'-0"

51'-0"

Baseline

Waterline

IN the late 1950's, the State of California's Department of Water Resources planned a dam across the Feather River at Oroville which would create a new water reservoir. The existing trackage of the Western Pacific RR. would be inundated by this reservoir, so WP relocated the line to the west over a 23-mile route. See fig. 1. The rerouting involved building five new tunnels and two bridges.

One of the new bridges was this massive concrete arch bridge built over the Feather River's North Branch. Its span is 1011 feet long and about 200 feet above mean river level. The structure is reinforced poured concrete except for the pipe and structural metal handrails. The deck is recessed and the track is laid on standard ballast.

This bridge is far too large to be modeled full size in most scales. Even in N scale it would be over 6 feet long. Few model railroads could scenically handle a bridge this large, as it would visually overpower the balance of most layouts. However, the basic design can be preserved and the proportions condensed. If the height and length are reduced to approximately one-fourth the prototype dimensions, the resultant bridge closely resembles the prototype. See fig. 2. The section thickness should also be

reduced to one-half or three-fourths those of the prototype to maintain the proportions.

A model bridge could be constructed of wood, styrene plastic, or plaster. Plaster will produce a most realistic concrete-type surface. Separate forms for the arches, deck, and vertical supporting members can be constructed of wood or plastic sheet. Wood forms should be sealed to prevent the plaster from sticking to the surfaces. The finished components can be filed and sanded to fit and then joined with white glue. The arch form will be the hardest to cast. The mold can have side members cut from wood on a bandsaw. The bottom can be made of wood also. I suggest you use .100"-thick styrene sheet to make the removable top and bottom sheets. See fig. 3. All of the parts should be secured with panhead sheet metal screws which can be removed to release the casting. Molds for the vertical supports and deck can be constructed similarly.

The surfaces of the model, regardless of the material used, have to be properly finished and colored. Cast concrete has markings on it showing the outline of the various rectangular wood or metal panels which form the mold. These are usually

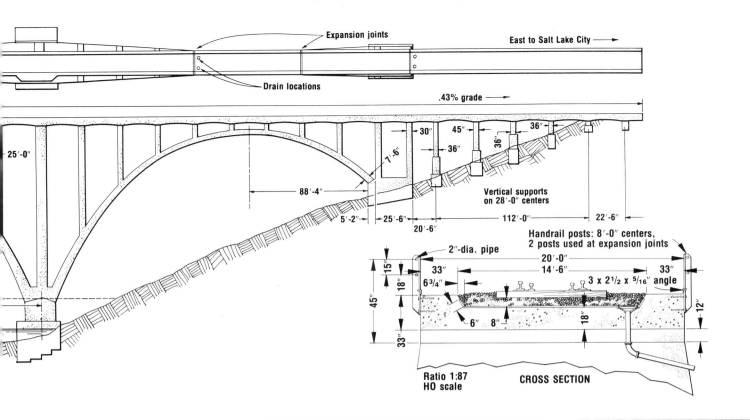

Expansion joints

East to Salt Lake City →

Drain locations

.43% grade →

25'-0"

88'-4"

7'-6"

30"

45"

36"

36"

36"

36"

Vertical supports on 28'-0" centers

5'-2"   25'-6"   20'-6"   112'-0"   22'-6"

Handrail posts: 8'-0" centers, 2 posts used at expansion joints

2"-dia. pipe

15"   18"

33"   6¾"

20'-0"

14'-6"

33"

3 x 2½ x 5/16 angle

45"

33"   6"   8"   18"   12"

Ratio 1:87
HO scale   CROSS SECTION

about 4 x 8 feet. Some seams are smooth but others are not, so the cast joints are not visible. A few scattered lines scored into the component surfaces with a sharp knife will suffice to simulate these seams.

Concrete is not the gray color purported by some model paint manufacturers. Actually, it is off-white with tinges of gray and some yellow. Concrete is not evenly colored, so any coloring should be applied as a wash or as a weak colored spray. A tinge of rust here and there is generally found on most concrete structures, but apply this weathering sparingly. A little time spent inspecting a prototype concrete structure will help in reproducing the color. An average model can be enhanced considerably with good coloring, but an excellent model can also be rendered mediocre with poor coloring. — *Gordon Odegard.*

Western Pacific RR.

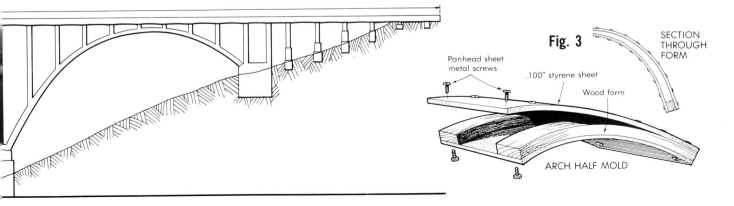

Fig. 3

SECTION THROUGH FORM

Panhead sheet metal screws

.100" styrene sheet

Wood form

ARCH HALF MOLD

B&OCT bascule bridge

BASCULE bridges date from antiquity. The medieval moat drawbridges were a simple type. Only slightly more elaborate bascule bridges were built in Europe in the early 19th century, especially over canals. Modern development began with the construction of the Van Buren St. Scherzer rolling lift bridge in Chicago, designed in 1893. About this same time,

Linn H. Westcott.

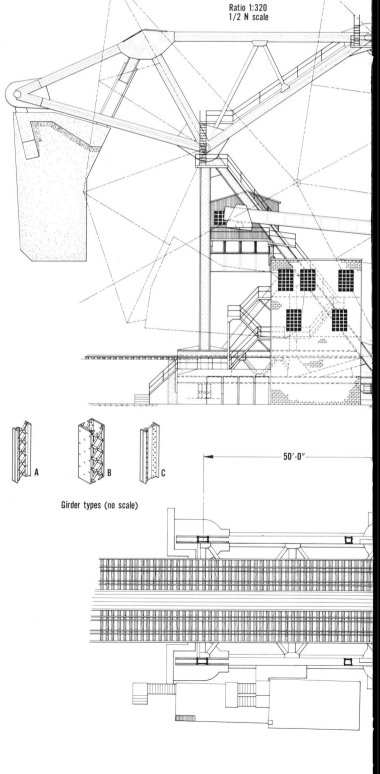

Ratio 1:320
1/2 N scale

Girder types (no scale)

A   B   C

50'-0"

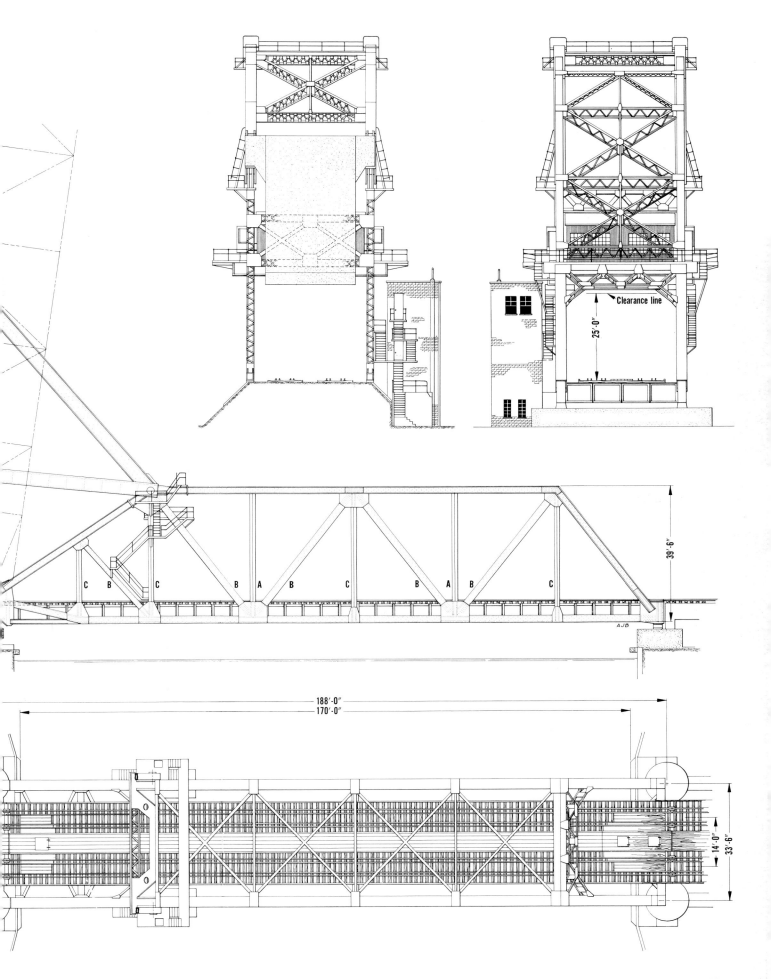

Clearance line

25'-0"

39'-6"

C B C B A B C B A B C

AJB

188'-0"
170'-0"

14'-0"
33'-6"

Linn H. Westcott.

completely dredged. A few hundred feet to the east, the St. Charles Air Line RR. had a longer bridge over the old channel. These two bridges played alternating roles in the handling of all traffic of both railroads while the following construction took place: First, the St. Charles Air Line bridge was moved to the new channel beside the B&OCT bridge. It was shortened by one bay. Second, the B&OCT bridge was then raised to accommodate a nearby grade-crossing elimination. Third, the St. Charles bridge was also raised to the level of the B&OCT bridge. Finally, both bridges were put into independent service side by side.

This B&OCT bridge is a reasonable size for a medium-size or large model railroad. In HO scale and larger it could be used to span an aisleway. In HO the clear opening is 23½". The model can be built of most common model materials: brass, wood and cardstock, or plastic. Structural shapes are available in wood, plastic, and metal. Solid structural members could be substituted for the latticed portions of the prototype, but open lattice construction has enough merit in the finished appearance to justify the extra work required.

Good alignment is necessary if the bridge is to operate. See the July 1973 MR Clinic for some ideas on alignment. Also, the approach tracks should be electrically interlocked to disconnect power to the tracks when the span is opened. A movable span presents a real opportunity for a working interlocking including signals, derails, bridge locks, and bridge movement controls. The July Clinic deals with these elements too.

Some mechanical lifting methods are discussed in the review of the AHM rolling lift bridge in the September 1973 Trade Topics. While the mechanics are not exactly the same, the principles using wire or gearing can be adapted. The simplest method is to attach a strong thin wire (such as Nichrome) to the moving parts and fix them to a rotating crank or wheel under the layout. One wire should be used for each side of the bridge to keep the span from skewing during the raising and lowering operations. Brass rack-and-pinion gearing as small as ⅛" square with 64 pitch is available through any supplier handling Boston Gear products. A suitable slow-moving pinion-gear drive could be mounted in the corrugated machinery shed, duplicating prototype practice. The underside of the moving rack mounted atop the pinion gear has gear teeth. These two racks (one at each side) move the lift section and the counterbalance frame. Note that the rack teeth on this particular bridge are covered with sheet metal on the top and sides.

The counterbalance should be built so that it actually counterbalances the weight of the lift section. It should be hollow and filled with lead shot or sheet until nearly balanced, but the lift section should be slightly heavier so it will not lift when a train passes over. A solenoid or mechanical lock can be used to anchor the lowered bridge if desired. If the counterbalancing is done correctly, a small motor will be sufficient to lift a large, heavy structure with ease. The prototype takes about a minute to raise or lower all the way.

the Tower of London bridge, a roller-bearing type, was erected in England.

The bascule bridge has several advantages over other movable spans. Construction and erection costs are generally lower than for other types. A swing span must be moved a complete 90 degrees for the passage of almost any vessel, whereas a bascule bridge need be raised only enough to clear the particular vessel passing beneath it, saving time and operating costs. The bascule requires about half the space of a swing span to provide a comparable channel clearance. Also, a swing span requires a massive single pier at the center of the waterway, often an awkward place to provide, not to men-

tion construct, a footing. With a bascule bridge, the load is divided between the two end piers, which are more easily built.

The bascule bridge has better alignment and lifting control than the vertical lift type, and requires and uses less material and has simpler construction.

The Baltimore & Ohio Chicago Terminal RR. bridge over the south branch of the Chicago River is a trunnion-type bascule with a 188-foot lift span over a 170-foot-wide channel. The bridge was constructed in the late 1920's as part of the Chicago River straightening project. (See *Railway Age* magazine, February 28, 1931.) It was a new bridge begun over dry land before the new channel had been

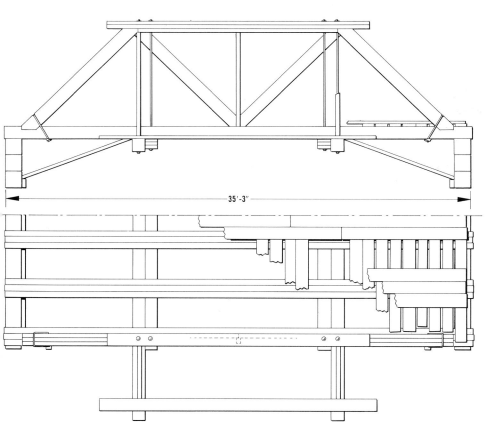

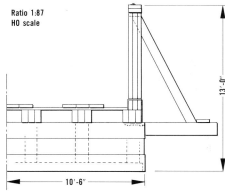

Ratio 1:87
HO scale

13'-0"

10'-6"

35'-3"

Simple truss bridge

THE prototype of this simple truss bridge stands in a remote corner of Wyoming, near the village of Four Corners. It was built in the late teens or early twenties as a highway bridge. The span will not handle heavy loads but could be used near any turn-of-the-century right of way, or, in a rundown condition, in a more modern layout. Construction is fairly easy, and the size can be adapted to fit any location.

The model and photos are by Mel McFarland, who also furnished the information about the bridge.

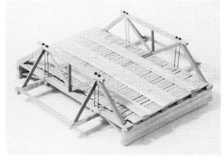

145

Photos by Harold Russell.

Add a covered highway bridge to your layout

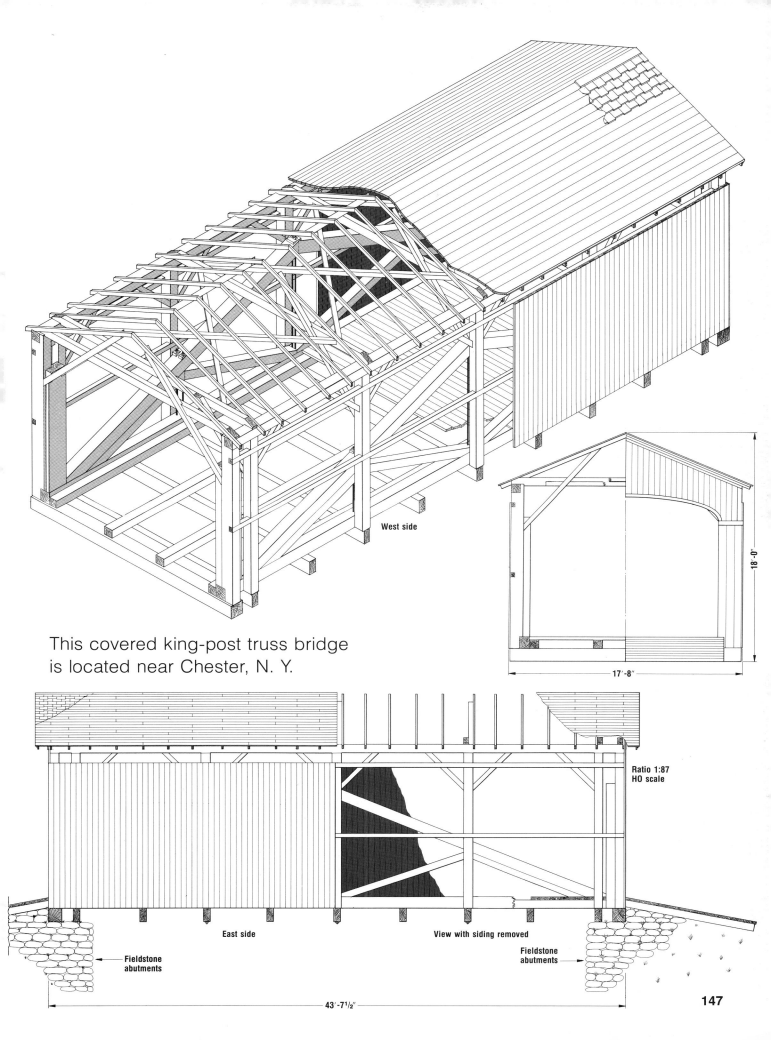

West side

This covered king-post truss bridge
is located near Chester, N. Y.

18'-0"

17'-8"

Ratio 1:87
HO scale

East side

View with siding removed

Fieldstone
abutments

Fieldstone
abutments

43'-7½"

147

Covered railroad bridge

St. Johnsbury & Lamoille County RR.
structure is of a convenient size
for modeling

THE bridge of our prototype drawing on the following pages is still in existence on the St. Johnsbury & Lamoille County RR. where it crosses the Lamoille River in the town of Wolcott, Vt. It was built sometime between 1898, when the first covered bridge of the then St. Johnsbury & Lake Champlain RR. was built at Swanton, Vt., and 1909, when the road built a covered bridge at Hardwick. The exact date of construction is not known to us. The lattice used was a design developed by Ithiel Town, one of the greatest of the New England covered bridge builders. The bridge was of all-wood construction except for

the metal bolts supporting the floor beams; wood pins connected the other components.

Why were so many early road and railroad bridges built as covered structures? We quote the answer given by an old New England carpenter reported in R. S. Allen's *Covered Bridges of the Northeast*: "For the same reason our grandmothers wore petticoats — to protect their underpinning. They covered bridges likewise."

Those early bridges were built of wood; and the greatest enemy of wood is moisture. Wood that is alternately wet and dry soon rots, so the bridges were covered

to keep the internal structural timbers dry — particularly the trusses which gave the structure its strength. The roof, sides, and flooring were considered expendable, although these were protected to a considerable degree by painting.

While time and the elements are fast taking their toll of the few remaining covered bridges in the country, trains will continue to race through this one. When the StJ&LC was recently taken over by new management, it embarked on an improvement program which included replacing the road's covered bridges with steel structures. The Wolcott bridge was

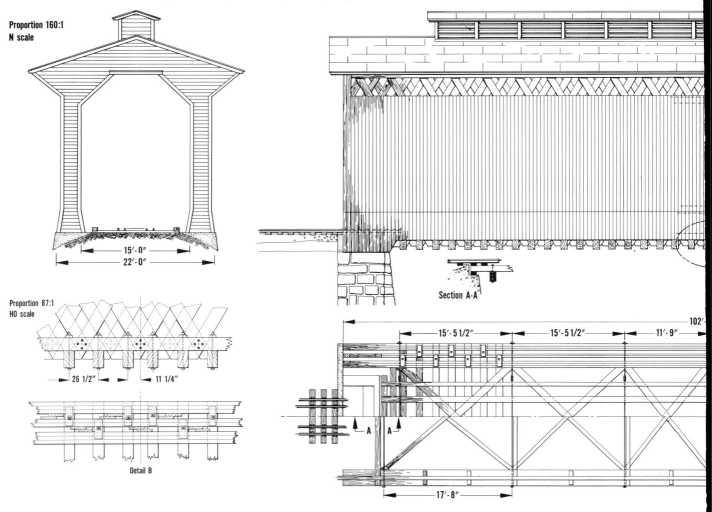

Proportion 160:1
N scale

15'-0"
22'-0"

Proportion 87:1
HO scale

26 1/2"   11 1/4"

Detail B

Section A-A

15'-5 1/2"   15'-5 1/2"   11'-9"   102'

A   A

17'-8"

scheduled to be so replaced, but Vermont's Board of Historic Sites became interested. With the help of the Lamoille County Development Council it raised the money needed to save the bridge — money to allow the railroad to adapt the bridge for the greater strength desired.

The StJ&LC did this by installing steel spans inside the structure with their centers resting on piles driven into the riverbed. These carry the weight of StJ&LC trains. Thus the covered bridge now bears only its own weight. It is the only railroad covered bridge in service in Vermont, and one of the few covered bridges left in the U. S. in daily use.

The accompanying photos were taken by Bob Hagerman before and during the installation of the steel spans. The hole in the roof showing in the closeups was where part of the roof and cupola were temporarily removed to allow the driving of piles under the center of the bridge. Our thanks to the Lamoille County Development Council and Mr. Hagerman for the photos.

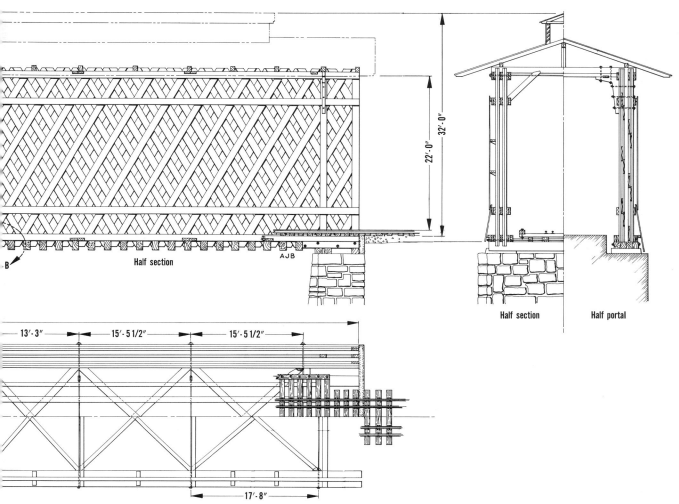

Half section

Half section   Half portal

13'- 3"   15'- 5 1/2"   15'- 5 1/2"

17'- 8"

22'- 0"   32'- 0"

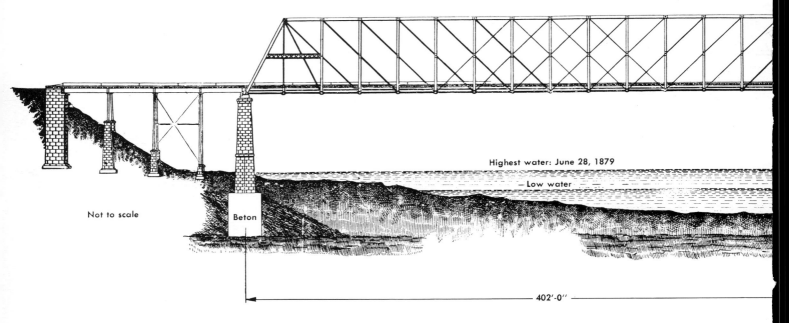

Highest water: June 28, 1879

— Low water

Not to scale

Beton

402'-0"

Old Plattsmouth truss bridge

THE Burlington & Missouri River RR. in Nebraska (the company name ends here) built this truss bridge across the Missouri River at Plattsmouth, Nebr., in 1879 and 1880 to connect with the Chicago, Burlington & Quincy RR. Previously connections had been made by means of transfer boats. While the bridge was under construction the two companies consolidated, and what

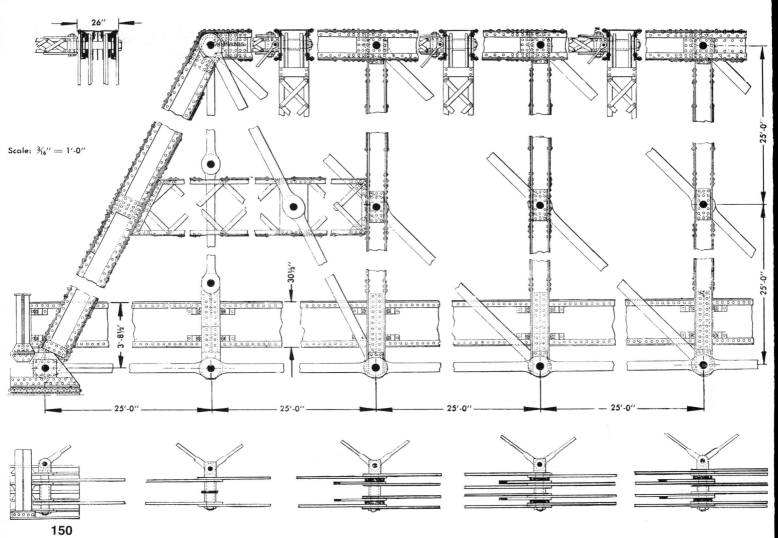

26"

Scale: ³⁄₁₆" = 1'-0"

30½"

3' - 8½"

25'-0"

25'-0"

25'-0"

25'-0"

25'-0"

25'-0"

25'-0"

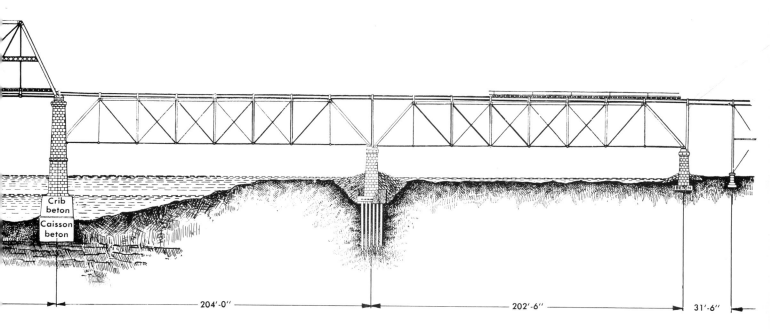

Crib beton

Caisson beton

204'-0"   202'-6"   31'-6"

had been the Burlington & Missouri River RR. in Nebraska became the Nebraska Division of the CB&Q.

Our plans show only three of the bridge's five spans, but the other spans were identical in appearance: another through span and one more deck span. Each through span was 402 feet long; the decks varied slightly: 205½, 204 and 202½ feet. Besides the 1416 feet of bridge spans there were also 1440 feet of iron viaduct at the east end and 120 feet of iron viaduct at the west end. We doubt that many modelers will have space for even one 402-scale-foot bridge, but we'll leave the shortening to you.

Our plans and illustrations are from 1880 editions of the *Railroad Gazette*.

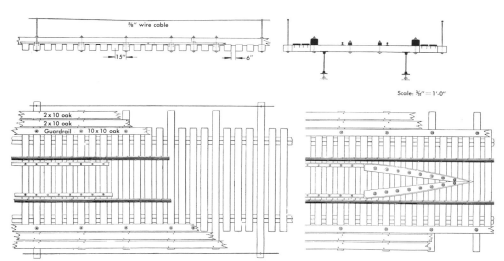

⅜" wire cable

15"   6"

2 x 10 oak
2 x 10 oak
Guardrail   10 x 10 oak

Scale: ³⁄₃₂" = 1'-0"

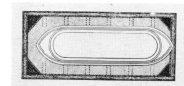

Plan of pier

Index

Investigation 2 pages D66–D76

Write the term in each pair that correctly completes each sentence.

7. A magnet that is made when electric charges move through a coil of wire wrapped around an iron core is called an (electric circuit, electromagnet).

8. Electric cars have rechargeable (batteries, magnets).

9. Refrigerators, hair dryers, and ceiling fans all contain (electric motors, dry cells).

Complete the following exercises.

10. Describe some of the developments in the field of telecommunication.

11. How is an electromagnet different from a permanent magnet?

12. Why is the statement "don't mix electricity and water" good advice?